Return to Oneness

Principles and Practice of Spiritual Technology

Zivorad Mihajlovic Slavinski

authorHOUSE®

AuthorHouse™
1663 Liberty Drive
Bloomington, IN 47403
www.authorhouse.com
Phone: 1-800-839-8640

©*2009 Zivorad Mihajlovic Slavinski. All rights reserved.*

No part of this book may be reproduced, stored in a retrieval system, or transmitted by any means without the written permission of the author.

First published by AuthorHouse   8/7/2009

ISBN: 978-1-4490-0206-0 (sc)

Printed in the United States of America
Bloomington, Indiana

This book is printed on acid-free paper.

This book is the product of work of Zivorad Mihajlovic Slavinski and Jadranka (Alda) Stilin Mihajlovic. The investigation of this information took many years. As do all honest people, they earn their living through their work. To copy this work without compensation to the owners is to violate the economic, legal and human rights of the authors and means stealing their products. To copy it is a failure of personal and Spiritual integrity. He/she who does so affirms himself/herself as dishonest, as a thief. Stealing burdens karma. Thank you for not doing so.

Gratitude

I am grateful to the people who have contributed to the publishing of this book with their donations: Perica and Jelena Popovic, Alek and Mirjana Sirbegovic, Mile Jerkov, Lilian and Vladimir Besevic, Drazen and Andreja.

I am grateful to Mirjana Sirbegovic who helped me in translating parts of the book into English and to people who edited this English edition: Carol Saito, Karen Gould, Judith Daniel, Reg Reynolds and Phil Rothenberg.

I am grateful to Vladimir Stojakovic for his texts which I have included in the book and to my daughter Ivana who is the original creator of the Ivana End of Words method, which I only polished a bit.

Beograd, 2005

Table of Contents

1. Introductory Remarks 1
2. Dual Universe: Our Fundamental Playground 3
3. The Concept of Duality in Eastern and Western Thought 12
4. The Path to Oneness 20
   Oneness and Opposites in Alchemy
   Leonardo da Vinci on Neutralization of Polarities
   Good in Evil and Evil in Good
5. Symbols 28
6. Systems, Methods and Techniques 42
   Tantra and Hatha Yoga
   Journey into Integrated Awareness
   Fear and Love
   Turning a Problem
   Healing into Wholeness
   Tao of Chaos
   Exceeding the Self-image
   Alchemical Meditation Ouroboros
   Oneness Meditation
   Hammer or H.A.M.R.
   How to do the Hammer Exercise
   The Symbolic Polarization Method
   The Technical Procedure
   Polarity Therapy
   Polarities in NLP
   Gestalt "Communication on the Pillow"
   Psychosynthesis

    Psychology of Dual Brain
    Marriage of Spirit
    The Sedona Method®
    Flemming Funch: Integrating the Polarities of the Self

7 Two Brain Hemispheres 100

8 Ida, Pingala and Sushumna. 104

9 Neutralization of Energy Polarization 110

10 Creation and Discreation of Subjective Reality 114

    The Duplication of Experience
    Three Ways to Discreate the Primary
        Decision (Alpha)

11 Spiritual Technology. 125

12 The Basic Principles of Spiritual Technology 132

    A Holistic Approach to Phenomena
    The Alternating Technique
    Solve et Coagula
    The Principle of the Hologram
    Duplication or Recreation of Unwanted Experiences

13 Spiritual Technology: Systems, Methods and
    Techniques 150

    Gnostic Intensive
    Individual Gnostic Intensive (IGI)
    Excalibur
    Excalibur-2
    Aspectics
    Entities Processing
    Entities Work Procedure
    Filling the Empty Space

Expansion of the Being as Light
Holographic Life Repair
Deep PEAT
Nothing or Nothingness
Sudden Turn of States in Consciousness and in Body
Looking for the Opposite State
Creating Consciousness of Polarization
Symbols of the Deeper Contents
The Container and its Content
The Duplication of the Decision of Defeat
Pleroma and the Neutralization of Polarities
Circular Processing
On the Importance of Exact Verbalization of Primes
A List of Primordial Polarities
Fundamental Polarities
DP2 (Deep PEAT Second Level)
The Practice of DP2
DP3 (Deep PEAT Third Level)
Theoretical Foundations of DP3 Method
Essential Conditions for the Successful DP3 Process
Important Details of DP3 and the
    Preparation of the Client
Instructions
How the Integration is Attained
Stabilization
The Opposition
Forgiving
Circular Processing
Mistakes in the Application of DP3
The Practice of the DP3 Method
DP3 and Soul Retrieval
Application of DP3 on Eight Life Dynamisms

The Procedure of Integration of Life Dynamisms
PAST/FUTURE RUNDOWN
SPACE RUNDOWN
Other Applications of the DP3 Method
Some Observations on the DP3 Process
Hui-Neng's Platform Sutra
FINGERTIP TECHNIQUE
LITTLE MAGICAL METHOD

14 Identities..................................273
    Working with Identities
    Elimination of Identities
    Fingertip Method
    Application of DP3 to Unwanted Identities
    The Creation of Positive Identities using DP3

15 The Money Game and How to Play it...........282
    Identities and Acquiring Money
    Identity of a Successful Person - Using DP3

16 The Dynamics of Polarities...................293

17 The Evolution of Processing 296

18 Levels of Consciousness and Processing.......299

19 Polarization and Integration 302

20 Inner Magic of Words........................308
    Ivana End of Words (IEW)
    The Procedure of IEW
    Verbal Reduction & Expansion (VRE)
    Reduction
    Expansion
    Things to Look for in this Process

Observations
   Possible Mistakes in the Application
      of these Two Methods
   Possibilities for Application of VRE
21 The Shadow and its Integration................343
   Shadow Integration: The Magical Mirror
22 Left Hand Paths and Right Hand Paths.........355
23 Caution with Depression.....................357
24 Duality in a Session 362
25 "The Freedom For" and "The Freedom From".....364
26 Permanency of Processing Results.............366
27 Spiritual Honeymoon 371
28 On Being a Processor 375
   The Story of Two Friends
29 Paradox and Humor in Spiritual Work..........379
30 LAST WORD 382
LITERATURE 385

1

Introductory Remarks

This book is the result of the common efforts of my wife Jadranka (Alda) and me. We spontaneously shared the work on it. Originally, I created all of the Spiritual technology systems (except the **"Ivana the End of Words"** method, which was created by my daughter Ivana)**,** but Alda has contributed greatly to their fine tuning and polishing. Participants of our workshops witnessed how the two of us work together as a harmonious team in which each of us has our own role. However, for the sake of simplicity, the text of this book uses the singular "I", because it would be a bit complicated and confusing to use the plural "we". This remark serves to correct the possible impression that the book was exclusively produced by me.

The second important remark concerns the change of the term **"neutralization"** which I used in my previous book ***"PEAT and Neutralization of Primordial Polarities".*** In this book, instead of the term "neutralization" I mainly use the term ***"integration".***

The reason for this change is as follows. In the Serbian language, which is my native language and which I wrote the book originally, the term "neutralization" is adequate and proper but not in English. In English it often has a negative meaning. In English to "neutralize" something often means to make it passive and passivity never happens in the process of resolving polar opposites. On the contrary, a person who has neutralized or integrated two polarities becomes able to express either one or the other at his own will in a given situation. The more adequate term to describe the process in English is **"integration"** and that is why I used it in this book. Sometimes I use the term "neutralization" as well. If I publish the new edition of my previous book, its title will be ***"PEAT and Integration of Primordial Polarities"***.

2

DUAL UNIVERSE: OUR FUNDAMENTAL PLAYGROUND

In more than 50 years of my studying and practicing many different systems, methods and techniques of Perennial Philosophy, I had a domineering impression – there exists one hidden goal which all these individual procedures lead to. A few years ago (I am writing this in 2005) I realized it was the gradual movement from the world of duality, separateness and opposites to the state of Oneness, unity and harmony. It was strange how much time I needed to understand that simple and evident truth, because the majority of valuable teachings and wise men constantly point to it in one way or other. At the same time blindness of such clear and evident truth is the explanation for why a huge majority of the human race lives their whole life in a state of separateness.

We also find similar situations in the sphere of the exact sciences. One of the avant-garde theoreticians of modern physics Dr Fred Alan Wolf writes about it: *"One of the hidden axioms of physics is that the foundation of everything is simplicity. Whatever the secrets of universal laws are waiting to be discovered, those secrets will be simple."*

The situation in science and Perennial Philosophy is a paradoxical one. First we see the complexity and try to explain the world with twisted and complex explanations. It is the long way around to simple laws presented with a couple of basic lettered symbols. Before that phase, for a long time, we had to remove thick layers of different contents in our own mind until finally, under the dense deposits of barren soil, shines the golden grain which we were searching for.

Until that happens, the dualistic universe is our predestined playground which we are playing our life games on, from year to year, from life to life. It fundamentally makes polarities, opposing forces of life inside us and in the universe outside of us and the latter are the reflections of states of our consciousness. To experience duality means to see and experience these opposing forces. In duality, we see the differences of life. In everyday life it enables us to analyse, describe, compare, and put in different categories, to set goals which differ from our present state, to experience success or failure.

From time immemorial wise men have taught us there exists the state of Oneness and the whole manifested universe longs for it, primarily human beings, whether they are conscious of it or not. In Oneness there is no comparison, there are no two things, states, phenomena or beings to compare, because there is nothing outside of it. To be in duality means to ask questions. To be in Oneness means to know the answer, which to all questions is the same. As Daniel C. Matt states in **"The Essential Kabbalah"** in his discussion of absolute undifferentiation: *"At the deepest levels of divinity, all opposites and distinctions vanish, overwhelmed by oneness."*

To be in Oneness does not mean to be in a neutral position, because neutrality is neither one nor another polarity. Oneness means that both polarities are inseparable united. As long as we are in a neutral position between two polarities we are not able to comprehend each one in another.

Some wise men said duality is necessary because it enables twice as many experiences, either in the outer or in the inner world. A well known Muslim mystic from the 13th century Jalaluddin Rumi says, speaking about the existence of pairs of polarities:

> *God turns you from one feeling to another*
> *And teaches you through opposites,*
> *Thus you have two wings to fly*
> *Not only one.*

But when two polar forces inside an individual are in strong conflict, they often make a neurotic structure. Then we define one component of such an experience as good, the other as bad, we identify with the good one and fight against the bad. The dualistic nature of this universe sets the stage for many splits in our mind, as well as for many neurosis which are the most frequent disturbances of our time. Dichotomies like I and Others, We and They, Good and Bad, Light and Darkness...constantly draw us into in one or the other side of such a split. To transcend such states of inner breaks, wise men, shamans and practitioners of Spiritual practice created and applied, since ancient times, techniques of uniting opposites into higher synthesises of wholeness.

Such practical knowledge does not come easily. Only through permanent use and application can practitioners advance on the Path of integration and self-relaization. Every moment is a test because dual forces tempt us permanently, trying to pull us into themseleves, into separation and suffering.

For our practical life this is important: In every pair of polarities that manifest inside us we estimate the dominate polarity as less valuable. The moment opposing forces enter reconciliation, when they unite into one, all conflicts, awkwardness and neurosis coming out of them vanish.

We feel this world from the stage of dualities, because we learned from early childhood to experience it that way. We have a strong tendency to experience some people as good or bad, some situation as favorable or unfavorable, a point of view as right or wrong, self and others as valuable or worthless. The world we live in is built on duality, as an arena of opposites inside, which most of us live our life through. In the universe of matter, energy, time and space (MEST) it is not possible to find one phenomenon or state, without their opposites being there. Light does not exist without darkness, warm without cold, good without the idea of bad, happines without suffering. The old proverb says that not one picture is painted just with light, there must be shadows on it as well.

In many situations it is important to know the difference between good and bad, but to live forever in a dualistic world is evidently a limited way of life. Such a life is inevitablely painful, filled with suffering and fears and most of the time there is the feeling of helplessness and uncontrol. We are thrown from one polarity to another, and their number is countless. We experience such happenings as the result of outer forces, unable to understand there being reflections of splits and duality in our mind. Elimination of duality, through transcendence, neutralization and integration of polar opposites, which happens in one moment of our Spiritual evolution, make them simultaneously vanish in the outer world as well.

Dualism in essence is the act of cutting human consciousness in two and from that cutting comes subject and object, one which sees and is seen, one who is getting the knowledge and knowledge itself. The line of cutting is actually splitting the outer and the inner world. At the basis of this splitting of human consciousness is the human Ego. Ego has got two main characteristics: It has an irresistible desire to exist and it creates the split between man and the rest of the world. It is the creator of the division of "I" and "Non-I". From this duality comes numberless others.

Judging from the historical point of view, in the mythologies of many people, primordial dualism is represented as the separation of heaven and earth, sun and moon, male and female, the cosmic principle. In epistemology (the study or a theory of the nature and grounds for knowledge) it is the separation of subject and object, an observer and the observed, knower and an object of knowledge. In ontology (a theory about the nature of being or the kinds of existence), dualism is presented as separation of "I" and "Non-I", "I" from other beings, in essence "I" from everything else. In religion we can see duality of creed and infidelity, grace of God and demonic seduction, God's omnipotence and human trifle. All our social values are experienced in pairs of opposites: success is opposite failure, strength and weakness, agressiveness and tolerance. Polarity is also evident in esthetics: beautiful and ugly, acceptable and unacceptable, decent and indecent, adequate and inadequate.

Because neither phenomenon, nor thing exist without it's own opposite, the world seems to us like an endless field of opposing forces, polarities and dualities. But in the womb of a mother and some time after birth, a child is in a state of wholeness or unity. In that state there is no difference between the being and its surrounding, because I and No-I do not exist. In time, out of the formless sea of Unity certain elements start to separate. In the beginning it is connected with the appearance and disappearance of mother. In synergy of internal urges and contacts with mother and other beings from the surroundinsg in that seamless field of consciousness, I is forming gradually and simultaneously No-I as well. Connected with such differentiation is the game of hide and seek which we can find in all nations, because in the small measure it is the game of loosing of Oneness and finding it again. Its beginning is the game of a mother hiding from her child and her sudden reappearing in its visual field: There is no mother...there is no...there is no...here is mother again!! The game begins that way and later on all children play hide and seek, illusory disappearance and finding the lost again.

Although the basic and the strongest polarities seem to be irreconcilable opposites, they are not. Polarity consists of a pair of opposite poles of One, they are two extremes of the same concept, which create and define each other. In this universe the existence of one polarity is impossible without its polar opposite. There is no advancing without retreating, weight without lightness and having without non-having. A man is able to appreciate a positive polarity in the measure in which he experienced the negative one and vice versa. This law has great importance for every kind of therapy and Spiritual development. It explains why pain, suffering, sickness and death must exist as long as there exist well being, joy, winning, health and living. For humans it is impossible to experience one polarity without experiencing the other, because they are One, experienced from different points of view. Therefore, the attempt to forever remove any kind of negativity is the sign of the absence of wisdom. Why it is impossible to attain the permanent domination of one polarity over the other, in spite of the efforts we are making during our entire life? **Because they are not separate opposites, but complementarities, two sides of the same.** Is it possible to increase one side of a coin so much that its other side completely vanishes? Of course, not!

Between two extremes, or polarities, there is the whole spectrum of shades in which two polarities is mixed more or less. Between light and dark there are many shades of light, between warm and cold all shades of temperature.

Both polarities and the shades between them is one and the same thing, separated in two directions by energy invested in them. Many people have difficulties, or it is completely impossible for them to understand polarities as two sides of one and the same thing or phenomenon. For some of them, the teachings of Perennial Philosophy and quantum physics could help in understanding this, i.e. the concept, All is One.

If a man does not understand the laws of the dual universe, he has the tendency to resist and confront negative polarities and the experiences which follow them. The resistance to any negative experience means we are trying to make it weaker, and such resistance just make it stronger and more persisting. *Resistance causes persistence!* The **resistance** is the investing of energy to prevent some manifestation, in other words, to stop it, change it or destroy it. When you invest energy to stop, change or destroy some manifestation, you invest energy in it, and therefore make it stronger and more real.

The teaching of polarity is spreading widely. It has also entered into the humour of intellectually oriented people. A joke which Hall Stone, well known creator of the Inner

Voice method, gives us shows this. He published it in an article **"Consciousness and Spirituality"**. In it, God says to Adam: *"I have got two wonderful gifts for you. You will be extremely happy to get them. However, there is a problem."* Adam, without thinking about the problem, asks God, what are those wonderful presents? And God tells him: *"One present is consciousness. With it you can think, choose in life and to live an ordered way of life under your control."* Impatiently Adam asks God at once, what is the other present? God tells him: *"The other present is a penis. With it you will have great joy and pleasure, for yourself and for others and you will be able to prolong the human species."* Adam is enthusiastic about this and says to God: *These presents are wonderful. I don't seem to see any problem."*

Then God told him: *"Here is the problem, Adam. From now until eternity of these two magnificent gifts you will only be able to use one at a time."*

It is the experiment God devised for us, said Stone. On one side we have the divine gift with all its beauty and high nature. On the other side we have the penis, the body, emotions, relationships, instinctive life and a very complex psychology. What a pair of polarities! We wrestle with these polarities for thousands of years. Stone adds:

> *"Our solution is mainly to label body, instincts and emotions as negative, and the God's side as positive. Thinking about God in such an archaic way, we become judgemental and all that does not come under the label "divine things" we judge as bad. Things connected with God are good. That split, that dichotomy, which tortured us for aeons, can not be solved that way any more. Their*

reconciliation must come from individuals being able to live their lives connecting these two realities."

This book is written, mainly as a practical manual for such people. Writing it, my goal was, as Moshe Feldenkrais nicely said, to make the impossible possible, to make the possible easy, and to make the easy elegant and very quick.

3

THE CONCEPT OF DUALITY IN EASTERN AND WESTERN THOUGHT

The history of human civilisation presents the permanent preoccupation with the concept of duality, positive and negative, active and passive and the always present good and bad. The way of understanding duality brought about a difference between Eastern and Western philosophy.

In Eastern philosophy all aspects of duality are understood as mutually complementary forms of expressing fundamental Oneness. They are complementary values supporting each other which cannot exist one without the other. The East teaches us that at the deepest level of truth everything is One, but the forms of its manifestation are different. Sri Aurobindo in his paper (**"Upanishads: Texts, Translations and Commentaries"**) piše sledeće: *"Brahman in his manifestation embraces both Vidiya and Avidiya. In Sanskrit vidia means* **Oneness**, *Avidia means* **multitude.** *If they are both present in manifested existence, the reason for this is necessity of both of them for the existence to be. Avidia exists because Vidia supports it and embrace it..."*

On that topic Lama Anagarika Govinda (Anagarika Govinda) wrote: *"The perfect mutual interpenetration of forms, processes, things, beings, etc., and the presence of the experiencing of subject in all of them - in other words, the simultaneity of differentiation and oneness, of individuality and universality, of form and emptiness - is the main thesis of the great Buddhist philosopher Nagarjuna, who lived in the second century. Where, however, everything is in flux...the relationship of form to emptiness and vice-versa cannot be conceived as a mutually exclusive nature or as absolute opposites, but only as two aspects of the same reality, co-existing in continuous co-operation. Because "form" (rupa) must not be confused with "thing-ness" or materiality, since each form is the expression of a creative actor or process in a beginning-less and endless movement, whose precondition, according to Nagarjuna, is precisely that mysterious "emptiness" (or "plenumvoid," as it has been aptly called) expressed in the term Sunyata."*

We would do injustice to ancient Greek philosophy if we omitted pointing out it's philosophers which felt the world was One. Heraclitus and Parmenides claimed that the universe is One and dynamic. Heraclitus believed that unity of all things is in their essential structure.

We would do injustice to philosophical thought of Ancient Greece if we do not point out to its philosopher which saw the world as One. Heraclitus taught that the universe is in a constant change. The change is the basic principle of existence and its main mechanism is the relationship of the water and fire polarity. These two elements represent all dualistic opposites in nature, starting from the most evident such as day and night, increasing and decreasing of the moon, ebb and flow of the tide and other less noticeable changes.

Parmenides taught his followers that One is endless and indivisible. It is not "...*unity of opposites, because opposites do not exist.*" He thought that "cold" means just "no warm" and darkness means "no light". But One can not be divided, because the whole is present everywhere.

Probably both of them exceeds Pitagora, one of the greatest mystical philosophers and a matematician. His whole cosmogony is based on the relationship between Oneness and duality. One exceeds all dualities, uniting opposites. Uniting them yields Oneness. Outside of Unity, there is Multitude, and the whole cosmos is built on their relationship.

The dualistic teachings of the dominant majority made for the basis of one of the essential characteristic of contemporary Western society – seeing all spheres of thought, belief or activity in the dualistic way, either positive or negative. We see individual experiences and social happenings through interactions, competitions and conflicts. It happens mainly by directing our attention to one pole of duality and at the same time we ignore the other, or treat it with hostility, or we integrate duality into some structure which bypasses the conflicting situations.

Western society is built upon the basis of dualism, on irreconcilable confronted polarities. Between the good, which we should aspire at any cost and bad, which we should avoid uncompromisingly, there is an insurmountable gap. It expresses itself in the philosophical understanding of life, in the moral orientation of Christianity and, until recent times, in science.

In Christian teachings, the problem of opposites starts with the appearance of man on the world stage, when God created him. It is interesting that there are two different things about genesis. Let us see the first one: *"And God said, Let us make man in Our image, after Our likeness: and let them have dominion over the fish of the sea, and over the fowl of the air, and over the cattle, and over all the earth, and over every creeping thing that creeps upon the earth. So God created man in His own image, in the image of God created He him; male and female created He them."*

In the second story it is said: *"And The Lord God formed man of the dust of the ground, and breathed into his nostrils the breath of life; and man became a living soul."* Based on these two stories the duality of the human nature is evident, because the man is the field of war between his divine nature, the copy of God, and *his* inferior substance, dust, which he is made of.

In the chronology of Christian teaching, duality is even more emphasized with the coming onto the stage of the first human beings, Adam and Eve. They live innocently and happily in the Garden of Eden. Their God let them do whatever they want, except one: They were not allowed to eat the fruit from the tree of the knowledge of good and evil. In that innocent world suddenly the serpent appears. It is evidently evil and it tempts Eve, stirring her desire for the power and the knowledge. It said to Eve – if you try that fruit you will be equal to God. The question comes to mind – who created that evil serpent? It is clear God did it, because He is the only creator. Eve leads Adam astray and they eat the fruit from the tree of the knowledge of good and evil. In that moment they find out what is good and evil and in Adam a fear appears for the first time and shame as well.

The Bible story of the genesis of the world and man, points out the braking down of the first Unity. With everything existing in the moment, the appearance in Adam's consciousness of good and bad (see later on my method **"Ivana End of Words"**) was the first duality, that consciousness splits man's Oneness into two seemingly inimical opposites. It causes the feeling of guilt and fear in him, and causes the Human Being to be thrown out of the state of Oneness and since that time man suffers in the dualistic world of opposites. Nevertheless, simultaneously human autonomy appears and man gradually gets control over his world. In other words in a small measure man takes over the role of God. We can read in the Bible: *"And the LORD God said, Behold, the man is become as one of us, to know good and evil: and now, lest he put forth his hand, and take also of the tree of life, and eat, and live forever. 23: Therefore the LORD God sent him forth from the garden of Eden, to till the ground from whence he was taken."*

The rest of Christian teachings show the effort to eliminate the problem of good and evil forever, which means the problem of the polarity of human nature, is an impossible. In the Bible story of Noah's Ark the good beings should survive separated from bad ones, which should die. But even after the deluge man is the same, torn apart with opposite forces inside himself, the good and evil still exist in him at the same time. How to come back to the state of All-Unity? That process does not evolve in Eden, but on the lower level of consciousness, in the world of opposites. Throughout the development of the human race some wise men have appeared who taught such possibilities and point out different ways of accomplishing that goal: reconciliation, neutralization, integration of opposites in the human being, the realization of his totality.

Christian teaching has great power, because during the last 2,000 years it has penetrated Western philosophical thought as well as Western science, though the dualistic teachings of ancient Greece existed before it. Until recently the dualistic point of view was dominant in this part of the world. A crack in such a vision of the world appeared in modern physics in 1925. Before that time Western science presented the universe as a material creation consisting of smaller and smaller particles of matter. At the other side, energy was considered to consist of energetic fields or waves. The dualistically oriented logic of the West stressed the mutually exclusive nature of these two states of existence – matter and energy. Then the discovery was revealed of matter and energy being two manifestations of the same.

In that year (1925) there was a surprising scientific discovery, which is even today is widely unknown to masses of people. That discovery, Quantum Physics, points out that the smallest material particles are not material at all; they are just forms or manifestation of energy. They simultaneously appear as waves and particles as well. This opinion, substantially the same as Oriental philosophy, pointed to the Oneness of basic polarities the substance of the material universe and caused far reaching changes not only in science but in the understanding of the world in the Western civilisation. The father of quantum mechanics Erwin Schrödinger wrote: *"Subject and object are one. We can not say that the barrier between them was broken down as the result of recent discoveries in physics, because that barrier actually never existed."*

In the first half of the 20th century interest in studying polarities and opposites moved from philosophy to psychology. Noticing the tendency of the human mind to think in terms **either/or,** psychologists started developing theories and systems of therapy which directed the individual to embrace aspects of their psyche which were ignored and suppressed.

Sigmund Freud with his psychoanalytical theory was the first to embrace consciousness and unconsciousness, socially acceptable feelings and at the same time aggressive, impulsive and destructive impulses.

K.G. Jung continued where Freud stopped. Self, he said, realized through the process of individuation, means merging and uniting of contradictory values and states. Leaning on the teachings which, in the history of Western thought, were suppressed and rejected, as Gnosticism, Kabbalah and alchemy, and crossbreeding them fruitfully with Hinduism, Taoism and esoteric Christianity, Jung created the vision of humanity in which depolarization of individual and collective consciousness will be realized.

It could be said that the key element of Jung's teaching is uniting of opposites. In his interpretation, 'Self' unites in itself conscious and unconscious, personal and impersonal, individual and cosmic and all important archetypes, as animus and anima are, persona and shadow. He often pointed out that 'Self' manifests in opposites and conflicts which exist between them, but also in their merging into Oneness: *"Nothing can exist without its opposites. In the beginning two were one, and again they will be one at the end."* The level of individual development, and the development of the whole society, said Jung, is the capacity to recognize polarities and to merge them. Hegel (George Friedrich Hegel) was mistaken, Jung said, thinking that those processes take place on the intellectual level. These are insights happening inside human psyche: *"Unity of opposites on the higher level of consciousness is not a rational process, neither it is a matter of human will; it is the process of psychic development expressing itself through symbols."* Unity of opposites is the symbolic and psychological truth which should be experienced, not only speculated about: *"The perfectly wise man sets himself free from opposites, seeing the connection existing between them."*

4

THE PATH TO ONENESS

The ego is the center of our dualistic experience of the world. It is our instrument to survive in every day life. It compares things, events and situations telling us what is good for us or warning us to avoid danger situations when they occur. In short, it helps us to survive in an optimal way.

At the same time, having a feeling of I, feeling strongly separated from the rest of the world as a polarized I, Ego is the basic source of our emotional and spiritual problems. The consequence of this fact is that Ego is the bases for a polarized being to have a dualistic experience of the world.

For many people is very difficult to accept that different manifestations of good and evil are two complementary sides of the very same thing. For clarities sake, I shall repeat what has already been said, since it seems there can never be enough repetition of these things because human consciousness, which is strongly polarized from childhood, resists evidence about the truth of Oneness. That is why in life, as well as in religious presentations of salvation, there is a permanent effort to eliminate one of the polarized opposites that exist in pairs. Religion tries to solve the polarity of good and evil by conquering evil once and forever.

In everyday life people try to solve the polarity of wealth and poverty investing all their efforts toward eternal wealth. In philosophy, materialism has been trying to present that the primary principle of the world is matter and other idealistic philosophy systems try to present spirit, or ideas as the primary principles of the world. It is very evident that there are many manipulations with opposites as if the difference between them was real and changeless.

As Ken Wilber says, many people believe life would be wonderful if we could delete all negative and non-wished polarities from our existence, keeping only positive ones. In science, medicine and human relationships, it is generally accepted today that progress means approaching positive polarities by leaving negatives. But as he says: *"...in spite of the evident advantages that agriculture and medicine show today, there is not the slightest proof that, after so many centuries of forcing positives by eliminating negatives, mankind is happier and has found inner peace. In fact, all evidence demonstrates that today's situation shows the opposite results. Our time is full of fear about the future, frustrations and isolations, boring and senselessness in spite of all that wealth."*

In an attempt to eliminate all that is negative we forget that positive could only be defined in relation to negative. The idea about polarities evidently points to the fact that these are descriptions of the same thing, seen from different points of view.

By destroying negative we destroy every possibility to experience positive. That is why we have a tendency to live with polarities like irreconcilable opposites, completely separated so that the presence of negative could only mean complete exclusion of the existence of positive. But, this is not the truth and wise people have been trying to teach us that for centuries.

There is a certain difference between giving and receiving, but they are irreconcilable, because in order for someone to receive there must be someone who gives. They are, therefore, like all others polarities, complementary aspects of the same reality.

We shall view, in short, different philosophy systems and personal teachings that have pointed out the true understanding of universal duality. Then, we shall demonstrate how we can overcome them.

There are different names for the experience where polarities are merged or when duality becomes Oneness. Some call it polarity neutralization, or integration of polarities, or Janus's experience, trans-dual experience. They all show the same things - that opposite polarities appear from the common oneness.

Saints, mystics, spiritual teachers and unique individuals in all spiritual traditions and societies have had the same experience. Those experiences were expressed by different terminology depending on cultural, religious and lately even scientific situations. But what is common to all these approaches is the consciousness that the integration of opposites makes unity, not a negation of any of them.

It is evident that absence of stimulus intensifies its existence; without pauses between tones there wouldn't be rhythm in music; without them musical tones would be just noise. In The Far East, that which is not said or done is equally important as that which is said or done. In music, poetry, painting, architecture or everyday talking we intensify details by contrasts. Classical painting insists that figures come from a dark background like from deep water; dark interiors of cathedrals intensify light impression and the feeling that this place is different from other places.

There is probably, no other philosophy like Taoism that expresses so clear the idea that the universe is based on the harmony and complementarities of polarities. Primordial polarities of Yin and Yang are inherent in everything around us: there is a masculine principle, which is the source of light, motion and energy and a feminine principle supporting Yin energy. Dynamic synergism of these two complementary opposite principles is well presented in the popular symbol of Tai-Chi-Tu, which is a Mandala of Yang and Yin. Dark feminine half of Mandala is like a big tadpole with a white point within, and white masculine half of Mandala is with a dark point within, which demonstrates that each of them have a seed of the other.

Taoists emphasize that all the opposites of the universe are polar complementarities in which each polarity is dynamically connected with another. Only together do they represent unity. Harmony, integration or neutralization is possible only through the connection and unity of both poles of existence. The Chinese culture doesn't give moral importance to Yang and Yin. Neither Yang nor Yin represents "good", but dynamic harmony between them does; where as disharmony between them represents Evil. They only seem to be opposites of each other. In fact they are two poles of the same unity. There is no separation between them; they are harmonized making unity pervading each other. The No-Being is pervaded with Being without any resistance, desire or refusing.

To be in Tao means to be non-reacting "I", with my permanently conscious self within the reactive mass. When I penetrate into the void with all essentiality, extending through everything that exists, it merges with existence, like color put into a pot with water coloring all the water in it.

It has already been said, in my books **"Sunyata"** and **"PEAT",** that in the 20th century many prominent physicists noticed a big similarity between the old eastern philosophy tradition and modern Physics. Talking about the symbolism of Yang and Yin, it is interesting what Danish physician Niels Bohr says about them. When in 1947 he was proclaimed as a knight for his extraordinary contribution to science, as a motif for his solemn close he chose a symbol of Yang and Yin commenting: "Contraria sunt complementa" meaning "Opposites are complementary".

Oneness and Opposites in Alchemy

The so called Emerald Table (Tabula Smaragdina) is the mysterious manuscript that influences generations of alchemists and occultists. It was ascribed to Hermes Trimegistous (Three Times Great Hermes) until 1614, when Isaac Casaubon discovered that it was created by a group of authors in the second or third century BC.

There are three motifs emphasized by mystics in Tabula Smaragdina: The idea of Oneness or Unity, the idea of separation or duality and the idea implicit in unity of opposites making alchemical connection or unity.

As alchemical scripts permanently emphasize Unity, it is logical to conclude that it is one of the most important ideas or concepts of alchemy. Some other mystics that were not alchemists also talk about this idea calling it by different names. Paul Tillich calls it **the fundament of a being,** Mirca Eliade calls it **a sacred centre** and for mathematician/philosopher A. N. Whitehead it is the **ontology principle**. This unity is the base of everything, making limitless potential from which comes everything else that belongs to nature and experience. In "Tabula Smaragdina" there are words that describe it well: *"All things come from one…"*

Leonardo da Vinci on Neutralization of Polarities

Between many sources in my research I have recently found a very informative book: "Da Vinci Decoded" by Michael J. Gelb. In this book he reveals spiritual secrets from Leonardo's Seven Principles. He has published two other books: "How to Think Like Leonardo da Vinci Workbook" and the companion volume two "How to Think Like Leonardo da Vinci".

Gelb studied da Vinci's methods of thinking, his problems solving and researches. In his last book, as the fifth Leonardo's principle of spiritual growth, he discovered neutralization of polarities or integration of opposites. As the most important he emphasizes a neutralization of male-female principles.

In his dairies Leonardo points out that we all come from pure potential, from Eden's Garden, bringing with us from birth both principles, masculine and feminine. Only by harmonizing these two energies can we return into The Garden of Eden from which we have been expelled. This truth has been known in many ancient traditions like Yoga, Taoism and recently Jungian psychotherapy. Gelb shows that Leonardo's masterpiece, Mona Lisa's Portrait, is a visual and artistic presentation of matrimony between feminine – masculine principle within enlightened being. There have been many discussions between art theorists about the symbolism of the Mona Lisa Portrait and a significant number of them think that this portrait is Leonardo's self-portrait. It is well known that many of Leonardo's figures on his paintings are bisexual or androgynous, presenting the harmony or unity of opposites or polarities within the human being.

Michael J. Gelb quotes well known authorities who have been able to see the same thing. One of them is Lori Dechar, a well known professor of Oriental healing in New York: *"Leonardo was a Taoist. Through Mona Lisa's smile and androgyny of many of his figures on his paintings, he reminds us that the inner matrimony of masculine and feminine energies, the balance of Yin and Yang, can deliver infinite worlds of spirit and rediscovery of paradise on earth"*.

Evidently, Oneness is an ever present goal of all mystical traditions. But there is also a place for humor. Among the many facets, social styles, and traditions within the general Zen practice, one characteristic that is most intriguing and unique is its relationship to humor. Zen distinguishes itself from the many religions of the world by being able to laugh at almost everything, including its most precious values. Among the many facets, social styles, and traditions within the general Zen practice, humor stands high. So, there is a question: How many Zen Buddhists does it take to change a light bulb? Answer: None, they are one with a light bulb.

Good in Evil and Evil in Good

There is an educative Taoist story about good and evil as inseparable parts of life. The only wealth a Chinese farmer had was one mare. Once the mare ran away and his neighbors said*." What a terrible thing that your mare ran away."* And the farmer answered: *"I don't know if it is bad or good. That's life".*

His mare turned up the next day bringing a whole herd of wild horses. The farmer's neighbors came and said: *"What luck. Your mare brought you so many horses. Now you are rich."* And the farmer said: *"It is difficult to say if it is good or bad. That's life."*

The farmer's son wanted to train horses so he rode one. But the horse threw him. He broke his leg and became lame. Their neighbors said: *"It is terrible what happened to you, your son has become lame."* But the farmer said: *"It's neither good, nor bad. That's life."*

Soon after that a war started and all the other sons from the village were taken to the army except the farmer's lame son. Then neighbors said: *"Maybe we shall never see our sons again. But you are a lucky man; your son was not taken away."* The farmer said again: *"I don't know if it is good or bad. That's life."*

The story continues the same way always with new events from life, always finishing the same way. Do you know how? A wise farmer always says: *"I don't know if it is bad or good. That's life."*

5

Symbols

Unity of opposites frequently appears throughout all religious symbols. All such symbols, seemingly opposite, are combined in a dynamic whole – from one come two and after some time from two comes One. It is an eternal game of creation, expressed through all human beings. It is the main message of all religions, if we are able to read their symbols. What follows here are the most frequently met symbols of Unity and duality.

The star and the crescent in Islam symbolize the unity of solar and lunar energies.

The Cross is probably the oldest symbol in the world. Centuries before the Christian era ancient crosses were in use as a symbol among the Chaldeans, Phoenicians, and Aztecs. The ancient Greeks, the Babylonians, the East Indians, and the Egyptians used it. In Christianity the cross is the symbol of Unity and oneness of Spirit and Matter.

Ankh is an ancient Egyptian tau-cross with a circle on the top. In teachings on polarities it is called Nem Ankh as well, which means "the key of life". The circle at the top of the cross represents the macrocosmos (the sun and the heaven) and at the same time it is similar to a man (microcosmos). As a symbol, ank expresses the neutralization of opposites or integration of active and passive characteristics. In the horizontal position it represents male and female sexual characteristics, but some people interpret it as a symbol of eons which are going to come. As I said before, the circle being the symbol without the beginning and the end represents the eternal soul. For many initiates ankh also represents the key to hidden mysteries. One possessing it is able to understand the hidden knowledge of eternal life and to penetrate to the kingdom of the dead.

Circle (or Ring) is an ancient and universal symbol of unity, wholeness, infinity, the goddess, and female power. To earth-centered religions throughout history as well as to many contemporary pagans, it represents the feminine spirit or force, the cosmos or a spiritualized Mother Earth, and a sacred space. Gnostic traditions linked the unbroken circle to the world serpent forming a circle as it eats its own tail.

Circle with a dot in the middle represents unity of male and female energies, because dot represents the male force. Together, the circle and the dot symbolize the merging of male and female forces.

Compass and T-square: The compass represents spirit. The ruler (part of a square) represents the physical level of existence. Together they represent movement toward perfection and a balance between the spiritual and physical worlds.

Caduceus was an old Hindu symbol. Latter on it became the symbol of medicine. In Hinduism it represents the juncture of Ida and Pingala (for more information on Ida and Pingala see other parts of this book). They are wrapped around the fire energy of Susumna, which flows through the middle canal of the spine and represents their integration. In the West, Caduceus is the sceptre of Hermes, the god of alchemy. In Western tradition it is presented with a golden stick surrounded with two serpents, which represent two opposite principles, which must be integrated, such as sulphur and quicksilver, warm and humid, spirit and matter. They neutralize each other in the integrative gold of the stick. Lately, Caduceus stands for the basic dualism of existence which must be integrated in unity of the stone of wisdom or Elixir of Life. Therefore Caduceus is the symbol of balance attained by uniting of opposite forces. Symbolically they can represent the inner conflict of biological or moral forces.

The **Labyrinth** is an ancient Celtic symbol of wholeness. It represents a pattern of initiation into the Celtic sacred mysteries and the path to the deepest core of Being, the sacred place of renewal and self-transformation. It combines the imagery of the circle and the spiral into a meandering but purposeful path. The Labyrinth is a journey to our own center and back again out into the world. It has long been used as meditation and prayer tools.

A labyrinth differs from other symbols because it is an archetype with which we can have a direct experience. We can walk through it, thus it is a metaphor for life's journey. It is a symbol that creates a sacred space and takes us out of our ego to our True Being. A labyrinth has only one path. With a labyrinth there is only one choice to be made. The way in is the way out. The choice is to enter or not. The choice is whether or not to walk a spiritual path.

A labyrinth is evidently a right brain task (see "Two Brain Hemispheres"). It involves intuition, creativity, and imagery. A more passive, receptive mindset is needed. At its deepest level the labyrinth is a metaphor for the journey to the center of your True self and back out into the world with a broadened understanding of who you are.

Hexagram: In Judaism, the Hexagram or the Star of David with interlaced triangles, one points upwards and the other points downwards, symbolises Oneness of laws of earth and heaven, of material and Spiritual world. Dr Cathy Burns writes: *"The Hexagram is formed by uniting the Water Triangle with the Fire Triangle, which is the Six-pointed Star, Star of David, Solomon's Seal, etc. When the two triangles (the 'Water Triangle' and the 'Fire Triangle') are joined together into one symbol, it forms a six pointed star known as a double triangle, hexagram, Crest of Solomon, star of the microcosm and the Shield of David, among other names."*

Uniting of water and fire, or male and female energies in this universe is one of the greatest secrets. When they unite on the physical plane of existence, their unity is steam, which is the symbol of uniting principle, because it goes upwards and disappears into nothingness. On the mental plane it is the meditation which brings us to the transcendence.

The Wheel is a universal symbol of our cosmic unity, astrology and Spiritual evolution. The pagan sacred circle plus any number of radiating spokes form the wheel - a Wheel of Life in India and Medicine wheel to American Indians. It symbolizes unity, movement, the sun, the zodiac and reincarnation.

The Winged Globe is an ancient Egyptian symbol of unity but it is found in the religions of other races. It represents the relation existing between Spirit, soul, and body. Soul gives wings to body. Spirit is the enveloping principle, like the atmosphere in which both soul and body exist, and from which they draw their original inspiration.

The Serpent, with his tail in his mouth, is as significant as it is forbidding. It indicates the conjunction of male and female, also the ring or unit; it was at the same time a sign of eternity.

Pyramid: There are countless interpretations of this old symbol. One of the best was given by Bulgarian mystic Mikael Aivanhov (Omram Mikhael Aivanhov): *"The pyramid is a symbol of the hierarchical structure of the universe; a symbol that teaches us, in every area of life, to rise above the plane on which we find only multiplicity and dissemination to the higher plane of unity. For it is thanks to this progressively simpler and more lucid point of view that we shall be able to grasp the true reality of things and find the best solutions to our problems.*

"If you want to learn to find your bearings and act with determination, you must not tolerate any inner states of division in which two contradictory thoughts or desires occur simultaneously. You must work to create unity, and you will only achieve this if you unite yourself with God, with the divine centre within you. Unity exists when all parts cooperate for the smooth running of a whole or, symbolically when all points on the periphery converge towards the centre. Only then is it possible to act effectively. Observe life around you, and you will see that divisions dislocate and destroy, whereas unity builds and strengthens. Whether it is a matter of atoms or of human beings, everything must converge towards a single centre."

The etymological meaning of the pyramid is very interesting. That word consists of two words from the old Greek language: "Pyros" which means fire, and *"amid"* which means *"in the middle"*. So the full meaning is *"the fire in the middle"*.

Unicorn: We meet the unicorn as a symbol in many legends, myths and fairy tales. In one of the oldest legends it is said: *"There lived a fierce, horse-like beast that roamed the earth. Its savage spirit could only be tamed by the touch of a virgin (this is evidently integration of two opposite forces). In such integration the beast is transformed into a noble white steed marked by a singular horn at its head. In its spiritual ascent, a pair of wings appears to free the Unicorn from its earthly bondage forever".*

In different traditions the unicorn has multiple symbolic meaning. In ancient China it was the symbol for royal attributes, in Europe the symbol of divine declaration and later on, for psychoanalysis the symbol of phallic power. But mainly it was the symbol of surpassing the dual nature of a man.

Vesica Pisces: Vesica Pisces means "fish bladder" in Latin. The symbol appears frequently in medieval art and architecture, but its roots go back further still. It is made by linking two circles together, bringing the outside edge of each to the midway point of the other.

When the Vesica Pisces is displayed vertically, there appears the shape of a fish. Early Christians adopted the fish symbol as their own, and used it as sort of secret code to identify themselves to one another and avoid persecution. This symbol has been much used in art and architecture as a frame for Jesus and the saints, or as the passage between heaven and earth through which Jesus went to heaven.

When the Vesica Pisces is viewed horizontally, however, the Mandala becomes the symbol of the Divine Feminine, and in this context the Vesica Pisces is the vulva of the Goddess. Almonds are a primeval fertility symbol, but in the Middle

Ages, Christ as a child is often shown inside a Mandala, superimposed over Mary's womb.

Gregg Braden writes in "Awakening to Zero Point" (Bellevue, WA, 1977): *"The figure illustrates the act of projecting the known into unknown from the vantage point of the edge of the sphere. As the two perfect spheres are formed in close proximity (each contains half the diameter of the other) a zone of commonality is created in the overlap. The form of the vesica was used as both the Egyptian Glyph for the "mouth", as well as the Creator. Additionally this glyph is also very similar to the Mason glyph for zero, associated with our galaxy of the Milky Way."*

Vesica Pisces is also called The Eye of God. One out of many interpretations is that two circles represent heaven and earth, or spirit and matter and they are united in Christ which is the intermediary of two worlds. For us it is most important that Vesica Pisces is the simultaneous symbol of duality and unity.

J. Johnson points to the appearing of the Mandala symbol in a well structured sentence. That is the reason why a man burdened with many problems has a need to speak more then usual and the speech has a healing function. Well articulated speech takes in oneness in a fragmented world. Johnson says that to make any well articulated sentence means to create oneness. When we are under stress, speech used in the proper way is a healing process. Also, he says, all instructive stories are Mandalas. As we are telling them a merging of polarities happens and at the end they are the same. Using such and similar ideas as a guiding thought, I recently created (and describe it for the first time in this book) a method called **Verbal Reduction and Expansion** (see later on).

Spiral has a number of remarkable properties. Spirals are a dynamic expression of natural and cosmic forces, a dominant universal fractal evident in everything from the form of seashells, whirlpool movements inside atoms, embryos, and our DNA code to the spiralling galaxies that inhabit the universe. The spiral is a timeless glyph of nature's design alphabet. The spiral is the symbol of fundamental movements in the cosmos. It both comes from and returns to source. It is a continuum whose ends are opposite and yet the same. And it demonstrates the cycles of change within the continuum and the alternation of polarities within each cycle. It embodies the principles of expansion and contraction, through changes in velocity, and the potential for simultaneous movement in either direction towards its two extremities. On the spherical vortex these extremities, the centre and periphery, flow into each other; essentially, they are interchangeable. Spiral Dynamics posits that the evolution of human consciousness can best be represented in this way: by a dynamic, upward spiralling structure that charts our evolving thinking systems as they arc higher and higher through levels of increasing complexity. Perhaps the greatest message of the spiral in nature is that it arises out of the reconciliation of opposites.

Chandra Mandala is full moon, without moon spots. It is a symbol of spiritual purity. Chandra Mandala is the passage to Freedom, because it declares the aspirant is almost finished with the process of removing veils of ignorance and clearing his mind of spiritual dirt. When this happens, the usual human tendency to classify everything in pairs of opposites vanishes and we become completely conscious of the unbroken Oneness of true reality.

Sadha Shiva is the eastern symbol representing freedom of consciousness from polarities. It has a form of androgyny, half man and half woman. It sets on a white bull and has five heads, representing five senses and five elements, cleared and united in Oneness. That way this symbol gives us the vision of an aspirant which has finally found his/her center and who understands human existence in totality.

Astrological symbols: The majority of astrological signs have a double nature. It comes from the original Oneness, but points to polarities and dualities in the manifest world: Two horns of Aries and Taurus, double nature of twins, double pincers of a cancer, two pans of a scale, two parallel lines of Aquarius, two fish swimming in opposite directions, centaur of Sagittarius which is half man and half horse etc. All these symbols of duality grow out of the deepest Oneness.

Quetzalcoatl is a feathered serpent, ancient deity and legendary ruler of the Toltec in Mexico. The name is also that of a Toltec ruler, who is credited with the discovery of corn, the arts, science, and the calendar, so he is the god of civilization. His nature – feathered serpent points to his double nature united in one. Today we have Freud's and Jung's stressing of the double nature of a man, but less known is the knowledge of the dual nature of human consciousness in the ancient civilization of the Toltec during the Middle Ages in Mexico. The dominant symbol of Toltec was Quetzalcoatl or feathered serpent. It was a symbolic notion of the dual nature of reality and human consciousness. Merging of two opposites, an eagle and a serpent, a being which flies and a being which crawls was the symbolic presentation of human evolution, individual and social. Through the symbol of Quetzalcoatl, Toltec pointed to fundamental human need, transcendence of the separation of the individual and the rest of the world.

Yang / Yin: The Tai Chi symbol, Yin and Yang, is the sacred symbol of Taoism and is used extensively in philosophy and in martial arts. Yin represents eternity, dark, feminine, left side of the body, etc. Yang is it's opposite and represents history, light, masculine, right side of the body.

The cyclical and alternative nature of Yang and Yin, two fundamental polarities of the universe, mean many things. In a cyclic change all existing phenomena and states transform into their own opposites. Because one fundamental polarity creates another, complementary one, all phenomena have inside themselves the sprout of the opposite states. For example, expansion has in itself the inception of shrinking; advancing has in itself the beginning of retreating etc.

When the opposite state or phenomenon seems to be absent or nonexisting, such an impression is wrong, because one polarity actively creates another, because in their essence they are One. Neither a phenomenon or a state can be deprived of it's opposite polarity. Some people call this **presence in absence.**

Ideas which originate from higher levels of consciousness are Yang, and material shapes and manifestations which come from them are Yin. Yang begins every entity, and Yin complete it. One of them can not exist without other. Yang and Yin illustrate the dynamics of opposites and complementarity. They are two extreme poles which are expressed in all polarities: good and bad, male and female, I and non-I and similar polarities. One polarity does not operate visible at the same time as the other. When one dominates the other retreats into a potential state. In time its potential grows until it comes to the critical point when it transforms into an actual manifestation, and the second one starts to retreat. The image of a seesaw illustrates them well: As one polarity grows and grows in strength the other goes down and vanishes from the visual field, then the opposite process starts...and so on into eternity.

Yang and Yin are the fundamentals of duality for the whole universe, but it would be wrong to take them as good opposite of bad, especially because one holds the other in itself, as a part of its inner essential nature. This transformation of one into another is cyclical and incessant, so its impossible for one of them to dominate permanently with the other. Every strain to attain such domination is doomed to failure. Because between them tension exists, but they also balance each other as complementary parts of the whole. They penetrate each other and exist inside each other.

Even though they are complementary polarities, they point to Oneness which is in the basis of the world, because they are inseparable connected and mutually conditioned. Knowing their fundamental Oneness, we can understand them simply as phases in the eternal cyclic process. In that process each of them is bound to another and transforms into another during its own development.

Hermaphrodite or androgyne: For the great ancient Greek philosopher Pythagoras the universal hermaphrodite or divine androgyne is the symbol of Primordial Oneness. From his time to now androgynous is used in western mysticism and alchemy as one of the fundamental symbols of integrated polarities. But it is also present in Eastern mystical tradition.

The majority of Eastern philosophical systems see the Highest Consciousness as bisexsual. In China, it reflects simultaneous existence of basic polarities of light and darkness, two aspects of one and the same reality which is alternatively visible and invisible.

We can find the same idea in the gnostic texts. In cosmogonies of different traditions androgyne, as undivided Oneness, is present. The genesis of the world, and humanity later on, is only possible when that ornifinal Oneness divides into separate, opposite parts. That process of separation happens in the middle phase, and at the end, as well as in the beggining, there is inseparable Oneness, when all opposites are reconciled and merged.

Mircea Eliade, an eminent researcher of mysticism, takes it as a symbol of neutralization of two fundamental principles of the cosmos – male and female in divine unity. He points out the existence of this symbol in old Egyptian, Chinese and Indian religions and in European alchemy.

At the beginning, opposites are just potentials for manifestation and at the end they attain final reconciliation and integration. In the eschatological vision of final salvation the individual is integrated into the whole in which polar differences do not exist. Such outcome in alchemy is called "mystical wedding". God must be free of polarity, because He is self-sufficient, coming from Himself as the only source. Tending toward perfection as the highest goal, man will attain an androgynous state in the future, because his perfection could be made only in the image of God.

In everyday language Hermaphrodite or androgyny means bipolar being, union of man and woman. The term *"androgyny"* comes from Greek *"andros"* – man and *"gine"*- woman, and *"hermaphrodite"* is the blending of names of Greek gods Hermes and Aphrodite. Historically taken androgyny is the union of all attributes, not only sexual, in divine unity or the "cosmic man", either such being existed in time immemorial or will as such time in the future. It was usually presented with two faces, or with a body with two heads. Shortly, androgyny contains two basic principle of life and points out to a bipolar state of being.

Androgyny represents, at the same time, both united aspects of the being. Either the opposites are merged within the potential state of the not yet manifested being or the manifested being has realized their re-integration and rejoined the primeval Unit.

Originally, the "Being" stood beyond the opposites merged into the Unity. Established above polarities, it was neither masculine nor feminine and evidently has nothing of the physical features of the hermaphrodite. In reality, he was standing outside of this physical universe, at the spiritual level of Oneness. Splitting of the "Being" symbolizes the polarization of the primeval Unit, at the beginning of the manifestation of any thing or appearance. We should notice that in the Bible the original Adam was an androgyny who only became male when he gave birth to Eve, from a part of his body.

The Greek philosopher Plato, in his text *"Symposium"* told us that in the ancient time there were only androgynies, consisting of two connected beings of opposite sexes. Because they boasted with their double nature, they provoked the gods and Zeus punished them and split them in two. So human beings came into existence and love is just the eternal striving for attaining past wholeness. From then on man and woman look for each other and feel nostalgia for their complete nature. Unity, which man and woman attain in sexual relationship, is a reflection of attainment of that lost Oneness.

Fascination with androgen does not belong only to ancient times. Many modern thinkers recognize the need of integrating all polarities inside us, which will make us a kind of evolved androgyny. For example, a modern philosopher and the father of surrealism Andre Breton writes in his book "On Surrealism in its Living Works" (1953): *"It is of essential importance to ...make the reconstruction of primordial Androgen inside of us ...which all traditions speak about."*

6

Systems, Methods and Techniques

All religions and most of the systems of psychological, emotional and Spiritual development tend toward Oneness, unity or wholeness as the highest goal. Such Oneness means the integration of all elements and components of a Being, which by previous development and through many traumatic experiences was split, divided and fragmented. Oneness has the attributes of harmony and perfect balance. The Spiritual Technology which I created is an assembly of systems, methods and procedures which has such a goal. Contrary to Oneness, everyday reality is experienced as a field of opposite dualities, conflicts and imbalances.

Though Spirituality is mainly understood as Oneness and wholeness, people often do not understand that in its manifestation Oneness is a developing and dynamic phenomenon. When Oneness manifests, that manifestation happens through different phases, aspects, opposites, paradoxes, conflicts and their solutions. Everything is in permanent change and Spirituality is no exception. It is not a static synthesis, a state once attained, unchangeable for ever, but the process in which different forces confront each other inside a person, pushing and pulling in different directions and transforming into new forms. Transformation, says Lama Anagarika Govinda, contains inside itself, change and stability, multitude and singularity, movement and stability. By its own nature, it connects polar opposites and unites them in the all-embracing rhythm.

We will take a look at how different systems achieve that goal and after that I will describe my systems and how they are designed to achieve this goal. I will give an overview of my previous systems and I will explain extensively those systems and methods which I will be describing for first time in this book.

Tantra and Hatha Yoga

Tantra is an ancient spiritual discipline that calls on us to embrace all aspects of our being - including personality, emotions and physical drives - in the process of achieving spiritual transformation. Rather than withdrawing from the workaday world rejecting the physical and emotional sides of human nature, Tantra seeks to recognize the positive aspects of physical reality. By incorporating all of our being in the spiritual endeavour, we achieve integration, fulfilment, and eventual liberation. Although the philosophy is expressed in sacred writings known collectively as *Tantras*, Tantra itself focuses primarily on personal experimentation and experience. According to Yogini Padma Ushas Suryananda, *"The Tantras and their teachers do not say 'withdraw from the world. The flesh is evil. All is Maya [illusion]. Rather, they tell the practitioner to seek with a sincere and pure heart for Liberation, enjoy the pleasures of the world you live in, always keeping the spiritual intent alive, and you will come to live in the Oneness of Pure Being.'"*

Tantra acknowledges that the world (as well as the individuals who inhabit it) is made up of polarities and opposites: male and female, soft and hard, negative and positive, static and dynamic. The relationship and interplay between the polarities is the source of both suffering and change. By seeking to explore, understand and integrate these polarities, we are able to reach a state of spiritual transcendence.

Journey into Integrated Awareness

In the book "Ask Anything, And Your Body Will Answer" Julie J. Nichols described the account of her first hand experiences with Integrated Awareness as a method for integration of polar opposites which we attribute to parts of the body.

The basis of this technique is as follows. Everything is the consciousness and energy in movement, therefore our body also partakes in all processes. The workshop leader told Julie to divide (in her imagination) her body into left and right halves and asked her to imagine one part of her body vibrates quicker than the other. Then to find a third level of vibration, different than the first two and asked her is it a higher or lower rate of vibrations compared with the first two levels?

When she did that, the following ideas came to her: She was able to divide herself in her thoughts. She was able to identify a separate experience of vibrations in each half of her body. She was able to create the third vibratory phenomenon which includes both halves and is neither one of them.

"I feel the first vibration which is of a low frequency, stable, predictable, monochrome, like vanilla ice cream...Then I concentrated on the other half, the vibration I go to secretly, the one I hide. It is maybe thirty to fifty percent higher, definitely more exciting. Just enough variation to draw strange attractors in, there's an undercurrent, perhaps, of fear. I might get caught. I realize that at this frequency, I love. At the other, I just keep on working.

So I'm lying on the floor in this safe and expanded place, this blue-carpeted light classroom, playing with two unlike vibrations, ordinary and extraordinary, mundane and miraculous, the story of my life. (Maybe of everyone's life and I haven't known it.) And I'm supposed to create a third vibration, make something new. This is the planet of polarity and paradox; transcending duality is how we expand, how we create. Do I go for a higher or lower frequency? What kind of vibration will embrace both parts of me?

The workshop leader tells Julie not to analyse, to let her body tell her what she should do. And she does it. "My body (or my energy?) seems to want to come to something which is neither high, nor low."

The leader asks her to imagine her two halves as male and female and to go up and down the scale and note how many male and female tunings there are for her.

"And it does. I can feel myself checking not just different frequencies but whole different measuring cues. My body (or my energy?) seems to want to arrive at--well, something neither higher nor lower. It's different than either of the other two energies I'm holding. It's like a full guitar chord riff instead of a one-string melody, a three-dimensional iridescence replacing one flat piece of construction paper, a seven-course meal following a fast. It's got more dimensions, more flavor, than either half alone."

The leader gives her the instruction to imagine her two halves to be anything she wants: Her health and other people's health; current time and past time; performance vs. authenticity. To travel through these possibilities and notice differences between the two halves in each case. To notice where in her body the different vibrations occur. Then to pause to create a third harmonic for each pairing, and tune both halves to it, to transcend seeming incompatibilities."

"In some instances, what 'transcends seeming incompatibilities' is easy and pleasurable. When I check "my health" (a strong, earthy energy) against "everyone else's" (less strong, more like the "ordinary" I took on earlier), I can make a third harmonic (wide and yellow) that pulls everybody out on the running field with me, lifts them into the sunshine, feels the joy of moving fast, all of us together in a well-run race. Yet other times I can't get to a third vibration, I get tied up in rule-knots. Rule-knots as if my body were saying, 'Hold it, Jul--trust me. It's not time yet."

When the thoughts that you allow to form in your mental field are matched to an expanded body state and an expanding emotional state, the thoughts take on a greater vision and encompass more. When that takes place your life force, your vital energy becomes strengthened and expanded and you have the ability to impact in the world and to inspire others and to serve others at a greater level. Surely all of this somehow must be related to the deepest desires of the soul.

Fear and Love

Both this world and our experiences are the play of the polar opposites of **Love** and **Fear**, says the therapist and researcher Edward Francolini. There is nothing else! The foundation of experience consists of these two aspects of being in a combination of varying shades of each which fuse together to incorporate within themselves all our experiences. All other emotional states and phenomena are just guises which mask these two fundamental polarities. We can only respond in love or in fear, or we can respond anywhere in between with a little of one and a little of the other.

Emotions are the backdrop to our experience in this polarized world. They are the inner tapestry that is woven as we move through our experiences in response to them. Emotions are signals from our inner being, signals brought to consciousness that serve to tell us where we stand in balancing the polarities of love and fear within ourselves in any given moment. As such, they are forerunners of knowledge, serving to inform us of our relationship to Self at any given moment of time through the responses we have to our every experience. Each emotional response tells us how far away or how close we are to being in alignment with our own Self.

This is quite a different perspective of the emotions than we are taught yet this is what the emotions do, Francolini says. They are a conscious signal sent from the center of our being which bring us information about our relationships. We can misinterpret the signal and the information being sent, but we cannot miss the signal itself because we definitely feel it within the body. We feel the emotional responses that we have and we register them within the mind. They are the road map home, to our True Being.

So what happened? The life we live every day seems far from following a road map home. Most of us cannot read the signs so we end up getting lost. If we can't even read the signs, what hope have we for a successful arrival back home? We've not been taught to view our emotions from this perspective. We have been taught to label them and in doing so place a value on them which is based on the desirability of feeling and experiencing them. It is, as you know, the old game of "good and bad" in this universe. We want to feel 'good' so we pursue that which we think will bring this emotional response into our being. We don't want to feel 'bad', so we attempt to avoid that which will bring this emotional response into our experience. We tend to view emotions as either, good or bad, desirable or not desirable and in this way we get lost because we have mistakenly taken the signs as the experience itself and in doing so we do not see what the real message is all about. And it is in this way we continue to cycle from one extreme to the other, over and over and over again, and become trapped in the polarities of expression.

Francolini continues his story of this polar world. We get trapped easily because we are reluctant to feeling emotional pain. This is a learned response. We have been taught to avoid feeling pain and that pain is bad and undesirable. But pain is simply a sign given from inside, just like every other emotion and it has great value. All it is saying is that through these experiences, within which I feel pain, I am not in alignment with who I really am, that I am not in keeping with my true nature. Pain says that through this experience, within which I am feeling a painful response, I am not in synch with my desire and need for growth and development, period. That's all pain is saying. It took me a long time to figure this out.

Half of this world is the arena of darkness and it is all about the pain. Pain is the garment of fear, one of the two extremes of polarity. Pain masks what we fear, and fear is the realm of darkness. Beneath pain lies fear, manifested in many guises, a web woven of negative emotions like anger, guilt, shame, remorse, failure and the like, all of which are sensed through pain. The dark emotions are 'fear itself', exploring itself and its many ways of expression. It has got its own value.

It is the experience that allows Self to know itself on deeper levels than are available without it. In our aversion to feeling pain we avoid looking at and embracing what we fear. If we let the pain of an experience stop us from looking at and examining our experience any further, we cannot recognize the underlying fear to integrate it into our beings and we remain immersed in darkness. The darkness repeats one theme over and over again and it is powerlessness.

Unfortunately, Edward Francolini does not give us sound advice on how to stop this confusing game and find a way out of it.

Turning a Problem

Another practitioner, Charles Thompson, did not create a system for integration of polarities, but his article **"What a great Idea"** gives practical advice on how to see and experience things in opposite ways. Even though he does not show how to merge polar opposites he at least provides a way to make us aware of them. He quotes words of Lao Cu from the classic book **Tao-te Ching:** *"To learn how to lead people the wise leader learns not to follow. To prosper, he learns to live simply."*

Starting from these proven ideas, Thompson gives the practical advice: Learn to see things backwards, from inside and upside down. In a nutshell, this is his practical method:

1. State a problem in the reverse. Turn a positive statement into a negative.

2. Define what something IS NOT.

3. Figure out what all others DON'T DO.

4. Start using "What if..."

5. Change your perspective.

6. Turn results from one side to the other.

7. Transform a victory into a defeat and defeat into a victory.

This is simple advice and could be fruitful especially as a problem solving activity. Using this approach one can find guidance for developing creative thinking.

Healing into Wholeness

Lisa Sarasohn is the author of "The Woman's Belly Book: Finding Your Treasure Within" and creator of Honouring Your Belly, a project supporting women. She created the following technique for resolving conflicts of opposing needs and tendencies. Her method is very simple. Take a look at it.

1. Take a few moments - through journal writing, meditation, or reflection - to identify some of the apparently conflicting needs and desires operating in your life at this time. Part of you may want to have or do "this" and at the same time another part of you may want to have or do "that." Distinguish these polarities as clearly as you can.

2. Sitting comfortably, with your back straight and your feet flat on the floor, place your hands upon your knees, palms facing upward. Deepen your breath, allowing your belly to move out and in with your inhalation

and exhalation. Let your eyes close to focus your inner awareness.

3. Choose one of the polarities and, focusing on your right hand, imagine you're holding its essence in your right palm. What does this polarity look like? See its shape, color, degree of gloss. What does this polarity feel like? Feel its weight, density, texture, temperature, degree of stillness. What does this polarity sound like? Listen for its music, its voice. Thoroughly immerse yourself in the sights, sensations, and sounds of this polarity.

4. As you're ready, shift your attention into your left hand and imagine you're holding the essence of the other polarity in your left palm. Repeat the same process as you did above in step three.

5. Now shift your awareness so that you can see and feel both hands, and what they each contain, at once. Still breathing deeply, letting your belly move with your breath, slowly lift your hands from your knees. Gradually bring your hands toward each other, watching and feeling the images and sensations in both hands.

6. Very slowly and gradually, bring your palms together so that their surfaces come entirely into contact with each other. Continue to breathe deeply and relax as you wait and watch, without expectation or demand, for whatever new images and sensations may emerge. (If no new image emerges immediately, that's fine; it may become apparent to you in the next few days, perhaps when you least expect it.)

7. With your palms in firm contact with each other, rotate your hands to bring your thumbs to your chest, your fingers pointing upward. Bring whatever new images and sensations that have emerged into your heart of compassion, surrounding them with your love.

8. With your palms still in firm contact with each other, rotate your hands to point your fingers downward and bring the heels of your hands to your belly center, a point about two inches below your navel. Bring whatever new images and sensations that have emerged into your belly--your heart of creation--infusing them with your pro-creative power.

9. Then rest, absorbing and appreciating your experience of uniting polarities into a greater whole.

Tao of Chaos

In his book "Tao of Chaos: Essence and Enneagram", Stephen Wolinsky describes a "quick" method of neutralization/integration of opposites: *"For centuries, since the dawn of the development of Yoga, the question of oppositions has persisted. Simply stated, how do we bring together the pairs of opposites, i.e. hate/love, yes/no, feminine and masculine, together? In the land of 20th Century Psychology, this has been seen as an attempt to integrate pairs of opposites, or certainly to access, by choice, one opposing pole and then the next. These polar opposites, however, have never fully been integrated. Why? Because there is a presupposition that these polar opposites are essentially different. Quantum Psychology says, polar opposites are not different, but at the quantum level are the same undifferentiated substances."*

To convince the reader of his statement, he describes the following exercise:

1. Notice a pair of polar opposites, for example love/hate, man/woman, strong/weak, dependent/independent etc.

2. Notice the dimensions and shape of the two opposites.

3. Remove labels from these two polar opposites and see them as created from the same kind of neutral energy.

4. Notice what occurs.

"Here we can see, Wolinsky says,*" that when the two polar opposites are seen as being made of the same essential substance, there is no contrast – hence there are no polar opposites... Actually, seeing them as made of the same substance dissolves the conflict and hence dissolves the problem."*

Unfortunately, Wolinsky's claim is too optimistic. When you do this exercise it is true that two polar opposites will merge, but the effect will be short-lived. Five minutes after doing the exercise there will not be much left of that integration and the two separate opposites will exist again. For the person who understands the mechanism of DP3 (Deep PEAT 3) the explanation is easy. In the exercise described by Wolinsky what has happened is only one of the four elements that make up a polarity has been removed. Wolinsky's technique only removes the pictures from each of the two polarities. But what separates two polarities in our dualistic world are multi layered mind masses, which are made of 4 elements: pictures, emotions, body sensations and thoughts. Until we remove all 4 elements there will not be a true and permanent integration.

Exceeding the Self-image

In his article "Self-Image" Tibetan Lama Tarthang Tulku gives advices on how to go around self-image: *"As soon as we know self-image for what it is, we know that we can change, that we can develop flexibility in attitudes without giving up anything. This change is possible because our consciousness is by its nature not fixed, but flexible."*

We develop this flexibility by adopting new perspectives, the lama says. For example, every time you feel unhappy, you should say *"I am happy."* You should say it strongly to yourself, even if your feelings contradict you. You should remember it is your self image that is unhappy, not you. It is possible to switch instantly to a happy, balanced attitude and to stay there by believing it. There is this choice when you are open to a positive attitude. Your whole inner quality can change, even if the external conditions do not.

Another way to counter self-image is to become immersed in the unhappiness, feel it and believe it, and then switch it swiftly, electrically, like a fish darting in water, to happiness.

Tart hang Tulku emphasizes: *"First, be the experience, completely accept it. Then, jump to the opposite extreme. How is it? It is possible to clearly see the differences between the positive and negative experience both at the same time. By jumping mentally from positive to negative and back again, it is possible to see that both are manifestations of awareness and as such have a 'neutral' energy which can be used in any way. In the beginning, try to gain skill in this switching technique. You can see what you are feeling now and how it was before, sometimes feeling the two different situations simultaneously. The technique thus teaches acceptance, making it possible to have positive feelings about any experience that occurs."*

Alchemical Meditation Ouroboros

Adam McLean, well known contemporary alchemist, created a very simple method, or a technique, of neutralizing polarities. Its name is Ouroboros and its technique is "alchemical meditation". One should not be surprised with this. Karl G. Jung first discovered the dominant tendency of alchemy – neutralization of all polarities. In alchemy the opposites are called the King and Queen, the Sun and Moon, Gold and Silver, or Sulphur and Mercury. In every case, the idea is the same: there are two chief principles in Nature. One is masculine, active and positive; the other is feminine, passive and negative. The uniting of these two principles is, in one sense, what constitutes the Magnum Opus or Great Work of alchemy. Their union produces a secret stone which partakes of both principles in essence, yet it is also independent of them. This stone is the Secret of Secrets and the Mystery of Mysteries, the highest neutralization. Here is this alchemical technique. McLean does not describe his "retort exercise" but one could guess how it goes.

One should go into his inner space performing that retort exercise. Concentrate to a point, that point should be either the place of calmness inside of you or just visualize being in the point in the middle of a retort. Because it's difficult to concentrate this way for a long time, you should let "the natural forces of the soul play into the existence."

When polarities appear, you should visualize this as the point becoming a line. As the main point in the process of neutralization, McLean says: *"Try to keep your consciousness as long as possible at the centre of this line of polarities. One will feel swaying from the centre on either side the polar forces of positive-negative, above-below, active-passive etc. Let one's being run through as many possibilities as one feels comfortable with."*

After you exhaust most of the possibilities, bring that mental image into the focus of your attention, using the Solve et Coagula technique, and inwardly feel that line as a snake with its head towards your own head, and tail at the base of your spine. Feel the serpents head and tail as polarities and let its forces fully develop. *"This picture reflects the natural structure of one's inner being"*, says McLean.

To finish the process, you should build an Ouroboros (the serpent biting its own tail) by uniting the two polarities. Just visualize the serpent's head grasping the tail and focus it around your own heart. McLean's further instructions may be not completely clear to the average reader, not versed in alchemy: *"Using Solve et Coagula one can allow this symbol to rise into the higher part of one's interior being. As the snake grasps its own tail, so on the higher level one's soul takes hold of itself, and begins to work upon its own substance, uniting the polarities, uniting conscious with unconscious, positive and negative, spirit and body etc.*

"One can use this exercise in a general way, or in order to work through particular polarities one has encountered in one's study, or through the experiences of life. One must not reverse the process in the case of the Ouroboros exercise. Once one has formed

the symbol inwardly, do not take it into pieces, but finish at this point, letting the unity remain in one's being."

Oneness Meditation

I tried to find who the author of the Oneness meditation is, but could not. It is probably Frank Sant'Agata and it is based on two pairs of polarities: One is **Good and Evil/Bad** and another is **I and others.** The author maintains that these four entities make up the basis of human existence. This meditation method has as a goal to collapse the polarities **good/evil** and **I/others,** which should lead the practitioner to an altered state of consciousness. Some people have told me this method is efficient in calming down negative emotions.

These are steps of the Oneness Meditation:

1. Find a place where you will not be disturbed for 10 minutes.

2. Close your eyes, notice your breathing and concentrate your attention on these four polarities one after another: god and evil/bad, I and others. Remember them visually or emotionally. For example, remember something which you evaluate as good, then something which you experienced as bad, then yourself in some situation and finally others experiencing something.

3. Remember at least five places, objects, moments or persons which represent good for you. In your imagination direct these thoughts (memories) into the left side of your visual field and concentrate on one after another of those chosen entities until you get to the peak of emotional intensity. At the same

time become conscious of you physiological reactions: feeling of warmth, breathing, skin sensations, tension of mucles etc.

4. At the right hand side of your visual field place several thoughts connected with evil or bad (thoughts about some people, moments and objects which represent evil or bad for you). Stay with them as long as you need to attain the noticeable level of intensity of those emotions. Become conscious of the body sensations following them.

5. Since your memories are left and right, start alternatively getting into one group then in another. Do it as long as you are not able to shift quickly from one group to another, oscillating between these two opposites.

6. Now change the value of these memories. Memories from the "good side" shift to the "bad side" and memories from bad side to the good side. Concentrate, trying to feel their values are changing.

7. In this step you should make an effort to become conscious that good and bad are not truly separate. Feel those two groups mixing and merge into one whole. Imagine that good is bad and bad is good and that they are one.

8. When good and evil collapse significantly and merged, start working with the polarity of **I/others.** Direct your attention to yourself, and then to what characterizes "others". It could mean the whole universe and everything you don't consider "myself". This is by its nature a more direct process and therefore the process

Return to Oneness

of accumulation which you used with polarity good/bad is not needed.

9. Now imagine that "I" is really "others" and the opposite. Start changing ideas and thoughts and do it as long as you are not able to do it pretty quickly.

10. Finally merge yourself and others and feel that you are one. What will be "one" as the result of this process can not be described, it can only be experienced. When you attain that state, remember the results you got in collapsing good and bad. Now try to collapse both ideas into "one" the end results of both pairs of polarities. That means in the final phase all four elements should merge into one (**good and evil/bad,** and **I and others).** Stay in that state as long as you feel the need.

11. Slowly bring your attention to your surroundings and concentrate on the here and now. The goal of the Oneness Meditation is the feeling of being in the center, free from all delusions. Every time you do this meditation use another group of new memories, you will gradually remove the charge from all of those memories and make them unable to influence you.

Hammer or H.A.M.R.

This is one of the new methods and therefore it is not widely known. David Kenyon Nelms created it and presents it in his book *"**Inner-Fire Kindling"*** published in 2004.

This is the basic idea of this system: People with positive attitudes toward life and other people who get along better in life have such good attitudes because of the optimal way they think. This system teaches people and trains them to think in an optimal way. It does it through a progression of easy exercises.

First you should find out which thought models are most officious (the author of the systems help you with that) and then to strengthen those models and keep them permanently in place. Each exercise, called a "Hammer", lasts on average less then one minute and enables you to strengthen one thought and keep it as your own. With just one repeating, Nelms claims, the practitioner will established and permanently keep the new positive attitude. The exercise is very simple and quick and after some time it becomes automatic.

If you want to get maximum benefit from the Hammer technique, you must observe the following two rules:

1. In one period of time (past, present or future) you must strengthen and keep just one positive thought.

2. In one day do just one repetition (see later how to do that).

The new adopted thought is just one a day so you will give your brain enough time to assimilate the new thought model. But you can approach the same problem from another angle, from another side and install a similar, but not exactly the same thought. For example, if you feel unloved by people around you, one day you can do the Hammer installation of a new thought model *"I feel loved"*. Next day you can approach that problem from the other side, which means to embrace another aspect of the same problem: *My associates love me"*, and the third day *"Members of the opposite sex like me very much"* and so on.

How to do the Hammer Exercise

Hold your hands half stretched out in front of yourself, with your palms open upwards and imagine the sequence of thoughts in them. In one hand you imagine one thought in three periods of time – past, present and future – and in the other hand imagine the opposite thought. At the end of the process take the assembly of these thoughts and impress them into your chest with your hands kept them together.

The exercise starts with imagining in one hand the old thought which reflects the old, negative state, and in the other hand you imagine, new, positive thought. Kenyon Nelms says: *"You can not remove the basic thought models which cause your negative reactions, but you can combine it with new thoughts and change it drastically that way so that they create a completely new positive reaction."*

Then simply imagine the new positive thought overflowing from the hand it was in to the other hand, and then overflow back to the first hand and the thoughts mixing. Now the old (negative) thought and new (positive) thought are mixed in both hands, which cause the mixing of these thoughts in both brain hemispheres which the hands are connected with.

Now for a short period concentrate on any thought connected with the past time, imagine it in the first hand and tell yourself *"Past"*. Then concentrate on the other hand and again think about the past and tell yourself *"Past"*. Then repeat the process with the future. Let it be one quick thought about future, any kind of thought, you don't have to pay attention to its correctness. Simply point your attention briefly to any of the future days, months or years and feel them in that hand and tell to yourself *"Future"*. Then without waiting, concentrate on the other hand, again thinking the same thought about the future, or some other thought about the future, and tell to yourself *"Future"*.

Now take a look around, feel the present moment and concentrate on that feeling in your first hand and tell to yourself *"Present"*, and repeat that process at once with the other hand and tell to yourself *"Present"*. Keep in mind that the process must be quick and simple.

Finally install the contents of both hands in the "I" center in the middle of your chest this way: Your hands, open and turned upward, put one over the other, wait in that position about two seconds and then press them together to the center of your chest.

Then repeat the same process, starting with other hand. That means to imagine in the other hand the same old thought, and new wanted thought in other hand, and repeat the procedure.

I personally checked the Hammer process and can tell it is a worthy one. The basic thing is the neutralization and integration of both brain hemispheres. Statements of its efficiency are partly exaggerated. Some exercises need to be repeated, approaching the problem from many different points of view. Some new contents are not permanent as the creator of this method asserts. It is possible though, that different people will get different results using it.

The Symbolic Polarization Method

In the words of Steve Mensing, the creator of this system, the Symbolic Polarization Method is an intuitive process of integration of polarity targets. His hypothesis is that the intuitively created symbol, because it is rooted in unconscious processes, will mirror the beliefs, emotions, and sensations for which they stand. The advantages of using intuitive symbolic targets are these:

a) They greatly reduce resistance, making for easier integration.

b) They can stand in for polarized or opposite beliefs, emotions, and sensations.

c) A symbolic target can stand for larger items like a body or our felt sense of almost anything. Whatever you can intuitively create a symbol of (that for which you can intuitively create a symbol) you can integrate.

A good rule about creating symbols for targets: They have to be made intuitively and not intellectually or logically. The reason: We want our symbol fully rooted in our emotions, feelings, sensations, and unconscious processes.

The Technical Procedure

1. Breathe through your left nostril – twenty deep inhalations and exhalations while you keep the right nostril shut. As you breathe that way, let your tongue and face be relaxed. Resume your regular breathing after the 20th exhale.

2. Place your right palm on the region of your heart and keep it there for the remainder of the process.

3. Direct your attention to your body and try to detect any polarized or opposing feelings, beliefs, emotions,

or sensations. To get such feeling you can ask your body how it feels toward a problem or a certain situation. Give it time to respond. Notice the overall felt sense – You will get a foggy feeling about some polarized state. If you wish you can label your polarized beliefs, emotions, or sensations as: "Polarized beliefs", "Polarized emotions", or "Polarized sensations". This will provide you a slightly outside perspective of what you're working upon – --the "just back" position.

4. Then, allow your unconscious mind to create two separate intuitive symbols one for each side of the polar opposites. Create a symbol for one side of the polarity and then create one for the other. Give them some time to become clear. In that period, you are an interested observer, observing how those symbols appear from murky depths.

5. When the two separate symbols give you a sense of being fully formed, allow them both to be beside each other on the visual screen of your awareness. If you wish, you may allow these polar opposite symbols to dialogue with each other, or you can shift your awareness back and forth between the two opposite symbols, spending time on one side and then the other. Pay attention to intuitive messages of both symbols. Then observe them together without trying to get rid of them or keep them. At some point they will vanish. Perhaps they will even visually fuse.

Steve Mensing says that symbols can give us valuable information about our deepest conflicts. You can form polar symbols of entire dreams you've had, areas of ambivalence, or any area of your life where dichotomies exist. You can take polarities like love and hate, pleasure and pain, being and nothingness, wholeness and fragmentation, or life and death and intuitively make them into a symbolic polarization.

I'm not able to judge the value of this method, because I did not apply it in practice, neither do I know anyone who has done so. Personally, I don't find it easy to accept that polarities will vanish just like that in the last phase of application of this method. What make them opposite polarities are great masses of energetic charge between them, and to remove them one needs an efficient method. In Mensing's description of his method, such a procedure is not given. Also, it is a pretty unclear how one should come intuitively to polarity symbols. But perhaps the procedure will become clearer when one applies it in practice, which is the reason that I have described that method.

Polarity Therapy

Polarity therapy was created and developed by Randolph Stone as he was searching for the fundamental process of healing in man. It represents a valuable synthesis of Oriental systems of healing (such as Ayurvedic medicine, acupuncture, and yoga) and systems created in the West (natural healing, chiropractic, craniosacral therapy and similar). It is a holistic system which operates with life energy in all of its forms, using a very complex combination of work with the body, physical exercises, nutrition and psychotherapy. Its goal is to integrate body, mind, emotions and spirit.

It is interesting how Stone created his system. He understood that there is a similarity between the human body and a magnet – a magnet has a positive pole and a negative pole and a magnetic field spreading around them. Electric currents create these fields. Similarly, the human body may be viewed as a bio-magnet, whose energetic currents create magnetic fields both around and in the body. Subtle energetic fields and currents are present in every cell, tissue and organ. That life energy manifests itself not only throughout the physical organism, but also through our thoughts, emotions, personal relationships, and Spiritual experiences.

To be able to function, all atoms which constitute an ordinary magnet must be oriented in one direction. That way, small magnetic fields combine and create a great magnetic field. Atoms of the human body must also be harmonized and polarized; otherwise, the bio-magnet of the human body would be disorganised and would not be able to function well. If we strike strongly a magnet with some hard object, the magnetic field becomes destroyed, because the common direction of its atoms becomes disturbed. They become depolarized and get into an unbalanced and mutually conflicting relationship. A similar disturbance happens in the human organism as the result of a trauma or a stressful situation. Recently it was discovered that there are similar effects on human beings when one is exposed to the strong electromagnetic fields which exist around contemporary electronic devices.

When energetic currents are not blocked and flow undisturbed, a man is healthy; he functions optimally and his thoughts and emotions are harmonized. Traumas and stressful situations disrupt those flows and our emotional and bodily functions become devoid of necessary energy. Such energetic disturbances manifest as physical pain, sicknesses and emotional disorders. Practitioners of Polarity Therapy use their hands to sense energetic flows, and so they discover existing blockages. The final goal is to set the blocked energy free, so that normal flow is restored and self-healing happens spontaneously.

Characteristics of the energetic field in the human being and around it are well known. In oriental medicine, energetic polarity concerns the universal pulsating contractions and expansions, or attraction and repulsion. Life energy, in Chinese medicine, Chi, and in Ayurvedic medicine, Prana, is the foundation of the whole life. Randolph Stone pointed to the symbolic meaning of the old Egyptian symbol the caduceus or Hermes' stick, two serpents twisted around the middle pillar. Two wings at the top of the caduceus are symbolic of the two brain hemispheres, and a small ball above them is the pineal gland. Those two serpents represent two main energetic currents, Ida and Pingala (see later on), and the middle stick symbolizes Sushumna or the middle energetic current. When Ida and Pingala are well synchronized, energy circulates at the optimum in the energetic field and the result is harmony and health.

Polarity therapy embraces all dimensions of the human being: body, mental, emotional, and spiritual. *"Health is not only the expression of body well being, but also the harmony which allows the free expression of the soul through the mind and body of the individual,"* Stone says. Today, his system is in strong expansion -- the American Association for Polarity Therapy (APTA) is penetrating medical schools, hospitals and colleges. Many therapists of different orientation adopt its techniques. It reputation is based on the success which its practitioners attain in removing stress, chronic fatigue, arthritis, traumas and cancer.

Polarities in NLP

When they speak about polarities, the adherents of NLP system (Neuro Linguistic Programming) usually use the term "parts". They say that people sometimes experience being "incongruent," in an "inner conflict," or "of two minds". These issues do not relate so much to external pressures, but primarily to the deeper structures being in conflict within the person.

There is more then one definition of a conflict. A simple one is that **a conflict is a state of disharmony or imbalance between opposing individuals, or in the case of inner conflict, between ideas and desires inside one person.**

In NLP, they make a clear difference between internal and external conflicts. In therapy and Spiritual work, inner conflicts are of greater importance. Logically, they always seem like opposing polarities or opposites. For example, they happen often in behavior. A person may want to enjoy the food and at the same time may want to be slim. Almost everybody has opposing believes or values. Another example: A person can think that writing good poetry is a very desirable ability and at the same time strongly believes he/she does not have that ability.

Freud believed such internal conflicts were ultimately at the root of many psychological problems. He said: *"One side of the personality stands for certain wishes, while another part struggles against them and fends them off. There is no neurosis without such a conflict."* If there is an internal conflict, the battlefield shifts inward, and a battle begins between the two parts of one's self. As Freud points out, *"...the external frustration is supplemented by internal frustration."* And when the fight is between two parts of one's self, one can never win, and Freud adds, *"This conflict is not resolved by helping one side to win a victory over the other...one side in either event will remain unsatisfied."*

Attempting to solve this type of conflict by suppressing one side, as one would do with typical opposite ideas, creates a double bind in which, Robert Dilts says, you are damned if you do and damned if you don't. It is as if the struggle is between two conflicting intentions rather than between an intention and the uncertainty as to whether it will be achieved. In the first case, the resolution involves finding the intention behind the conflicting behavior and generating alternative solutions in order to achieve the individual's intended outcome. In the case of conflict, however, it is the confrontation of antagonistic intentions that is at issue. Because the parts have opposite intentions, no alternatives can be produced which satisfy both intentions directly.

Furthermore, because the internal conflict is not grounded in external events or results, the conflict cannot be resolved by anyone outside of ourselves. In such a situation, anything can become another stimulus for a fight. Even the simplest decisions lead to a struggle, a struggle which is never resolved because it is not really about the content of the decision but about the deeper cause underlying it.

The constant stress coming from such internal conflicts may cause different symptoms, very often physical ones. These symptoms also become a battlefield for the parts in conflict. Robert Dilts point out that *"Since systems attempt to reach balance or homeostasis, however, certain symptoms may actually provide a potential point of "compromise" between the conflicting parts."* But Sigmund Freud was the first to point out that *"...The two powers which have entered into opposition meet together again in the symptom and become reconciled by means of the compromise contained in symptom-formation. That is why the symptom is capable of such resistance; it is sustained from both sides..."*

In NLP, conflict integration means the procedure by which contradictory or incompatible responses, or "parts," are defined, separated and resolved. Integration of conflict is one of the main NLP processes and it is routinely applied to the resolution of many mental, emotional and interpersonal problems.

According to Grinder and Bandler ("The Structure of Magic Volume" II, 1976, p. 45), the basic steps of conflict integration involve:

1. Clearly identify the key issues involved in the conflict. These issues will be expressed as either **opposites or polarities**.

2. Clearly establish distinctions from either of the parties in conflict.

3. Integrate the client's incongruencies by first making contact between the polarities, and then achieving a meta position from which to bring the polarities together in a new way.

4. Find the positive intention and purpose behind the issues of each party. The positive intention will necessarily be at a higher level than the issues creating the conflict. *("You cannot solve a problem at the same level of thinking that is creating the problem.")*

5. Make sure that each party recognizes the positive intent of the other. This does not mean that either party has to accept the method with which the other is attempting to satisfy the positive intention, nor does it mean that either party has to compromise his or her position.

6. From a higher position or so called 'meta position' find out a common intention which both parties share.

A key component to the process of Integration of Conflict is the identification and recognition of the positive intentions of both of the polar parts involved. Everything inside the human being has some positive intention, no matter how bad it seems on the surface.

For an average reader without a solid knowledge of NLP, some short description of their processes would not be enough. The method of Flemming Funch (see later) is mostly based on NLP conflict integration, so reading Funch's text, you can get the main idea about it.

Gestalt "Communication on the Pillow"

Western thought has been dominated by an attempt to conquer nature by developing a split between man and nature, good and bad, right and wrong, should and should not, reality and unreality? The frozen polarities which we have created in our rigid mind-body categories have all but crippled our capacity to appreciate ourselves as a part of the natural universe and the universe as a part of us. Ego rigidity occurs when we are unable to allow our awareness to emerge spontaneously, unwilling to trust the natural homeostatic permeability of our contact boundaries, and being incapable of owning all our parts.

The Gestalt approach to therapy, as developed and practiced by Fritz Perls, is a way of being with yourself and in relationship that enhances personal growth and healing. It is a phenomenological-existential therapy which teaches therapists and patients the phenomenological method of awareness, in which perceiving, feeling, and acting are distinguished from their interpretation. Explanations and interpretations are considered less reliable than what is directly perceived and felt. The goal is for clients to become aware of what they are doing, how they are doing it, and how they can change themselves, and at the same time, to learn to accept and value themselves.

The technique combines ancient concepts and modern exercises developed by Abraham Maslow, Carl Rogers, Moreno and Eric Berne. The goal of Gestalt therapy is awareness, or insight. In Gestalt therapy, insight is a clear understanding of the structure of the situation being studied. With Gestalt, we can increase our awareness of *what is* in the moment of Now.

In the context of this book, the most important gestalt teaching concerns dichotomies and polarities. A dichotomy being a split, such that the field is considered not as a whole split into different parts but, rather, as an assortment of competing and unrelated forces. Dichotomous thinking interferes with our wholeness because it tends to be intolerant of diversity among persons and of contradictory truths about a single person.

Organismic self-regulation leads to integrating parts with each other and into a whole that encompasses the parts. The field is often differentiated into polarities which complement or explicate each other. The positive and negative poles of an electrical field are the prototypical mode for this differentiation. The concept of polarities treats opposites as part of one whole, as yin and yang.

With this polar view of the field, differences are accepted and integrated. Lack of genuine integration creates splits, such as body-mind, self-external, infantile-mature, biological-cultural, and unconscious-conscious. Through dialogue there can be an integration of parts, into a new whole.

In Gestalt, we explore our dreams, visions, and hopes in dialogues between our polarities. As our dialogue becomes obvious, self discovery evolves out of choosing to be ourselves and touching the excitement and hope of responsibility.

Paul Reps speaks of a school in the Orient which teaches a game called "Pillow Talk" to groups of children. In Pillow Talk, one goes through five positions until you get to an integration. They go like this:

You start putting yourself, in imagination, into the **first position.** To be able to get into it, you use three elements to be **here and now:** Body sensations, emotions and thinking. First position means that you should become aware of what body sensation you have? What emotions do you feel? What do you think?

In the **second position,** you should identify with the polarity which is opposite to the first one. If on the first position you felt love and happiness, on the second you should feel hatred and misfortune. Choose all polarities important for you in this period of your life, and on paper write down opposites for every word which you wrote in the first position.

Opposite emotion for someone could be sadness, but for some other person it could be loneliness.

In your imagination you should imagine occupying the **third position** in which your two polarities merge. Close your eyes and imagine yourself at the apex of a triangle which at the bottom has your first and second position. Imagine yourself as one polarity, then as the second and then let both of them slip into you and merge. Pay attention to what you feel as it happens. Stay in that experience long enough to be able to define that experience by words. When you find a proper word for the state which you feel, write it on the third position. This process demands that you to take a look into yourself and become conscious of one of three possible attitudes: estimating, judging and observing.

Now it is time for the **fourth position.** In your thoughts, come above the triangle; take a look downwards and see what is happening. Write down whatever you feel. Give a name to your transcending place. Allow yourself to transcend your conflicting polarities. Just imagine yourself as something higher than those two polarities. When you find a word for it, close your eyes and withdraw into yourself. Repeat that word of yours and be conscious of your body, so that your body is able to know where transcendence lives in you.

Finally, go to the **fifth position.** This means you go into the middle of everything that makes you. Notice what you feel and how strong that feeling is. If something activates from your center, look for a word which is able to describe you at that place. When you are completely in your center, you are Everything. In the center of yourself you can be all things and appearances, you can search feelings which follow changes and you have the freedom for different choices.

Every reader who has gotten a proper experience with DP3 can compare these two methods and draw their own conclusions as to their value.

Psychosynthesis

Roberto Assagioli, the founder of **Psychosynthesis**, in his conception of the whole human being, included both the discoveries of psychoanalysis and well known spiritual traditions. He saw that, although psychology and spirituality are seemingly separate domains, those engaged in a spiritual search often need therapeutic help in integrating their experiences. Conversely, a psychology which does not appreciate the spiritual component of human beings cannot speak for the whole person.

The aim of his system is the integration of separate parts into one unitary whole. Assagioli describes it as *"Co-ordination and subordination of the various psychological energies and functions, the creation of a firm organisation of the personality."* In Psychosynthesis, this process is recognised as ultimately leading to transcendent states of pure awareness, joy, peace and love, and as extending beyond the "individual human being" as normally understood in the west.

Polarity is a fundamental phenomenon, Assagioli says, it is present in all cosmic manifestation. From the first cosmic manifestation, duality appears. The first and most fundamental duality manifests between Spirit and Matter, Unmanifest and Manifest.

Here I quote *in extenso* his well know article, "Balancing and synthesis of opposites":

"It is at once necessary to state that all polarity is a relationship between two elements, and that, as such, it is never absolute, but relative even to a particular pair of opposites: the same element can be positive in its relation to a certain 'pole' and negative in its relation to another. An instance of the relativity of the "polar relationships" exists in the fundamental polarity between Spirit and Matter. According to some, Spirit is the free and transcendent Reality which stands above the various pairs of opposites existing in manifested life. Such is the conception of Keyserling, contained in his book 'From Suffering to Fulfillment' (London; Selwyn and Blount) *by the same writer. According to others, Spirit corresponds to the positive pole, to the dynamic and creative element in all duality. Such is Jung's idea. In other words, Keyserling regards the "tension" between Spirit and the various manifestations of life as existing in a "vertical" direction, which he refers to as the 'dimension of intensity,' while Jung conceives polarity more as a horizontal relationship."*

Physical Polarity: As an example of physical world polarity, Assagioli takes the polarity between the positive and negative poles in electricity. This polarity is the basis of the constitution of material world. That electric polarity manifests itself in various ways with many practical applications, as in induced and alternating currents in an electric instrument. In the field of psychology, one can find good examples in emotional attraction and repulsion.

In the human body, one of the most important physical polarities is that between the sympathetic and the parasympathetic nervous systems; the sympathetic stimulates catabolism; the latter, anabolism

One of the most important and general polarities in the three kingdoms of organic life, vegetable, animal and human is the sexual. Assagioli points to that well known polarity: the positive pole is represented by the masculine element, the negative by the feminine element. But contrary to widely spread opinion, Assagioli says that this does not mean that the masculine is active and the feminine passive. Both are active, but in a different way, the masculine element being the initiating polarity, while the feminine element is the receptive polarity. This type of polarity extends far beyond the man-woman relationship to countless manifestations in life. *"It has been particularly and deeply emphasized by the Chinese who regard these two principles as the foundation both of cosmic evolution and of every aspect of human life. The creative aspect, symbolized by the father and Heaven, they call Yang, while Yin is the receptive and elaborative aspect, symbolized by the mother and the Earth. The well-being of Man depends, in the view of Chinese philosophy, on the harmonious accord between Man and the cyclic evolution of the Universe, woven from the innumerable relationships and interactions of Yang and Yin."*

Emotional Polarity: In the field of the emotions, the most obvious polarities are love and hate, excitement and depression, confidence and fear, pleasure and pain, and like and dislike. Evidently, the life of the average human being is based on his emotional reactions to things, to events and to other human beings. These reactions have a definite function of enabling different experiences within human beings; but if they are allowed to take over, which generally happens in everyday life, humans become their slaves. Assagioli says that his system of Psychosynthesis efficiently handles these opposites.

Mental Polarity: *"Consideration of the human personality in its totality discloses various fundamental polarities which have been extensively investigated by modern psychology. The knowledge about the human being acquired in this process has stimulated the development of important psychological, educational and psychotherapeutic techniques. The principle polarities here are: Body - Psyche; Consciousness - the Unconscious; the lower Unconscious - the Superconscious; Pathos (Receptivity, Sensitivity, Reactivity) - Ethos (Activity, Dynamism, Will); Eros (Feeling)- Logos (Reason)."*

Spiritual Polarity: The main and most basic polarity in the spiritual realm exists between the personality and the Transpersonal Self, a polarity which, in Assagioli's words, is the cause of many inner conflicts until increasing merging or unification are achieved. Such unification is spiritual psychosynthesis.

Interindividual Polarity: This polarity is not mentioned very often outside Psychosynthesis, even though there are many interindividual polarities which are of great importance. The first and fundamental one is Man and Woman, which is simultaneously sexual one, as we saw previously. Then there are the polarities between parents and their children, between different groups, between individuals and the different groups to which they belong. Assagioli adds: *"Two kinds of polarities which are of great importance are that between the northern and southern individuals and groups in each nation and continent and that between Western and Eastern peoples."*

Each of these numerous polarities demands from us that we balance them. The following is a survey of the principles and methods of balancing opposite polarities with the object of resolving their tensions:

1. **Fusion of the two poles.**

2. **Creation of a new being.**

3. **Adjustment of the opposite poles.** In Assagili's system one attains that by means of an intermediary center which is a principle higher than both. Action of this kind can be brought about through two processes. Either by diminishing the amplitude of the oscillations between the two extremes, at times even to vanishing point, thus inducing a more or less complete neutralization. An instance of this is the oscillation between excessive authority and uncontrolled freedom in education of children. Or by consciously and wisely directing the alternations so that the result is harmonious, in accord with the cyclic alternations of both individual and general, human and cosmic, conditions, which is the method taught by Chinese philosophy and particularly by the *I Ching*.

4. **Synthesis**, the fourth method, is brought about by a higher element or principle which transforms the two poles into a higher reality.

The different types of polarity also require different solutions. We have the freedom of choosing between different methods of balancing. We should keep in mind that the indicated solutions are not always as clear-cut as the above enumeration might lead one to believe. Many times, they overlap or are combined in various ways.

In the field of electricity, the simplest outcome is neutralization through the fusion of the positive and negative charges. In the biological realm, health can be defined as a balance between a series of polarities, which exist between the divisions of the nervous system, between various endocrine glands, etc. In the same way, Assagioli teaches his followers, *"...psychological life can be regarded as a continual polarization and tension between differing tendencies and functions, and as a continual effort, conscious or not, to establish equilibrium."* The most important psychological polarities are emotion and reason, and extraversion and introversion.

In sexual polarity, the union of the two physical elements has a creative effect. The dynamism of their fusion brings about the birth of a child which has characteristics of both parents. In the fields of drives, emotions, and body sensations, the balancing of opposite qualities requires the intervention of a higher regulating principle of a mental, or more often transpersonal, nature. One should prevent the drives and the emotions from overwhelming and submerging the reason and the will. *"The best way to achieve this is to learn how to disidentify oneself from them at will, in order to be free at any time to maintain the "I", the center of consciousness, on a higher level above them, in order to be able to observe and evaluate them, and to wisely regulate them as needed."*

Assagioli pointed out that to regulate does not mean to suppress, but on the other hand it does not lead at all to lack of sensitivity. As an example, he takes the best known polarity of pleasure and pain. As long as we remain under the compulsion of this duality, always compulsively seeking pleasure and running away from pain, we shall not find permanent peace or permanent satisfaction. *"On the other hand, a forced inhibition, an artificial impassivity, certainly does not constitute a satisfactory solution. This can only be arrived at by means of that clear insight which enables us to understand the causes, the nature and the functions of both pleasure and pain."* From his many experiences man can get true wisdom, and learn to keep the center of consciousness stabilized more and more at a level above the alternations of personal pleasure and pain. Finally we can identify with the Universal Life, with the Higher or, as Assagioli calls it, Supra-Individual Self, with the Supreme, which transcends all opposites in ineffable bliss.

Psychology of Dual Brain

Let me remind you about our body being energetically polarized in the following ways (see my book on PEAT): Left and right side of a body, upper and lower part, and front and back part. This was first pointed out in alternative disciplines, but even official medicine is starting to accept that knowledge. These findings served as the basis for the creation of methods for exceeding human fragmentation and attaining the complete neurological, energetic and psychological integration.

A few decades ago British scientist Roger Sperry received the Nobel prize for proving experientially the existence of two different "minds" in human beings who had the connection between the two brain hemispheres severed. He did experiments with the so-called split brain, i.e., those patients who had their connections between the two hemispheres removed. After the operation the behavior of these patients was normal in every way, except one. Both hemispheres functioned independently. These patients were able to walk, talk and do many other things undisturbed, but there were some surprising findings.

With their communications link severed (cut corpus callosum) each side of the patient's brain was functioning independently. The right hand and eye could name an object, such as a pencil, but the patient could not explain what it was used for. When shown to the left hand and eye, the patient could explain and demonstrate its use, but could not name it. Further studies showed that various functions of thought are physically separated and localized to a specific area on either the left or right side brain hemispheres.

About his findings Sperry wrote: *"The main theme to emerge… is that there appear to be two modes of thinking, verbal and nonverbal, represented rather separately in left and right hemispheres respectively and that our education system, as well as science in general, tends to neglect the nonverbal form of intellect. What it comes down to is that modern society discriminates against the right hemisphere."*

Fredric Schiffer, a leading Harvard psychiatrist and researcher, began his experiments from Sperry's findings and found out that we are of two minds, each one with a different degree of maturity, and each one associated with the left or the right brain. In his provocative book, "Of Two Minds: The Revolutionary Science of Dual-Brain Psychology" Schiffer gave overwhelming evidence that each side of our brain possesses an autonomous, distinct personality -- with its own set of memories, motivations, and behaviors. In working with his patients, Schiffer discovered that strategically altering someone's visual field can positively or negatively affect that person's sense of well-being. He showed how using this technique of visual stimulation can activate the specific regions of the brain that harbour both traumatic and joyful memories. This dramatic breakthrough demonstrates how it is possible to access, isolate, and work with the memories encoded on one side of the brain.

His most important finding is that changing the visual field which a client points his sight to influences his feelings. His technique of visual stimulation with spectacles constructed in a special way activates specific parts of a brain in which are accumulated either traumatic or happy experiences. Schiffer found that some patients reported strong differences in their emotional state, their perception of themselves, and their world view when the restrictive goggles isolated one hemisphere. In his analysis, the restrictive goggles enable the healthier, more mature parts of the mind to reveal themselves.

Using this technique with patients suffering from anxiety, depression, post-traumatic stress disorder, psychosis, addiction, and stress-induced heart disease, Schiffer illustrated how dual-brain therapy is able to reach out to the troubled mind and help it. He provided extensive lightly edited transcripts of his therapy sessions with these patients to document the process.

In a concluding self-help chapter, readers of his book can experiment by covering first one eye and then the other to see whether they can detect a mood change and, if so, to begin a dialogue between their healthy and troubled selves to bring about a more balanced, happy, and productive relationship between them.

Schiffer constructs a theoretical bridge between neuroscience and psychology the soundness of which remains to be tested. His work is almost the founding stone of a new psychological discipline – dual-brain psychology.

Schiffer states, *"The aim of 'dual-brain' therapy is to mend the archaic, destructive ideas and emotions of the mind on the troubled side, to teach it that it is safer and more valuable than it learned during some traumatic experiences.... I teach patients how to recognize and listen for the mind in their troubled hemisphere, and then how to speak to it -- out loud!"* On the basis of these experiences, he reasons that there are two minds, each with a distinct personality associated with one hemisphere, and that an imbalance between them is responsible for mental illness.

In the chapter on two brain hemispheres you will find additional material about this fascinating field.

Marriage of Spirit

Seventeen years ago Leslie Temple-Thurston created a system of psychological and Spiritual liberation which she called "The Marriage of the Soul". She started from Carl Jung's words *"Wholeness...is not achieved by cutting off a portion of one's being, but by integrating the contraries."*

Her system is not widely known at present, but in the narrow circles of the mystically oriented people it is very popular. Her basic idea was that one must first experience the Unity Consciousness if one wants to go over many divisions and splits inside oneself or between oneself and others, or if one wants to live harmoniously and to be able to really love. Living from the state of the egoic self or human personality tends to make us believe that we are all separate individuals. We run around unconscious of our true state of being and of our oneness with each other. Thus, we lock ourselves into a sense of limitation and forget who we truly are.

In her book **The Marriage of Spirit**, she sets forth the idea that our human personality is a matrix of interlinked energy frequencies forming a design that has shape, structure and density -- a design that humankind has ultimately come to call the human personality.

In truth, all separation is an illusion. It is a pattern of energy impressed upon consciousness that forces us to accept a false perception that we are living life as separate individuals, as human beings separate from each other. This sense of split and separation is impressed even more upon us through naming and labelling. We characterize our self with names in order that we might identify our self as different, within the context of our human personality. Then we take these identifications and further distinguish them with designations such as male/female, good/bad, and so forth.

Our true Self is who we truly are in a state of wholeness, integrated with previous shadow-stuff, without illusions of separateness. Connecting with our true Self allows us to realize that we are True Spiritual Beings, not separate personalities (one should keep in the mind that the word "personality" comes from old Greek word "persona" which means "the mask").

This system embrace a group of principles and processing techniques based on the mystical teaching of uniting of opposites. In her own words, those techniques are simple and quick methods for re-establishing balance in everyday life.

They help a contemporary person to bridge the gap between Spirituality and demands of the material world, and enable one to reach a higher level of understanding with oneself and others. They also they give one a greater strength and certainty in life. In a world split in countless polarizations, they offer one a third path - the freedom from extremes through their merging and transcendence.

The first condition of liberation is to understand that in our material universe everything must turn to its opposite sooner or later. Therefore, for the individual the big step towards freedom is the realization that he/she is neither her positive nor negative traits. Traveling towards liberation, we must stop binding ourselves to one side, either positive or negative and to rise in unpolarized unifying consciousness.

In the second part of her book, Leslie Temple-Thurston describes practical techniques from her system. She says that the first exercises, called **"Polarities,"** make a fundamental shift in consciousness, because they clear mental contents.

The second group of exercises, **"Triangles,"** results in a clearing of emotions. This group of exercises is more difficult to work with, because they often activate strong emotions deeply buried in the unconsciousness.

Working with the third group of exercises, which she called **"Squares,"** the practitioner has the opportunity to attain the deepest and most permanent changes in his/her consciousness.

Owing to embracing a very wide field of Spiritual life, this system represents a holistic approach to clearing of physical body, emotions, mental structures, and Spirituality. Polarity processing, Temple-Thurston says, represents an efficient instrument for liberating man from a compulsive game of opposing forces. It has several steps.

First step: Select experiences which should be processed.

Second step: Make a detailed description in a written form of those experiences with the method of stream of consciousness.

Third step: From the written text, the Processor should choose all words and phrases which are burdened with emotional charge. For example, control, rage, anger, helpless, victim, cause, misfortune, tricked, impatient, breaking the law, **underestimate, confused**...etc.

Fourth step: Make a list of those words and phrases.

Fifth step: Write down on the paper their polar opposites. What follows is an example of such pairing:

Hasten   Slow down
Block   Unblock
Behind   In front of
Curse   Bless
Kill   Save
Impatient   Patient

Sixth and last step: You should leave the solution to God (Spirit, Higher Force, Creative Force of the Universe etc.). You do it through prayer. In it, you ask God (Spirit, Higher Force, Creative Force of the Universe...) to take over from you those unbalanced states of consciousness expressed through polarities and bring them into a proper balance. When this happens, Temple-Thurston says, you will have a new, higher level of seeing of the situation. Then say, "Thank You" to

God (Higher Force...etc) with the full conviction that it will happen. She gives an example of such prayer:

O Eternity, take over these unbalanced states of mine, harmonize them and clear them. Do it so that I am able to see more clearly and to find a way to my Spiritual homeland. Knowing that it will be done, I am grateful to you.

What follows as a part of her process is – wait for the Grace! Wait for a couple of seconds. In that period, do something: make a tea, wash dishes...whatever. When the Grace comes down to you, perhaps you will feel a shift in your physical body or in your subtle body. Or some memories will suddenly come to you, or you will start getting insights. Maybe you will have a significant dream next day. Sometimes what happens is an appearance of some friend of yours which will give you some information. Higher Force will remove the veil which covers your undestanding and you will suddenly develop a deeper level of understanding of your experiences.

Finally, Temple-Thurston gives a strange statement: *"If you don't feel the shift happened in your consciousness, it's not important. The shift will surely happen, but probably you will not recognize it...This is important: After you defined the thing and offered it completely to Spirit, you don't have to do anything more! Leave it to Him."*

Evidently, this system has value. Especially the Second and Third Steps, in which one describes in detail experiences and chooses from a text the words and phrases which have in them some charge. Perhaps there is one objection concerning the most important element of that process. If a shift in consciousness happens, good and fine. But if a shift does not happen, says Temple-Thurston, don't you worry. It happened, but you are not conscious of it.

The Sedona Method°

This system of therapy and self-development has existed for longer than half of a century, but it became really popular in the last 10 or 15 years. Lester Levenson was forced to developed it because of his greatly disturbed health. When he was 42, in 1952, he had a stroke, a sick liver, kidney stones, spleen troubles and perforated ulcers. Medical doctors sent him back home to die. He became deeply depressed. Meditating about his life and seeing traumatic experiences he had, Levenson got a very deep insight that the cause of his illneses were his emotions. The other insight had a practical value – if we release emotions which limit us we will have a sound and calm life. He used those two insights for a period of three months. By the end of that period, he became totaly healthy again.

So those were the insights from which he developed his Sedona method of emotional release. The quintessence of his method, he expressed with these words: *"The key which will give you the permanent happiness is the knowledge of how to release your accumulated negative emotions. Releasing them, you will get a stronger feeling of happiness and other things important for you in your life will be better: Money, health...absolutely everything."*

The basis of all our experiences is emotional, Levenson said. Negative emotions start corresponding thoughts, and negative thoughts push a person to the wrong activity or force such one to retreat from useful activities. Watching people around himself, Levenson noticed the main types of behavior caused by negative feelings: suppressing unpleasant emotions, expressing them and releasing them or letting go of them.

Suppressing has the worst consequences as smoking, alcohol, drugs and other compulsive activities. Not only are people supressing their own emotions, they are often supressing emotions of their children. In the therapy circles, there is a popular joke: In the first two years of child's life, everyone around them is trying to get them to walk and talk, and for the next eighteen years, everyone is trying to get them to sit and to shut up.

Another way we try to handle unpleasant emotions is through their expression. There are some methods which try to attain human wellbeing through expression of unpleasant emotions. Workshop leaders of such methods tell participants: Share with others whatever you feel toward them, that is the way to set yourself free from such emotions. Such a catharthic approach does not give a permanent positive solution, however, because with such behaviour the person is likely to hurt others around him/her. It causes guilt feelings, and relationships with the closest people around become aggravated.

Only the release of negative emotions gives permanent results and leads to wellbeing and good relationships with surrounding people. Levenson supposed that removal of negative characteristics will automatically bring about positive states, but this has not proved to be true in practice. Consequently, his followers perfected the system. Basically it was the same as Levenson made it for simple negative emotions, but for deep negative feelings and negative beliefs, they use today's more complex procedures. That means – the

Sedona method is not a rigid one. It accepts contributions of followers and that is the reason it is in constant development. It is logical that such a constantly developing system can not bypass the polarities which make the fundament and arena of human life. Recently (in 2003) Hale Dwoskin, one of the most eminent practitioners of this system, published the book "The Sedona Method," which presents as a very worthy practical manual.

One of the main ways for people to cause misfortune and disappointment is holding onto their own limited beliefs and feelings. The opposite attitude, we would say the opposite polarity, is to let them go or release them. Holding for something and letting it go are components of the natural process of living. *"Such understanding is the basis of the Sedona Method,"* writes Dwoskin in his book, which is evidently emphasizing the polar nature our world.

The process of letting go or releasement of emotions has a few definite steps.

First step

Concentrate on the unwanted emotion which you feel in yourself in the present moment and let yourself feel it completely.

Second step

Ask yourself one of the following 3 questions:

Could I let this feeling go?

Could I allow this feeling to be here?

Could I welcome this feeling?

These questions are intended to ask yourself whether you could take one of these actions. Both "yes" and "no" are acceptable answers. Very often a man will release an emotion although now he answers with "no".

Third step

It does not matter which question you started with, now ask yourself: "Would I do that?" In other words, it means "Am I willing to let go/release that emotion?" If the answer is "no", or if you are not sure, ask yourself: "Would I rather feel this feeling or would I rather be free of it?"

Forth step

Ask yourself, "When?" This is really an invitation to let it go now. You will see that in this phase of the process it is easy.

Fifth step

Repeat the preceding four steps as often as needed until you feel free of that emotion.

Practising this simple procedure will cause the person doing it to have more and more internal freedom. Applying the Sedona Method on himself, Lester Levinson discovered that people are able to cast off the yoke of their past when they clear four fundamental needs which appear as polarities:

Wanting to control others – Wanting to be controlled by others

Wanting approval/love – Wanting to give others approval/desire to love others

Wanting security/survival – Wanting to die

Wanting to be separate – Wanting to be One with others

The final goal of the Sedona Method is the freedom to decide what to be, to do, and to have, and what you don't want to be, don't want to do, and don't want to have. It is the natural state of Being when we are not able to be disturbed with what happened in our past.

Flemming Funch: Integrating the Polarities of the Self

As I said before, the method for integrating Polarities which Flemming Funch developed from different disciplines, mostly from NLP, is, in my opinion, the best of all systems outside the field of Spiritual Technology. It can be learned quickly and it is easy to apply to oneself or one's clients.

Perhaps the only objection could be that Funch repeats himself more than once and has a tendency to present unimportant details which unnecessarily burden the description of his method. Therefore, I cut some parts of his description of the method. So, here it is in his own words.

Often we perceive a part of ourselves as unwanted, inadequate, or annoying. We don't necessarily always feel that way, but we may frequently have the idea that that part of ourselves needs to go. We don't like that part, so we try to "cut it off." We may experience this part of ourselves as alien or even as a separate personality. I have often looked back at situations in great wonder, flabbergasted at my own behavior. With age, I came to recognize distinct patterns of behavior that clustered together in different situations or with certain moods that appeared to both me and others to be at great odds with one another. Often one part of me seemed to watch the other in a kind of dissociation. One personality took the leading role in my self made play while the other became the audience. This is more common than I once thought.

Our natural state is to be whole, complete, balanced, and free. We assume we can't really lose it; we can only temporarily fragment ourselves and forget about some of the fragments. So, if we find that a part of ourselves is lacking, then we know right away that the lacking qualities are found in the "opposite" part of ourselves and that they will inevitably be there. If we can get them to work better together or to integrate completely, then we will become whole. An important rule here is that any part of a person is useful for something. Every part of us is "of the gods." There is no part that is not sacred and with purpose for the person. It is because the part is lacking other qualities or because its purpose got sidetracked or outdated somehow that it currently does something that isn't particularly welcome. If we can ferret out those useful and positive reasons, then any conflicts would tend to dissolve or become very easy to manage.

First we must determine that we actually have such a part of ourselves:

"Is there a part of you that (gets angry)?"

That lets us isolate it, and it makes us realize that it is not all of us. We differentiate from it at this point. We will usually have a small realization on that actually being the case. So, by the simple action of getting recognizing that a part of us is doing something unwanted, we have accomplished several things:

We have isolated that area of our personal reality.

We have differentiated it from ourselves.

We can now study it. We have implicitly admitted to being responsible for it. We have opened the door to handling it. We have excluded a lot of potential complexity about it.

Now, the next step is to get the part that is at odds with the first, unwanted part:

"Is there a part of you that is opposite to (the angry part)?"

We will also answer that quite readily. It is not particularly something to search for. We get a simple label for that part, e.g. "The calm part of me". Avoid going into searching for precise wording. We don't want a very precise label; we just want the general area.

We have now isolated the other side of the coin. We have to some degree recognized that that is also a distinct part of us. We have taken some sort of responsibility for it, and we have differentiated it from the self that is watching all of this, the self that we are currently talking with.

Differentiating this second part might take a little bit more work than the first part. The client might insist at first that it is simply "me". No problem, we just need to isolate which part of "me" that is. A little dialogue should produce a little bit more definition, such as "the calm part of me" or "the rational part of me". The client will naturally feel that this second part is closer to her "true" self, and that is quite fine. This second part is probably the one that feels that the first part is unwanted. Either one of them might be dominant, though. Also, both of them might be more or less unwanted.

Our underlying principle here is that something that was whole has been split into a dichotomy of two parts or polarities. That split creates an ongoing conflict or push-pull contest between the two parts. Our objective is to re-integrate those two parts with each other. Our plan is to first recognize that they are there and then work out what it is that is keeping them apart.

Neither Part A nor Part B is whole or perfect. We might initially feel that Part A is completely unwanted and want to get rid of it, that Part B is our own true self. However, that is one of the reasons we have the problem we have. The parts are separated by lack of acceptance, interaction, or understanding. The situation will persist as long as we can't accept both parts and as long as they can't accept each other. Despite our initial opinions, Part A will be found to have qualities that B doesn't have and Part B will have qualities that A doesn't have. We might regard both parts as unwanted, and that is fine too. That is actually easier to deal with than if we regard one of them as "Me." We are moving in the direction of recognizing that each part has its own portion of pros and cons and that the pros and cons will complement each other. Having differentiated the two parts, we can start working on them.

We aren't going to ask for any specific ultimate goal or purpose of the part. That would get us off into searching for labels. The part is most likely a composite; it doesn't have one single purpose. Trying to find one would mislabel and generalize a bunch of things in a way that isn't very useful. However, we should get a good idea of the general line of activity for the part, and what it is trying to accomplish. When we have gotten all the answers available for Part A, we can switch over to Part B and do the same thing. We can also get at what each part decidedly is not doing, what it is holding back or trying not to do.

"Are these two parts there at the same time, or are they taking turns?"

Get one part to actually say something to the other. Do it both ways, as with all of these questions. Encourage a conversation, get the parts to answer the communication, and so forth. It's not necessary to playact it to any great extent unless we want to. Mainly, we should get into the mode of listening to what each part of ourselves wants to say without trying to logically construct it. We also need to get the parts to like each other more by encouraging them to do so:

"Does (part A) accept (part B)?"

"Does (part A) appreciate (part B)?"

"Does (part A) like (part B)?"

"Does (part A) admire (part B)?"

"Does (part A) love (part B)?"

We want to get each part to open up to the other and exchange their secrets if possible. If nothing else, each one can appreciate something about the other for purely selfish reasons. Each side has something the other side wants. But we need to gradually move towards the recognition that the other part is a part of itself. Sooner or later we will start realizing the ridiculousness of splitting ourselves up into two imperfect packages that are in conflict with each other.

Once we have recognized that both parts have positive qualities, and we have put them on the road to being more willing to deal with each other. Now we need them to learn from each other.

"What could (part A) learn from (part B)?"

Each part has something the other is missing. They both need to recognize that, and they need to become willing to exchange what they've each got. It might be necessary to negotiate an arrangement by which it can be possible to exchange qualities. You might make it clear to each one that they don't have to give anything up. They can simply learn something more that will make them more able to do what they are doing. It might be necessary to clarify what each one wants, in order to make them understand that some of the qualities of the other side would be helpful.

Visualize the two sides exchanging energies.

This can lead to a variety of phenomena. Most commonly, we might find that an unpleasant feeling appears whenever the parts are getting close to each other. That would naturally lead to finding some incidents to re-experience. We would transform the feeling, and then return to the polarity integration and see how things proceed. We might also find fixed ideas which now need restructuring. It might be that time is needed, or that we feel overwhelmed by the speed of all the changes occurring, and that is fine. In that case, we simply need to plan how the process will continue. Perhaps the two parts need to feel each other out over the next couple of weeks to see how it will work. Maybe a full integration is too much of a change and should be done in stages. Either way, it isn't a problem. Our objective is to set a direction towards more integration.

Integration may perhaps be akin to what we refer to as Knowledge and Conversation of the Holy Guardian Angel (like in the Golden Down magic) in many respects. I think there are different levels of awareness and more than just two parts to be integrated. Integration seems to be an ongoing process that even once completed needs constant maintenance and strengthening. Once the parts of the self unite in friendship, they may find new conflicts as their friendship grows and deepens and as they change because, like all things, the self is not static but ever-changing and dynamic.

Flemming Funch's conclusions are evidently correct in the frame of his system. But they are mainly exceeded by the DP3 method, because it bypasses many of the difficulties he speaks about. I should point out that before I developed DP3, I used Funch's method for integrating polarities more than once and I had quite good results. But things are changing, better methods are coming up in all fields of human activity, and therapy and self-development are not exceptions.

7

Two Brain Hemispheres

"Intuitive spirit is a holy gift and rational spirit is only loyal servant. We created such a society that praises a servant forgetting a holy gift." Albert Einstein

The newest research confirms a teaching of oriental philosophy that the world is dualistically experienced through the body, nerves and energetic structure of the human being. For a long time, the human brain was understood as a unique organ through which we mainly experience ourselves and the world around us. Fairly recently, science has confirmed that the anatomy and function of two hemispheres of our brain are clearly distinguished. The functions of these two hemispheres are totally different. I have already quoted some significant information from Fredric Schiffer about the revolutionary science of dual-brain psychology.

The left hemisphere of the brain is rational, analytical and with a significant tendency to control the whole personality. It observes the world linearly. It responds to verbal instructions, resolving problems by logic and comparing different elements and characteristics of each particular part, searches for differences and tends to make detailed plans and logical structure. This hemisphere searches for facts, tends to express itself through logical talk and writing, controls emotions, and bases everything on cause and effect. It tends to organize sensory data in a logical way. For example, its language is linear and words come logically one after the other in a well thought out way.

The right hemisphere of the brain is the source of emotions, intuition, artistic experiences and creation. It is a foundation of general impressions, more oriented on the whole than on the integral parts, focused on forms and emotions. It is intuitive, resolving problems by presentiment and prediction, searches for similarity in different structures, tends to react spontaneous and unpredictably, accepts indications and not fully clear information, prefers questions not implying only one answer. This hemisphere prefers equality rather than authority.

Such classification makes clear to us that there are two basic ways of thinking directly connected to these two hemispheres. One is mainly verbal and analytical and the other is nonverbal and intuitive. Our mental processes are a combination of these two hemispheres, although there is alternating domination of one or another. All significant accomplishments come from harmonious interaction of these two hemispheres. All recognized achievements in different human activities seem to be a result of a stroke of inspiration. After intellectual and logical data analysis, with a dominance of the left hemisphere, comes a sudden intuitive breakthrough solution, with a dominance of the right hemisphere. At the end of this process, the left brain analytical hemisphere starts analyzing and balancing all given insights. Without the right hemisphere, there wouldn't be fruitful ideas; and without the left brain hemisphere, there wouldn't be a practical explanation for their use.

Some researchers claim that, generally speaking, the right brain hemisphere is specialized for our safety, which consequently means retreating, and the left brain hemisphere for aggression and new experiences, which means advancing.

It is well known that one hemisphere is able to have its own thoughts and emotions and to act with a high degree of independence from the other. That means that these two hemispheres are able to act in harmony or in conflict. If they are in harmony, brain activity is efficient. If they are in conflict, there are serious problems for that personality (see data from Fredric Schiffer). Consequently, there are two possible ways for these two brain hemispheres to relate to one another: reciprocal synergy or reciprocal inhibition.

Interactive harmony causes one hemisphere to intensify the activity of another. Inhibition means that one hemisphere of the brain brakes or reduces the activity of another.

If one of them is extremely dominant, it makes the other passive and relatively weaker. In such cases, roughly said, a person has only half of the brain at his disposal for resolving of life problems. It is optimal when those two hemispheres are so well balanced that the one whose processes correspond to the actual situation has dominance as well.

The relationship between these two brain hemispheres doesn't influence only mental processes happening in the brain, but the whole body. The left hemisphere controls the right side of the body, and the right hemisphere controls the left side. Even in ancient times, some people were consciousness aware of this. In mythology, the right side of the body corresponds to rational, masculine, and affirmative characteristics and the left side of the body to feminine, intuitive characteristics.

Western civilization generally emphasizes the left brain hemisphere's characteristics, neglecting the characteristics of the right one. Regarded from an historical perspective, the genesis of classical science is a result of left hemisphere domination. Right brain hemisphere's characteristics were ignored until Sigmund Freud introduced the concept of the unconsciousness in psychology, giving to it characteristics of sustained aggression and irrationality that to a high degree rule over human behavior.

The human brain is structured to act as a unique unity, as for survival it is necessary to use both brain hemispheres, depending on the actual situation. But, in most people only one of these two brain hemispheres has dominance in a given moment. There are people who are capable only of learned ways of thinking and application, incompetent for any creative approach to life; and there are people who tend towards an extreme emphasis on the right brain hemisphere, who live in their unreal world of personal feelings and fantasies. Well balanced people who have a complete integration of hemispheres reality live in both their hemispheres, rational and emotional, capable to reach the world in both a feminine and masculine way, not ignoring either of these ways of perceiving.

Although knowledge about the different activities of the two brain hemispheres seems to be a result of a new age, such an impression is typical only for Western civilization. Such knowledge was evidently present in Ancient Egypt and India. So called Sacred Geometry shows that ancient Egyptian mystics had been taught about the two sides to everything that exists, and which corresponded to the left and right brain hemispheres. It was emphasized that there was positive and negative thought in every life event, and both a feminine and masculine orientation in every life situation.

8

IDA, PINGALA AND SUSHUMNA

In some of the books about cellular consciousness that have appeared recently, there is a statement that the most significant ontogenesis' classification is the first division of the fertilized ovary which, by further divisions, causes creation of the whole being. This very first division, which is simultaneously organic and energetic, is the basis of polarization within human beings.

As I already said, there are three main energy polarizations in the human body: left and right, upper and lower, and front and back. The most evident polarization of those three is the one manifested by breathing through our left and right nostril. Although that was common knowledge in India over 2000 years ago, it was unknown in Western medicine until the end of the 19th century. Those who practiced oriental systems have known that this alternating breathing through nostrils is connected with dominant body activities of the left and right sides of the body, or the left and right brain hemispheres. Swara Yoga teaches that the dominance of each nostril in breathing changes regularly. The periodic alternation of the nostrils balances the whole system, which is very important for the application of Spiritual Technology methods, especially PEAT.

This phenomenon is quite late to be noticed in the West. In 1889, a German doctor R. Kayser named it "nasal breathe." Only in the 1980's, because of pharmaceutical research into nasal congestive problems, has Western Medicine shown a bigger interest in this phenomenon. That brought Swara Yoga closer to Western medicine. This phenomenon has been scientifically classified today into the Ultradian Rhythm (rhythmical changes that are happening daily in all people). In most people they are happening each 90 minutes. It is possible to observe personal ultradian rhythms by observing the way the average person's thinking alternates between clear thinking and its opposite, mental slowing down and dull-mindedness. During that period of confused thinking, people are not able to think fast and clearly. They usually have an empty look or their attention is not concentrated on that what they would like it to be. People who don't have ultradian rhythms behave like persons who are sleep deprived. They tend to be nervous and tense, to make mistakes, and to easily become ill.

There are some scientific studies (Rossi, "The Psychobiology of Mind-Body Healing", 1986) which point out that during stress and strenuous time, the intensity and regularity of ultradian rhythms change, leading to many psychosomatic illnesses. Rossi writes about it: *"I would like to mention that in my experience the onset of a disease is often signaled by a lack of a rhythm…"*

He says further about Debra Werantz (1981) and her researches: *"…who established that the rhythmical exchanges of dominance of brain hemisphere is connected with a similar periodic alternation of the nostrils' dominance through breathing."*

Such rare researches only confirm the ancient knowledge of Swara Yoga. It deals also with the various qualities of the flow of the breath in nostrils in terms of both cellular and cosmic import. The ancient Hindu sages believed that, by learning to read the breath and manipulate it, we can learn to read the outer and inner universe and also come into harmony and greater functionality. Swara Yoga teaches that there are many factors which influence these flows including the lunar cycles, the time of day, etc.

When the nostrils are balanced, the energy can flow into the Sushumna – being harmonized and synchronized and our latent non-dual dynamics becomes activated. This is the best period for meditation and spiritual practices.

Nadis is the name for nerves channels through which Kundalini energy is flowing. According to Swara Yoga, there are 72,000 Nadis and the main three are: Ida, Pingala and Sushumna. Originating in Muladhara Chakra, Ida and Pingala alternate at each chakra until they reach Ajna charka, Ida from the left side and Pingala from the right side, where they meet again with Sushumna, balancing and integrating in it. Continuing beyond the Ajna chakra, Ida and Pingala end in the left and right brain hemispheres respectively. They are complementary energetic streams that flow not through nerves but within the energetic field.

Ida is the left energy channel connected with a right brain hemisphere. It is passive, introverted, white, feminine, cold, also representing the moon energy or Chandra.

Pingala is the right energy channel. Pingala is extroverted, red, masculine, hot, representing the sun energy. Pingala is connected with left brain hemisphere. Prana, the all-pervading vital energy of the universe flows alternating through Ida and Pingala, activating our energy system on the right or on the left side of the body, respectively.

This alternate breathing through the left or right nostril lasts in a healthy person approximately one hour and half. In the moment of exchange of dominance, the breathing is balanced and the energy flows harmoniously through both body sides. In Swara Yoga, this phenomenon is called Sushumna breath, integrating and neutralizing both sun and moon energy, masculine and feminine, left and right. If the dominance of one nostril lasts for a longer time, it leads to emotional, psychological and energetic disorder.

It is established that different physiological and psychological states are conditioned with a dominance of one of nostrils. Deep sleep is more quickly induced by left-nostril breathing; appetite and digestive function are greater during right-nostril breathing. Sex is most satisfying if the male is breathing through the right-nostril and the woman breathing primarily through the left-nostril. During the dominance of the left nostril and consequently activated right brain hemisphere, we are more open to new ideas, and dominance of the right nostril and left brain hemisphere are very good for logical thinking and analyzing facts.

The intentional changing nostrils dominance can be learned very easily. The left and right nostrils should be closed by a finger alternately. A nostril which makes the highest pitch sound is the one that is most constricted. When the balanced breathing through both nostrils happens, then there is a shift in consciousness that directly relates deeply to the core nervous system. That creates a change from dualistic imbalance into non-dual co-operation, into harmony and unity. Such non-dual breath affects the mind profoundly, while the energy moves in the central, non-dual nadis Sushumna rather than in the polar nadis Ida and Pingala.

As it is very unpractical to wait long until Sushumna is activated, or at least Ida, which is connected with the right side of the brain, emotions and intuition, there are a few ways to change the course of breathing from non-favorable into favorable. The easiest way is by pushing the opposite nostril with thumb, breathing for few minutes through the one you want to open.

The next way is to push your underarm with the opposite hand. If you want to activate Ida breath then push your right underarm with your hand. If you want to activate Pingala then push your left underarm.

For the next method, you need more time. Lie down on the opposite side from the nostril you want to keep open. You should lie down for a few minutes, and if you don't have a deviated septum or a bad cold, your nostril will open.

The easiest way to change your nostrils flow is to sit quietly for few minutes and, without moving your head, concentrate your look on that side where the stuffed nostril is which you would like to open.

We can apply this knowledge about nostril activities in spiritual processing, especially with Deep Peat. One of the main difficulties during this process is that the client is not in an emotional but, rather, an intellectual state of mind. In such case, it is necessary to activate the right brain hemisphere by opening the left nostril.

As it is impractical to wait these short window of well balanced periods that last only few minutes, it is recommended that you apply the quoted techniques in order to open the left nostril. You may ask why is it better for Deep Peat to have the left nostril opened, having dominance of Ida? The answer is very simple. As already said, the main problem during Deep Peat is the client who intellectualizes the situation, trying to solve the problem rationally, comparing the present situation with similar ones, remembering previous experiences and methods that have already been proved in the past. And when a rational position is a dominant one, then a left brain hemisphere is activated. What we want is exactly the opposite, activation of an intuitive and emotional state in a client, as occurs when the right brain hemisphere is activated.

9

NEUTRALIZATION OF ENERGY POLARIZATION

Beside those methods that are used in Swara Yoga, there are a few very specific methods for eliminating energy disharmony within the body, or balancing its vital energy, which have been developed in the last two decades by meridian therapy practitioners. Polarization is not something bad. On the contrary, it is the basis for healthy body function. In order to have optimized life processes, it is necessary that energy streams alternatively from one body side to another one. When such a cycle is broken, the body suffers from energy blockages and confusion, leading to mental and emotional disharmony. And disharmony causes different personal problems.

Here there are some of the methods for the neutralization of energy polarization.

First exercise:

1. I repeat the exercise I have already written about in my Peat book as a method for normalization of disordered energy polarization. Put your thumb, pointer and middle finger of your non-dominant hand on your belly and, with two fingers of your dominant hand, rub alternatively the points of your collarbones, each for ten seconds.

2. Continue keeping the three fingers of your non-dominant hand on your bally and with two fingers of your dominant hand rub under your nose and under your upper lip for 10 sec.

3. Continue keeping the three fingers of your non-dominant hand on your belly and, with two fingers of your dominant hand, rub the lowest part of your spine.

End each of these or similar exercises by holding your hands like in prayer. It is a very simple technique. The inner dialogue between your two brain hemispheres stops when you do it this way.

I additionally advise this: Repeat the whole process so that the fingers of your dominant hand come on your belly and three mentioned zones are rubbed by the fingers of your non-dominant hand.

Second exercise:

Without moving your head, quickly circle your eyes in the shape of a big upright number eight. The number 8 should be so big as to fill up your whole field of vision. Do it few times.

Now move your eyes in the shape of a big horizontal number 8, again doing it a few times. Do it as fast as you can. End this exercise the same way as the previous one by holding your hands like in prayer.

Light and Heat

Take a comfortable sitting position and relax. Visualize your brain as two hemispheres connected by a big cable made of thick brain tissue. Imagine you are within your right brain hemisphere moving through it and notice everything that attracts your attention – little movements, concentrated energy fields etc. Is there any light within this space or shade or any color? Now try to lighten it, imagine a feeling of a big light within it, and imagine the feeling of big heat.

Imagine you are passing through the Corpus Callosum into your left brain hemisphere. Pay attention, if you notice any detail within it. Imagine that there is dark and cold within that brain hemisphere. Keep that impression for few seconds.

Turn back through the Corpus Callosum to your right brain hemisphere and imagine again that within it there is a bright light and a high heat. Be in this feeling for few seconds.

Return to your left brain hemisphere, imagining again a feeling of darkness and cold. Keep those sensations for few seconds.

Return again to your right brain hemisphere keeping alive an image of light and heat as strong as you can.

Now do the DP3 process on both your right and left brain hemispheres. Later in the text, there are instructions how to do the DP3 process. Feel as strong as you can your right brain hemisphere and notice 4 elements that you experience in that moment. Then feel as strong as you can your left brain hemisphere and notice 4 elements felt in that moment. Keep on doing this until all differences disappear. It will not be long until that happens.

Finish this exercise again with folded hands like in prayer.

Exercises with simultaneous tasks

The students of George Ivanovich Gurdjieff used to practice the following and similar exercises. In these exercises, we use the opposite movements. That is the reason why those exercises are not easy to do at the very beginning, but this feeling doesn't last for long. Many practitioners are very happy with the results they achieved in integrating the brain hemispheres this way.

1. Move your shoulder on the right side as much as you can and simultaneously move your head on your left side. Shoulders-right, head-left.

2. Then you change movements: your shoulder and your head on the same side at the same time; then shoulder and head simultaneously on the opposite sides…the same…the opposite…the same…the opposite.

3. Now make your exercise even more difficult. While your shoulders and your head are in the opposite movements, let your eyes move in the shoulder's direction, which is the opposite of your head direction. If it is difficult to do this exercise, overcome difficulties by step by step exercising. That means to forget your shoulders and move only your head right side and your eyes left side; then your head left side and your eyes right side. Try to keep your eyes' movements regular, avoiding leaps. When you can control these movements, take another step by moving your shoulders at the same time as you head and eyes movements.

Finish this exercise with a prayer gesture.

10

CREATION AND DISCREATION OF SUBJECTIVE REALITY

"When you are able to put your hand where your hand already is, you will enter the Kingdom." Jesus Christ in the "Gospel of Thomas"

This chapter is very complicated. I ask for your persistence in reading and studing it. Do not be discouraged if you are not able to grasp it at once. Follow examples from practical life, they will make it easier for you to understand the concepts. The sound advice is to read this text a couple of times. It will pay off. After you undestand it, you will be able to estimate the value of any therapeutic systems methods of self-development.

True Being creates its subjective reality through decisions and identities. Decisions are outside of this universe, but they start energetic processes in Being, which consists of 4 elements: mental pictures, emotions, body sensations, and thoughts. Discreation of that reality goes the opposite way, through dissolution or discreation of previously created elements and, finally, we have discreation of decisions.

Knowledge of the cycle of creation and discreation comes from Hindu philosophy a few thousand of years old. It points out that everything existing in this universe and human consciousness has its beginning, persisting and disappearing or the end. In Hindu philosophy, that cycle was personified in the substantial qualities of three deities: Brahma the Creator, Vishnu the Sustainer and Shiva the Destroyer.

Return to Oneness

In other words, the cycle of action, of creation and destroying, could be expressed this way: Creation, Persisting, Destroying.

Connected with these three fundamental processes, there are the four states of existence. I discussed them in my other books. Here I will shortly repeat it, because these states of existence are significant for an understanding of discreating (eliminating) unwanted states (problems), and also for the creation and maintenance of desired states and circumstances.

ALPHA or FIRST DECISION: This refers to the primary, original creation. The main characteristic of **alpha** or **first decision** is movement toward a goal and intention to attain it.

What complicates an easy understanding is that we must duplicate it if we want to discreate it. For a correct understanding, I will give here an additional explanation. In the **first decision,** we make a decision to create something new, if it does not already exist. But if something already exists and we recreate it, in other words if we create a perfect duplicate (copy) of our previous creation, it will vanish. With such an act, we will discreate, destroy or remove from existence the previous creation.

BETA or SECOND DECISION or DECISION OF DEFEAT: The main characteristic of Second Decision is stopping and retreating from the goal of creation. In essence, it is **the change of existing.**

The normal tendency of human beings is to maintain an existing state and circumstance which the person deems desirable. But for every phenomenon to persist in the physical universe, it is necessary to put some change in it. This could be produced intentionally, or such an act could be unconscious: but for persistence, there must be a change. For example, when a man experiences some trauma, many times he thinks and talks about it, he changes it unconsciously, connecting it with similar experience, taking into it his hopes, regrets, expectations, fears, etc. Old time Hindu philosophers used to say that the whole universe would vanish if changes in it were to stop for even one moment.

The problem for a human Being starts in the moment when Being, trying to realize its primary decision (alpha), experiences a defeat. In that moment, Being makes the secondary decision, the **decision of defeat** (or beta). That decision of defeat cannot destroy the first, primary decision, but the two of them coexist, one opposite the other until they are discreated. I will give you a detailed explanation of this mechanism latter on.

EXISTENCE or Reality is a state which exists in one moment in all existing worlds, and also in the subjective universe of the Being. Existence is the process of permanent change. Everything is changing, only the change is eternal. In the subjective universe of a Being, that state, existence, appears after the Being experienced a defeat, in other words after the **change of original creation.**

DENYING OF EXISTING (or Denying of Reality) is denying of some state, circumstances or appearance; it is an attempt to remove something out of existence with force. In his own universe, an individual does it through denying existing states or circumstances. However, no matter how illogical it seems to uninitiated people, denial is a sure way for something to continue existing. Here there is a law: **Resistence causes persistence.** Buddha expressed it with the following words: *"You become that what you resist "*

The Duplication of Experience

When we make the first decision (alpha), we try to create something new. But if something already existed and we create it again -- that means if we create the perfect duplicate or copy of the previous creation -- we will discreate it, remove it from existence. That act we call **duplication.** In essence it is **exactly the same as the first decision** (or **alpha).** It must be a perfect copy of alpha for discreation to happen. This is the general mechanism of creation and discreation of the metaphysical or subjective universe of an individual, which the majority of people do not understand. Using that mechanism of duplication in PEAT, we ask a Client to experience his/her unwanted state as completely as possible, in other words to **duplicate it,** and at the same time we warn him/her not to resist it, not to deny it, not to fight it, not to supress it... because all such acts mean change and will inevitably bring about its persistence.

In contemporary therapy, the process of duplication is almost unknown even though it is of vital importance for removal of unwanted states. I will repeat: **To duplicate some experience means to create in one's consciousness a perfect copy of it.** Such an act causes its discreation, which means its dissolution and vanishing from the existence.

Understanding of the process of duplication enables one to understand and apply correctly any kind of therapy. Simply said, when in our consciousness we copy some metaphysical creation exactly, in all of its elements, it gets discreated, which means it vanishes. But the partial duplication of some creation brings about its partial disappearance.

Such an approach is completely different from what we are taught from earliest childhood by parents, school, school teachers, books, ideologies, religions, i.e., to fight actively against our weaknesses, to overpower them, to suppress them, to reject them, cover or forget them. Experience shows that such conduct does not lead to removal of problems, but just to the opposite – to their persistence. If they seem to be resolved, such a solution is short-lived, because problems are just suppressed from consciousness and sooner or later they reappear.

However, in many systems of therapy or personal development, duplication happens more or less, but the knowledge of it is vague or completely is missing. What is a psychoanalyst doing during psychoanalysis which takes four full years? Demanding that his Client follow his/her free associations and report them, the psychoanalyst leads him/her to circle around a problem from a distance and from time to time to confront some of the many elements of the problem. That way, the Client needs four years to duplicate, bit by bit, his problem in totality. In other systems of therapy we see a similar approach but, luckily enough, the duplication is much shorter.

Knowing the principle and mechanism of duplication, we in Spiritual tehcnology lead a person to experience his/her unwanted state as it is, truthfuly and accurately, and to duplicate it that way. If a Client feels a fear, we ask him/

her not to fight it, neither to suppress and neglect it, but to experience it as completely as possible. Only then does it disappear. This applies to all unwanted states, of course.

In Deep PEAT, the duplication helps us to move down the chain of contents. Experiencing each one of them, we make them disappear, and the vacuum which appears in their place sucks into itself the next content. Experiencing one after another content on the chain of contents, we come to the All-Source; and it is the Void, or the Pleroma state, which exists immediately before Void. To prevent a Client from suppressing or forgetting some element of an existing state, we ask the Client to dramatize it, and that means to experience it stronger then it really is. That way, he/she will duplicate it more completely.

Although the mechanism of duplication of contents of the consciousness or of the body seems to be a new discovery, it surely is not. In the quotation from **"*Gnostic Gospels*"** found in Nag Hamadi, in the "Gospel of Thomas", Christ said to his disciples: *"When you are able to put your hand where your hand already is, you will enter the Kingdom."* Evidently this is a perfect metaphor of a perfect duplication.

Three Ways to Discreate the Primary Decision (Alpha)

Every creation starts with primary decision or alpha to create some experience, state or circumstance. Based on that decision, Being starts the cycle of creation: It creates, creates, creates…until it creates a perfect copy of its first decision, or until, in that creation, it gets defeated.

I have said that the primary decision could not be destroyed by the second decision. The reason for this is because any and every decision is a part of True Being, Atman; it is Atman's stuff. Decisions are outside of the physical universe, but they set into motion activities of the physical universe – mental images, emotions, body sensations and thoughts.

There are only 3 ways that the primary decision (alpha) can vanish from existence!

1. **Human Being can change or delete its own decision.** For example, a man decided to drink a beer, then changes his mind and drinks a juice. In that change of decision, he did not experience any defeat!

2. **Human Being can realize his/her decision in the physical reality.** This means the creation of a duplicate in the physical universe. For example, a man want to buy a car. After some time he buys it, which means he realizes his decision to have it. In the moment when he gets it, his decision to have it vanishes. If in that moment someone asks him, what does he want, he will not answer – I want a car. He can express some other desire – to have a house, better or more beautiful car, etc. For the Human Being, there is nothing more strange than decision – when Being sees it realized, it vanishes.

3. **Human Being can realize his/her decision in his/her consciousness.** On that mechanism many psychological and especially Spiritual processes are based. For example, when during meditation or psychotherapy a man recognizes and duplicates in his

consciousness his decision from a long time ago, that overgrown decision vanishes for good.

As I said before, a problem originates for one when one experiences a defeat of one's primary decision (alpha). In the moment of defeat, one makes a second decision of defeat (beta). From that moment on, there exist two opposite decisions within the individual which make an unpleasant seesaw, which means the existence of an unpleasant problem.

Let us take an example from life. A man fell in love with a beautiful girl and he decided to marry her and live happily. There are three possible variants in this story. In the first, after some time, the man fell in love with another girl and married her. In such a change of primary decision, there is no defeat! And there is no problem (except maybe for the deserted girl).

In the second variant, he married his girl and they "lived happily ever after." Be careful now – in the moment when he realized his decision in the real world, his decision vanished. If immediately after marriage some friend asks him what does he want now, **he will never answer – I want to marry my girl friend!** Having been realized, his decision to marry her disappeared. Now he can have other decisions: to have children, to buy a house, to advance in his profession, but he cannot have his original desire to marry his girl friend!

Even if it seems strange, we are not interested in happy outcomes, because in them there is no real drama, nor a beginning of a problem. For an understanding of how we create our world, our subjective universe, much more interesting is an unhappy version. In it our madly in love young man proposes marriage to that beautiful girl, but she turns his offer down, telling him she will marry another, much worthier person. In the moment of the rejection and humiliation our unhappy man makes his beta or the decision of defeat: *"Love is dangerous!"*, *"Love leads to humiliation"*, *"One should avoid women"* and similar. But that **beta** does not remove his original decision to marry the girl he loves. As I said before, decisions are part of True Being and they are **indestructible** until the Being Itself discreates them. Therefore, both decisions exist, one opposite the other, making an unpleasant and often very painful seesaw. Between them, an energetic ridge is created made of a negative energetic charge, and the person does not understand his own behavior. Whenever he is attracted to a good looking lady, he feels unpleasant body sensations, emotions, has inferior thoughts, mental images of possible rejection, etc. Later on, he will probably marry another woman, but his decision of defeat will persist. He can try to bury it in his unconsciousness, to forget it by smoking, drinking, taking drugs, having illegal love affairs which he does not understand, etc. Such a state of existence we call the **denying of existing**, but it cannot handle his problem, because denying, suppressing, rejecting, resistence always brings about persistence of the state.

Sometimes people ask, is it possible to eliminate the decision of defeat by creating an opposite positive decision? Some have got a mistaken notion that it is possible and use different ways to attain it, for example affirmations (autosuggestions). But I have to repeat once more, beta or the defeated decision is eternal until it is duplicated and that way eliminated from existence. True, we can cover it for some time with the opposite affirmations, but sooner or later it raises its head again and appears in consciousness. In some situations, the man can act against it and sometimes he overpowers it.

Return to Oneness

For example, even if he feels the tension in the presence of an attractive woman, he can force himself to communicate with her, but the tension will follow him as long as he does not duplicate that beta.

Experience shows that neither the changing of existing, nor the denying of existing, is the solution for unwanted states and problems of Human Being, but that only duplication gets that job done.

Usually such betas have been forgotten a long time ago; that is the reason we are not conscious of them. But in meditation or during a good process we can duplicate them. Usually we remove a lot of charge covering them, and when we strip all charge from them we are able to duplicate them and make them vanish.

Because this stuff is very important, I will repeat it, approaching it from a different angle.

Perennial philosophy teaches that decision always pops up from the Void, which is the deepest essence of the Being. If it is realized, it vanishes into the Void where it came from.

If the Being undergoes a defeat, the Being makes a disastrous decision (decision of defeat) which together with the first decision makes an unpleasant seesaw in ones life and is the basis of ones problem. Innumerable pairs of such polar opposites make the subjective universe of human being: to have and not to have, power and powerlessness, joy and sorrow, richness and poverty etc. People mostly are unable to understand a simple truth that opposing polarities are two sides or two halves of the same thing. In ones consciousness they are just separate with unpleasant and harmful charge.

Once that charge disappears, man sees both polarities as one, without any difference and after that polarities do not represent a problem for him. For the ancient Greek philosopher Demostenus who used to live in a barrel, poverty was not a problem, because he decided himself to live that way and he saw both richness and poverty as the same nonsense (which means, no polarities for him). But for a man which wants a comfortable life for himself and his family, poverty is a true problem just because he wants the opposite state, which means a secure and decent life.

That explains to us what happens in the majority of systems of Spiritual Technology. A problematic situation means the existence of harmful charge on its artificially separated halves. The duplication of an experience is the only way of charge elimination. **Owing to our inability to remove big charge from the whole of the problem, we do it part by part until all charge is eliminated.** In the DP3 method, we attain that alternatively repeating duplication of 4 elements which charge consists of (mental image, emotion, body sensation and thought) from both polarities; in Deep PEAT, we duplicate one after another layer of the problem until what is left is only the Void.

> When you check this knowledge in practice, it will be easy for you to estimate the value of some method of therapy or psychological and Spiritual development. The key criterion for that estimation should be this: **Does that method lead to the duplication of unpleasant contents in consciousness and body, or does it lead to change and denial?**

11

Spiritual Technology

Processing is a kind of concentrated self-examination. It is the deep penetration into our unbalanced conscious and unconscious structures burdened with harmful emotional charge, with the intention of reaching the true experience.

We process our consciousness and unconsciousness to free ourselves from unnecessary and unwanted layers of previous experiences, to supersede the splits and fragmentations of our Being and attain wholeness. Spiritual work on ourselves starts when we become conscious that in us there are dark parts and with our readiness to accept those parts and integrate them (see the chapter on shadow). K. G. Jung's attitude towards the process of individuation was expressed with the following words: *"We do not get the wholeness by cutting of parts of our being, but with the integration of its opposites."*

In another wise statement Jung points out that man does not become enlightened imagining beings of light, but by making conscious his dark and unconscious side.

A question may come up, regarding why we want to attain the integration of opposites in our being? There are two answers to that question. First, a man functions on the principle of pain and pleasure. Man wants pleasure and avoids pain. There are many unconscious elements that cause unwanted and unpleasant impressions, they create heavy problems, which burden man. Second, in every human being there is an innate and strong desire to know who he/she is and to connect to Oneness all of his/her separate, suppressed and split off parts.

We want to get to know ourselves, because we feel limited and alienated. We must set ourselves free from our unnecessary burden and from unworthy goals, we must harmonize our body, mind and emotions to be able to attain the optimal states of our abilities and energy, what constitutes self-realization, or using the words of Abraham Masow, it makes our self-actualization.

Spiritual processing gives us better understanding, wider consciousness and ability to move together with the river of life as an integral part of it. It frees us from the bonds of past experiences and the anxiety that comes from the future. A cleaned, clear consciousness, directed towards selected goals is the best thing we can have in this life. It gives us the needed strength to cope efficiently with life's challenges, substantially different with respect to the past, when we squirmed in the blind alley of no hope, enabling us to go after goals we reckon as valuable.

During Spiritual development, the individual that gets integration and neutralization of all opposites inside him/her – male and female, good and bad, activity and passivity, I and other beings – becomes the reflection of the whole universe. "I" disappears, and only pure and endless Void exists penetrated with the freed consciousness of a Being. The arousal of a liberated consciousness is free of expectations, wins and loses and opposite emotions. It means awakening the previously lost and now re-discovered Oneness in which the Being is the eternal self-observer.

Then the Individual is made whole because body and mind, consciousness and unconsciousness are not mutually exclusive polarities, but are integrated parts of each other. Our inner world reflects the outer world, and the outer world is reflected inside us, like two parallel mirrors reflecting each other. Mystics call such state "diamond body". Being now whole and completed the Being cannot be destroyed. There is nothing left to be created or to be destroyed because the Being is now outside of this physical universe, whole and eternal.

Before attaining such an elevated state, the Individual must discover all of his polarities and transcend them through integration. The Being must be both male and female, a child and a mature person, a creator and destroyer, an observer and the observed, on and on until there are no polarities left, becoming transcendent and whole, free of all internal contradictions and contradictions between the inner and outer. The liberation of "I" takes place through dissolution and it becomes one with all-existing. Then it is able to take over and reject any identity at will, it possesses nothing and all.

Coming back to processing, we can say it is a focused and conscious movement from ignorance to Gnosis or liberating knowledge, to the freedom from all reactive thoughts, emotions and behavior. Such insightful knowledge enables us to live here and now for the first time, so different from the past times when we were involuntarily pulled to our past or we lived feeling constantly fears from the future.

Spiritual Technology is a unique way of liberation from unnecessary burdens, a kind of psychological liposuction in which we set ourselves free from the unhealthy fat of the world we live in. We do not add to ourselves anything new, we just liberate ourselves from the old, until we start living in the whole consciousness of Oneness. We call this kind of processing Spiritual technology because it consist of principles, systems, methods and techniques, psychological, emotional and Spiritual, in which the goal is the reconciliation and union of opposites. The main principle is this: Integrating all opposites in our consciousness, we come back to our original state of unity and Oneness.

The strongest obstacle for such uniting activity is human Ego. I will repeat one of two main characteristics of Ego – feeling of separation from the rest of the world. Keeping our Ego separated, we project our unpleasant, negative and bad characteristics to outer world. Unavoidable consequence of such projection is our division and the unconsciousness of parts of us, which we project to others, feeling that we are blocked and limited, forgetting who we are as a whole. This feeling of alienation becomes even stronger when we label our experiences. Experiences become either good and desirable or bad and undesirable, more or less acceptable: mine and his, us and them, good and bad, love and hatred etc.

Becoming conscious of our rejected parts, enables us to start reacquiring and reintegrating them. As long as we are not ready to do that, as long as we have resistance to those parts and push them back into the darkness, the universe will repeatedly give us the same experiences, which we already lived, because their source is still active. Therefore we will go on passing through identical unwanted states, wondering what the causes are.

Return to Oneness

When we judge our polarity experiences we are in the state, which could be called **either/or**, and it is the state of duality. In the dual experience of the world good and bad, positive and negative always exists.

The ancient mystical tradition, in harmony with modern physics, teaches us that the universe is one huge hologram; we are all parts of the whole, the whole is in us and in our tiniest part. That means inside of us **we contain all and everything we see and experience in others!** It is part of us, no matter how unpleasant our estimations and labels we put on them are. The duality in our values and experiences limits us manifestly. It forces us to choose one pair of polarities, and that means just a part of ourselves, the one which we think is useful and desired. Evidently it means **we leave and reject the other polarity, which means part of us, because we are on both sides.** For example, when from polarities love and hatred the individual chooses love, the person cannot feel hatred and if it appears, the individual rejects it as a foreign body. When the individual feels hatred, the person cannot accept love and rejects it as well. That undoubtedly means that the individual missed one part of its Being and lives and functions just as a half.

Such conclusion should not create in us a feeling of inferiority, but make us conscious regarding what exists in us. With a widened consciousness starts the acceleration of the Spiritual evolution of our being (see **Circular processing, DP3** and **Shadow**).

That means we must accept the responsibility for all our split and hard to accept parts, for the time we spent pushing down those elements, which Jung called **Shadow.** Sooner or later, those suppressed beliefs, behaviors, emotions, thoughts, start to climb to the surface of our personality and with them we justify our faulty actions, manipulations, self-delusions and our behaviors, which are strange and often hard to understand for us. For example, the majority of us learned in childhood that expressing criticism, aggressiveness and rage toward elders is something bad, and we used to be punished because of it. The result of this is the suppression of such feelings and we make efforts to stay in harmony with family values, with socially acceptable behavior, to be "a good child". Before you know, such repressed emotions get great energy as the water accumulated in front of a dam. They start to function at unconscious level and instead of expressing our emotions when we are confronted with unpleasant situations, we recur to inferior and sometimes even harmful surrogates: smoking, overeating, alcohol, drugs, or we gossip others and criticize them.

Taking the responsibility for all our experiences and accepting their dual manifestation, through pairs of opposites, we, using Spiritual technology, learn to reintegrate hidden and repressed parts of ourselves. No matter how it may seem inappropriate and unpleasant for our Ego, this is the real way to self-discovery, individuation and wholeness. We must do it intentionally and consciously, because it is the part of us, but it is hidden in our dark shadow.

However, the attitude that unconsciousness contains only our unwanted aspects is one-sided and incorrect. True enough, everything we are not able to accept resides in our unconsciousness, but much of it is extremely valuable, sometimes even magnificent. Just because of its high value we are not to accept it as ours. A true development starts when we are ready to ask ourselves who am I? And to accept the answer no matter what it could be (see **Gnostic Intensive).** Our readiness to accept everything, which appears in such search, leads us into the other dimensions of our Being, in the negative sides of our polarities, those we projected in others, and opposite good ones, which we claimed as ours. We should not forget that unconsciousness is the inexhaustible source of understanding, a hidden treasure with pearls of wisdom. All such things await us on that path inside of us.

Making conscious our dark parts, our shadow, makes us understand we are not whole, but it also shows us the way how to become such: through the willingness and readiness to embrace and integrate all aspects of our Being, visible and invisible, positive and negative, insecurity in front of the challenges of the world and confidence, which is somewhere deeply buried in us, envy and admiration for others, love and hate...When all opposites are reconciled, man becomes enlightened and in words of Alan Watts, **an enlightened man is the one which is liberated from all contradictions.** Just that and nothing else. And how much efforts, time and suffering we need to realize such a state? From unmemorable time people speak about the thorny path they passed through to reach their goal. A few thousand years ago this was written in **Upanishads**: *" It is difficult to pass over the sharp edge of a razor. Therefore wise people say that the path to salvation is hard."*

12

THE BASIC PRINCIPLES OF SPIRITUAL TECHNOLOGY

Between the creators of certain Spiritual, therapeutic or self-developing systems and the system itself, there is a reciprocal relationship. A long time ago I wrote about it in my book *"Integral Excalibur"*. This book is not available to many people, so I will point out to that relationship once again.

Starting from the knowledge of the rules and laws of human nature, the previous research on the human mind, and perhaps owing it to a touch of luck, a man (the creator) created a system of Spiritual development having therapeutic intentions. When applied, the system changes the consciousness of people. After some time spent applying that system, the people who changed were able to observe the system from a new, higher standpoint, as less burdened beings, with a sharpened perception and better understanding of occurrences inside themselves. They were able to notice the limitations of the system and to correct some of its elements. This is the way the original system becomes advanced, perfected and more efficient. After it is changed and becomes more efficient, the system will influence people again and the system will become better changing them further. Changed people are able to continue developing the system, transforming it in an even more efficient instrument of human consciousness. This process of mutual influence between the system and man will last until the systems stop changing, coming to a stand-still and losing its ability of changing further.

While applying and improving my systems of Spiritual Technology we noticed the different operative principles they are based on. The principles are:

- A holistic approach to the phenomena, based on the insight that there are always whole, not separate polarities

- The Alternating Technique

- Solve et Coagula (Dilute and Condense)

- The hologram principle (the whole ocean exists in a drop of water)

- Immobility in time (the reduction of the whole event to one shortest moment of it in which there is no movement)

- Duplication or recreation of unwanted experiences, which we want to eliminate

Because most of the readers don't know these principles, I will spend some time describing them. Such clarification will help interested people to find an explanation for many phenomena of life and it will open the eyes of many professionals to the new dimensions of a therapeutic process and Spiritual development.

You will probably have the impression that all these principles are different approaches to the overall holistic view of certain experiences. Such impression is true. All aforementioned principles are just different paths to reach the same goal – to embrace all our experiences and all the phenomena of this world as undivided wholes, as they truly are.

Zivorad Mihajlovic Slavinski

A Holistic Approach to Phenomena

Be conscious of this proven fact: In this world of ours we automatically and unconsciously direct our attention just to half of the entire experience! To that half, which attracts our attention. Whether that half of experience is pleasant or unpleasant it does not matter much. While in the experience, we forget the other half and believe that it does not exist and we behave as such. As long as we are healthy we do not think about sickness, when we are in the middle of disaster we are not able to think about the happy moments we had.

A holistic approach to life phenomena requires us to include all sides and all elements, which participate in our experience. It directs our attention to the other side of our experience, which was pushed into the shadow, and to the full and complete experience of ourselves as the undivided part of the whole world.

For example, in Deep PEAT, when a Client tells us the he/she feels the lower part of his body as heavy or warm, a question always follows – Which body sensation have you got in the **upper part** of your body? Because it is very probable that in the upper part the Client has a different sensation, which he/she is not conscious of in that moment and that does not attract his/her attention. Besides, when a Client eliminates the emotional charge inside his own being, we should direct his/her attention to the charge, which exists in other people's position in his/her subjective universe. They are part of him/her, not so evident as an "I" position, but they exist. After few experiences man realizes that he created himself, that in his subjective universe he moves people like pieces on a chessboard during a chess party, which he calls "my life". In his life, he alternatively moves white and black pieces. To clear his experiences from the charge and to resolve his problem holistically, the Client must do **circular processing** in order to clear all relevant points of view, which means those points of view where there is some charge.

In the holistic approach to the phenomena what is also important is putting the future under control. All these elements are not present in the majority of other therapy and self-development systems. This is the reason of their short lasting effects. But such situation cannot persist long. The holistic approach is the idea that has to come.

The Alternating Technique

The Alternating Technique is an extremely valuable contribution to the rapidity and success of therapeutic and Spiritual processing. In it we try to approach and solve every experience from all sides, holistically. In current methods such attempts are rare, but they are necessary if we want permanent results and to shorten the time of processing. The Alternating Technique directs our consciousness to the neglected, forgotten and suppressed parts of the experience.

The weak point of many Spiritual, psychological and emotional development therapies, is the narrow and one-sided approach to phenomena, especially when related to the problems they try to resolve. In such attempts one always and exclusively wants to realize positive states, forgiving the other side of the coin. In creating the Alternating Technique my leading idea was a remark made by Ron Hubbard. *"When you are after the invention of some efficient process, you must not forget that we live in dual universe"*. I felt as if I had received a strong punch in my stomach. There was a jewel inside those words, but I still was not able to take it out from the mass of thoughts I had in my mind. Many times after that, I came across the same thought. Four or five years ago I created my Gnostic Intensive with the alternate technique and it hastened the process 7 or 8 times.

Unfortunately, Hubbard in his approach to the practical methodology forgot his own advice. Now, after I made my new breakthrough and created DP3 I can see why he was not able to do the same. As Ricardo Ragaz, long time follower and practitioner of Ron's Org of Capt. Bill Robertson, rightly noticed, Ron wanted to bring one always to the causative point. Always to be "the cause"! Never the effect! But the cause and the effect are just two sides of the same coin. This way of thinking, gave only half of the effectiveness to the processes. As G. Filbert rightly noticed in his "Excalibur Revisited", one should do the process until he/she is not only the SOURCE, but is the NON-SOURCE.

Geoffrey Filbert also stopped short at the verge of discovery. True, one should become conscious that one is both, but NOT one following the other, but at the **same time**. That means through neutralization or integration of source and non-source. Therefore, to make a long story short, one should take into account both sides, not just one!

For example, in the old technique of my Gnostic Intensive, before I discovered the Alternating Technique, the command was limited to "Feel who you are", "Feel life" and similar. In such approach the other side of the experience was evidently forgotten. A practitioner would get a mass of data, elements, and experiences concerning what one is not and what life is not! Trying to get just a positive polarity is not productive, because all the other stuff, which he tried to clear away, was following him as a shadow. It is not possible, or it is possible just for short time and what follows is a crash. When one applies Alternating Technique, in other words when one confronts with the positive as well as the negative polarity, mind masses are emptied much quicker and the desired goal is left uncovered. Then it is possible to experience it easier and quicker. It is even more evident in the DP3 method. Instead of hours, process lasts minutes. Therefore, whenever it is possible one should apply Alternating approach.

Some people know the story of my discovery of the Alternating Technique. For those who don't, I will go through it very shortly. All recent years I kept in my mind the statement of our living in dual universe. And couple of years ago I had a funny experience. Passing by a garden in the outskirts of Belgrade I noticed two men trying to pull down a large wooden pillar. Its lower part was buried deeply in the ground. They swung it left and right, forward and backward and in about 5 minutes pulled it down. A question popped up in my mind: "How long would they need if they had tried to do it by pushing the pillar in only one direction? Much, much more. Hours or maybe days." In that moment I had a valuable cognition and the whole idea of the new, more efficient alternating technique. I went home, called my family members and some friends and the next day I created a new kind of Intensive. I was right. The new Alternating Technique was extremely fast. Now instead of 40 dyads and many rigid rules for the participants, as in old time Gnostic Intensive, it lasted only 5 dyads and participants were allowed to drink coffee, eat whatever they wanted etc. which before was forbidden.

What is most important is that about 70-80% of the participants obtained Enlightenment in these 5 dyads. The reason that the Gnostic Intensive got such quick results with the Alternating technique lies in the extremely quick dissipation of mind stuff. After only 2 or 3 dyads participants are in state of empty consciousness and then it is easy to get the Direct Experience of Truth.

Solve et Coagula

From the earliest time eminent thinkers tried to discover the fundamental model of occurrences of social phenomena. Efforts to explain everything with one and only one element are too ambitious, because there is more then one key element. I will point out one of them, which seems to be omnipresent, because we find it in middle age alchemy, Spiritual development, psychotherapy and even in modern physics.

In quantum mechanics one of most fundamental phenomena is the duality of the wave and particle. Modern physicists say that light exists simultaneously as waves of light and particles of light. Physics is able to see it, but is not able to explain it. A wave has no limits, it spreads to all directions at the same time and we are not able to measure it. In the moment we try to measure it, it dematerializes from the whole space and appears only in the place it is measured as a particle, which has definite characteristics.

But long time before quantum physics, alchemy pointed out its most important operation: **Solve et Coagula**. Solve or solutio refers to the breaking down of elements and coagula refers to their coming together, in the process of transmuting base metals into gold or arriving at the Philosopher's stone. But it was a literal meaning. As a matter of fact, "solve" referred to the dissolution of hardened positions, negative states of mind and dissolution and disappearance of negative energetic charge. "Coagula" referred to the coagulation of dispersed elements into an integrated whole, representing the new synthesis on a higher organizational, psychological, emotional and Spiritual level.

Therefore, the real meaning of these three words ("Solve et Coagula") is a formula that the alchemists used to carry out this transformation. It could be described as a process in which something is broken down into its elements, which produces energy, and after that, its reconstitution in a more evolved form.

The same meaning is found in the well-known terms of science: analysis and synthesis. We first break something into its parts and then make a new, better or more acceptable whole. During this process, there is a release of energy.

Even in some particular occult systems, such as ancient Egyptian magic, we find this realization. There is the duality of Nuit and Hadit. Nuit is the "goddess of the infinite space (which means the wave)" and Hadit is the point (which means the particle).

What does all this have to do with Spiritual technology, therapy etc.? Very much! We are not able to work with a wave; we must transform it into a particle. We can't work with some indefinite problem, for example a fear. We do it after observing it and "measuring it". We ask our client, what is the location of his fear? Shape? Dimensions? Age? Color? Level of consciousness etc. Doing it, for example with certain types of fear, we will see that the endless and formless wave changes into quite concrete "particles", which is something we are able to operate with.

Asking for the details of our client's problem is the coagula phase. After this phase, applying an adequate method, we disperse it, freeing its energetic charge (Solve) and again we come out of the process with a "particle", which is a state that is positive and desirable.

The degree of someone's Spiritual and psychological development could be defined as the **limitation of his/her perception at a certain level.** Arthur Schopenhauer said this a long time ago: *"Everybody accepts the limits of own vision as limits of the world."* Dissolution (Solve) is the dissolution of those rigid limitations at a certain level, which enables us to expand our perception getting more experience connected with it. Coagulation means a new concentration of elements of the previously dissolved rigid structures and after that, the stabilization of a new perception of the higher level.

With every dissolution we have a transformation or change in the form. On the path of self-realization it is necessary to dissolve old experiences and only after that, we are able to concentrate elements into a new synthesis again. When dissolution occurs, the door of consciousness opens and therefore, it is possible to transform our attitudes, beliefs and convictions into the new whole, which is different when we compare it to the old one.

In life, when we encounter one-sided and petrified attitudes and apply a wider and all-inclusive approach (Solve) to them, those overgrown attitudes disintegrate. Very often, these are overgrown Ego structures, which are replaced with higher-level structures. Coagula means, I repeat, the coagulation and concentration of separated and dispersed elements into an integrated whole, which represents a higher synthesis. Therefore the true meaning of the formula "Solve and Coagula" points to the formula which alchemists used to attain the transmutation of lower level states, things and beings, into a higher level, to attain a new integration into more perfected forms.

Searching for the details of the Client's problem and concentrating on them is the coagulation phase. After it we apply an adequate method to disperse and dilute it and that way free energetic charge, which is bound in it. That way we free the space for a new "particle", which means for a new coagulation of better and more desirable experiences. A simple example of Solve and Coagula is in deep inhalation and exhalation in the Deep PEAT process. During the inhalation phase, the Client should be extremely concentrated on the content in his consciousness or in his body in that moment. When he starts exhaling, he relaxes and disperses his attention from that content and opens himself and is able to passively observe the following content. When it appears, the Client concentrates on it as completely as possible, which is a new process of coagulation.

In the Gnostic Intensive we also "collapse the wave" to a particle in both alternating commands. When Master of the Intensive explains the technique of the Intensive, he tells people that they must have objects in both commands. In the first command, "Feel who you are!" the participant is to find out who he is in that moment and feel himself/herself as such as strongly as possible. In everyday life, when a man thinks about himself, countless possibilities come up in his mind: thoughts about who he is, emotions, memories about who he was told he was, what he learned, read in books etc. He must find only one content, which means he must compress his consciousness into one point – which he is in that moment and to feel it. In the alternating command "Feel who you are not" the same procedure should be applied. Out of countless things and phenomena that come up, the participant should choose just one, which means compressing all possible contents into one, into whatever he is not, then feel it and report it to his partner.

If you want to throw a stone far away, you must squeeze your hand, but the moment you want to throw the stone away you must open your hand. Experience teaches us that most people try to solve problems using just the first part of the formula, which is **coagulation.** When they confront a problem, people usually invest conscious efforts in its solution. All the time, they are concentrated on the problem, they search in their memories similar situations and the way they came to the solution, or how someone else did it. In such attempts there even is physical strain. Their bodies are mainly tense; sometimes even a mild spasm is visible. As long as they are in the coagulation phase, their field of vision is limited and their perception is narrow. What is most important is that with such conscious effort, they make an energetic-like wall in front of themselves. It is a frozen wave of psychic energy, which doesn't let any new data come in. That frozen wall persists as long as people are in the coagulation phase and usually people tend to invest more and more energy in it.

To come to the solution of the problem, it is necessary (after investing energy in trying to solve it) to start with the dilution phase. It should be complete relaxation of thoughts, emotions and body. What we need to do is shift our attention from the problem we concentrated on to something else, or let our thoughts drift without a definite goal. What we need is a complete separation from the problem and physical relaxation. That dilution phase could last from a couple of hours (rarely a couple of minutes) to a few days or weeks. But it is the right way to come to the solution of the problem, which we were previously concentrated on.

Countless examples from literature and the biographies of many creators point out to the fact that such approach is well based. What really happens in the phase of **solve**?

The frozen wave of energy, which we created making conscious efforts, melts and is dispersed. In its place what is created is vacuum or an empty psychological field in which a solution can now enter. As a matter of fact, the solution is sucked into it. Previously it was impossible because of the concentrated energy, which we compressed there. Even though a person is seemingly passive, that vacuum actively sucks in itself new ideas and new connections between things, phenomena and ideas, which represent the solution to the problem, can also appear in the consciousness. As long as we are in highly tensed, we keep that energetic wall in front of the approaching solution and prevent it to manifest.

In the **coagula phase** our conscious mind is active.

In the **solve phase** our unconscious mind is active.

These two phases should not be mixed. If we are consciously concentrated on our goal, this is a signal to our unconscious mind that we want to realize our goal without its help and it has no space for its activity. On the other side, without the first phase of coagulation, the other phase, dilution, will not give adequate results. First we must squat if we want to jump high.

The old saying, *A morning is wiser than the evening*, points out to experiential observation that after making efforts, relaxation is needed, because sleeping during night, after a full day of conscious efforts, is the highest possible dilution. When we have a problem, experienced people suggest sleeping over it. Alan Watts, who is well known for oriental teachings, gives this suggestion: *"When you get the message, hang up the phone."*

This is a practical suggestion for the application of the **solve et coagula formula:** Spend some time to concentrate on how to find the solution to the problem. Then take distance, separate from it emotionally and thoughtfully. That way you leave to your unconscious mind the main part of the job.

At the same time, relax the body as much as you can. This is especially important when we have an urgent problem to handle.

I will repeat this procedure using different words. We should become conscious of our problem in its details and should feel it! Everything, which comes up in that process, should be completely accepted. There must be no suppression, no ignoring, flinching from its unpleasant elements. After that, we make conscious efforts to try to solve the problem. In this period of time, many similar situations will come to our consciousness, whether ours or belonging to other people. We will be conscious of the ways they solved their problems and will remember problems, which were not solved. In that phase, emotional, psychological and physical tension normally occurs. It is also good to put our goal on paper, writing down what we know about the problem and what we do not know.

Then we start the Solve phase. This means we will intentionally relax and separate ourselves from the problem. We could say to ourselves: This is a difficult problem, which seems to be unsolvable, **but I am relaxed.** Perhaps you should repeat this more than once. The bottom line in this procedure is separation and taking distance from the problem, like "intentionally forgetting" it. In literature, in developing creativity, writers point out endless cases of coming to the solution in a moment of complete relaxation. Probably the first time it was described was in the story of Archimedes bathing in the bathtub and how he discovered his law while relaxing in the warm water.

After straining a lot over a theoretical or practical problem, Thomas Edison used to take a nap on the couch in his laboratory. He solved the majority of his problems in these moments of drowsy relaxation.

Nikola Tesla used to intentionally produce the transition from the active to the passive phase. At the end of a day, after having concentrated on a problem, when he would become very sleepy, he would sit in an easy chair holding in his hands two metal spoons. Under his hands he put metal pots. When he fell asleep, he would relax and the spoons would fall in the pots from his hands, making a noise. That noise would wake him up. In that moment he used to put on the paper the first idea, which would appear in his consciousness and usually it was the solution he was searching for.

A good example for the need of relaxing is the story on catching monkeys. In the forest, hunters put a couple of pots with nuts and hazelnuts. The opening on the pots was so large that an average monkey could easily put its hand inside, yet it was too narrow to enable a fistful of nuts to come out. The hunters placed the pots on strong sticks, threw nuts around on the ground to attract the monkeys and went back to their camp. The monkeys watched the scene from high trees. Being very curious animals, they came down to pick the nuts, lurk into the pots and some of them pushed their hands to get the nuts inside. When a monkey squeezes its hand, and is not able to pull its fist out, it starts to jerk, fight and scream. When hunters hear the noise, they come and catch the monkeys.

All the monkey should do is to relax its hand. But, being in a "difficult problem" the monkey squeezes its fist more and more. That way it tries to solve the problem using force. But it is exactly that force, which imprisons. If in some happy moment the monkey relaxed its hand just for a moment (**dilution**), the monkey would find its way to freedom.

The Principle of the Hologram

1. **Whole ocean exists in a drop of water and**

2. **Immobility in time: The reduction of the whole event to one shortest moment of it in which there is no movement**

Every fool knows that a drop of water is in the ocean. Wise people know that the whole of ocean is in the drop of water.

These two principles are sub-elements of the previously described **holistic approach** to experiences, problems and goals. Because they are tightly connected, I will describe them together. In the field of Spiritual Technology they are very important because their application caused a great shortening of time in my processes and to an exceptional success.

Simply said, this is what they mean. Instead of great number of processed experiences, which we find in the majority of other systems (which make **the ocean of possibilities),** we do just one efficient process on one selected experience (which is just one **drop of water)** in **"frozen"** moment of time and all similar experiences vanish at once!

In other words, not only we choose just one experience out of the many possible ones, but also we shrink the time of the experience in just one narrow moment, lasting just a second, without any movement or changes in it. So, in a way, it is **"frozen"** in time.

People, which have got a practical experience with my systems, are able to understand this without problems. For those people who do not have such experience it is more difficult to understand it, so I will clarify this concept.

First, **the whole ocean in a drop of water:** It is unnecessary to process many similar experiences, for example, fear in front of people. It is losing time. It seems paradoxical, but it is true that it is more efficient to choose just one experience of fear and process it. When we eliminate that single experience, all similar experiences, which we are conscious of, will vanish.

Second, **immobility in time:** not only do we choose just one of the many experiences, but we limit its time to a minimum, to just one short moment. In other words, we coagulate the experience and stop the time of its existence.

The narrower the experience we choose for the process, the shorter and more efficient the process will be. We can obtain great results when we take the peak moment of that experience, which usually lasts just a part of a second, as it is an immovable part of it in time. Perhaps the following is even better for understanding the immobility principle: starting from a short movie picture (film), which presents that experience, which can last from a few seconds to few hours or days, we take just one moment and only one image, stopped in time, so that there isn't any movement, or any kind of change. On this short part we carry out the process.

The basis of this approach is the knowledge of the nature of human consciousness. **As long as we make changes in certain experiences, and movement is the change, the experience will persist.** Preventing the change of some experience gives us the optimal situation to discreate it. When we confront with it as it is, and prevent changes, which would cause its persistence in time, such experience will have the tendency to vanish. Such situation exists not only in human consciousness, but also in the macro-universe. Hindu sages say that this whole universe will vanish in the moment all changes come to a stop.

Such result is most evident in the Past/Future Rundown. When we delete one of endless number of experiences with the DP3 procedure, all other similar experiences, which we are conscious of that come from past and from the future, will simultaneously disappear.

Therefore, whenever it is possible we try to reduce all unpleasant experiences (the ocean) to one, and then select an experience reducing it to one representative moment frozen in time (a drop of water). When we empty all the emotional charge from it, we have emptied all similar experiences.

Duplication or Recreation of Unwanted Experiences

I explained this process in the chapter "Creation and Discreation of Subjective Reality", thus I will not repeat it here. Because it is very important, I suggest to you to study it in all details. Briefly said it goes like this: **Do it once, it persists. Do it again, it releases!**

13

SPIRITUAL TECHNOLOGY: SYSTEMS, METHODS AND TECHNIQUES

In this chapter I will expose my main systems and their procedures. Some of them came into existence as separate systems, others are more techniques. I wrote separate books on some of them. Some of those books are translated in English and Italian. I give information about the translated books in this text. My desire is to get as many of them translated in foreign languages as possible. It is the most efficient way to offer them to people. How many of them will be translated depends on both myself and my associates, which are helping me. It should be an act of synergy. Anyway, I will do my best to give these valuable instruments to as many practitioners as possible.

Gnostic Intensive

The question "Who am I" is certainly the oldest question for all people. It is said that Socrates was first to point it out (*"Man, know thyself"*), this it is alpha and omega of the human evolution, the beginning and the end of the knowledge. The same thought, expressed in other words, is attributed to Mohammed: *"Who knoweth himself, knoweth his God."* This question persisted in all systems of Perennial philosophy and a great number of methods, techniques and procedures were created to find the solution of this problem.

Just exactly who are you? You may say, well... I'm XZ, I'm 35 years old, a father of two children. I love my children very much, but sometimes I lose my temper with them. I often ask myself, am I that tolerant father, or am I the one who looses his temper with them?

You should understand that the essence of who you are is not your name, profession, your parents, your job, your career, your title, your age, your marital status, you possession, your religious affiliation, your fears or courage and good features... Moreover, it is neither your mind, nor your intelligence.

When you are angry, who is it that says "I'm angry?"

When you think about yourself as a tolerant and good person, who is it that thinks that? Who is it that speaks of his mind and the body and the feelings? Well so many people fought to discover it and so many concluded it is impossible to find out the answer to that question. Fortunately enough, that conclusion is not true. One can find the answer to that question, not in books, not on TV or on lectures of famous lecturers but in the last place where one looks for it – in himself. There are some methods serving that purpose and among all of them, Gnostic Intensive is most efficient, as far as I know.

As I said in the chapter on the Fundamental principles of Spiritual Technology, my work was influenced a great deal by the remark of a person, a valuable and far reaching remark, which in the creation of therapeutic systems and systems for Spiritual developments, we should always keep in mind, which is that **this is a dual universe!**

Working in pairs or dyads during a Gnostic Intensive is using this dual principle par excellence. Instead of having an individual fight with his own unconscious mind, which we see in many meditation systems, in the Intensive we have two consciousness's (the active and passive partner) fighting alternatively with the unconscious mind of the other.

The goal of Gnostic Intensive is Gnosis, Enlightenment or most clearly said, the Direct Experience of Truth. The final goal is a permanent state of enlightenment or Meuna, but real Intensives have more modest ambitions: to attain a Direct Experience on more narrow segments of reality, defined by questions or koans as *Who am I? What am I? What is life? and What is another?*

On so called special Intensives participants work on questions *what is God? What is love? What is Truth? What is my true will?* On some other Intensive people try to get Direct Experience on sound formulas, chakras (the tip of the nose, third eye, nape) or sometimes participants work on classic Zen koans, as *What was your original face before your parents were born?*

The Gnostic Intensive is a group technique. The Intensive Master (usually with Assistants) explains the technique, makes sure people observe the rules of the Intensive, gives moral support to participants and "validates" Direct Experience when participants get it.

The technique of the Intensive is dyad, which means participants work in pairs. In every pair, during the exercise, one participant is active, the other is passive. The passive partner gives the command to the active one: *"Feel who you are"* and after it *"Feel who you are not"*. The active partner accepts the command and starts to feel who he is. He must be completely open to all contents, which come up to his consciousness and his body as the result of his intention to feel himself. Whatever comes up he must communicate it to the passive partner. When he finishes the communication, his partner gives him a "polarity" command: *"Feel who you are not!"* Those two questions alternate in a period of 10 minutes. Then partners change roles – the passive partner becomes active, and active one becomes passive. One exercise takes 40 minutes.

The goal of the Intensive technique is to empty consciousness. In an empty conscious there are no contents that can prevent the participant to experience his objects: himself, another, life, sound, God...

The Intensive, which I brought from USA to Serbia in 1980 lasted 3 days, 7 days, 14 days and there were some lasting 30 days, even 6 weeks.

When I introduced the Alternating technique, which involves both polarities – what IS and what IS NOT – the time needed to attain a Direct Experience of Truth dramatically shortened and the percentage of enlightened participants increased. Now three to four dyads are enough and the percentage of success is almost absolute: 95-100% get a Direct Experience. In that short period, some participants get more them one Direct Experience. Incredible but true!

What is the essence of a Direct Experience of Truth, which is the only and one goal of the Intensive?

First we should say what a Direct Experience is not. It is **not catharsis**, whose main characteristic is a discharge of suppressed emotions, which happens more or less in an uncontrolled way. After catharsis people feel better, sometimes euphoric, so there is the possibility to mix it with a Direct

Experience. True, sometimes Direct Experience is followed by a catharsis, but they are essentially different states. In a catharsis **duality persists,** there still remains a difference between the subject and object.

At the same time, a Direct Experience is not an **insight.** An insight is a mental phenomenon, the sudden understanding of new relationship between existing elements. It is mainly followed by an **aha experience!** When a person understands new relationships that before that moment were outside of his ability to realize.

A Direct Experience is not an **occult or parapsychological phenomenon,** although Intensive participants sometimes have such phenomena: telepathy, precognition, feeling expansion into cosmos, remembering past life times etc.

The essential characteristic of Gnosis, Enlightenment or of the Direct Experience of Truth is **the disappearance of the differences between subject and object!** This differs from all other experiences which are dual: the Direct Experience of Truth is **the state of Oneness!**

From the moment a new human being is born it will experience an endless number of **indirect experiences.** To clarify this, I will give you a couple of examples. You read these lines. Between you as the subject and the text as the object, the **process of reading,** is a mediation. An intellectual process of understanding is probably present as well. While you are reading it is possible that you will remember something similar, which means that the process of remembering is present as well. All these are processes mediate between the subject and object. Sometimes it is possible to understand intuitively what the writer wants to say. But even intuition, a very subtle process, it is still a process and in a Direct Experience of Truth there is no process at all.

While communicating with a person, the listening process is mediating and probably other processes as well. If you experience that person directly, neither process would mediate; you would experience it without any process at all, which means that you and that person would become **one** for a short time. **The difference between the subject and object would vanish.**

Sometimes people ask why one cannot have Direct Experiences all the time. The answer is simple: because of his mind stuff, the masses of his mind (in yoga terminology it is called "chita"), charge or negative emotional energy. **Human mind is the sum of traumas, wrongly understood things, messages which have not been communicated completely, cut off communications, questions left without answers, unpleasant experiences that block the human being, and portions of knowledge we got.** So, when one wants to experience oneself and asks himself, *Who am I?*, instead of a Direct Experience of Truth, he will get and answer from a part of his mind mass: memories on what his parents told him about who and what he was, about human nature that he learned in school, heard from other people or read in books. All this data causes the alienation of human being from himself.

During a Gnostic Intensive, when the person empties his conscious from all mind masses, the person is left empty and is able to experience him/herself. In that moment one stops being a stranger to himself. Between the person who is asking *"Who am I?"* and the one who finds the answer…

there is no difference. A similar process takes place in the participants when they work on other questions during the Intensive (*What is life? What is another?* and similar).

In the traditional systems of Perennial philosophy such as Zen, Taoism and Sufism, besides different kinds of meditation, Teachers use stories and brainteasers as stimulating metaphors, which indirectly, most often by means of humor, orient the followers toward Truth, because direct talk about it is impossible. There is an anecdote about Mula Nasrudin, a Sufi wiseman, I used to tell participants during my old-time Intensives. In those Intensives, the participants had to struggle for days to experience matters which are evident and have always been present – as the answer to the question Who am I? This is how the story goes: One morning, Nasrudin woke up and suddenly realized that he did not know who he was. Hoping someone else would tell him, he went to town. He walked for some time, but it seemed nobody knew the answer to his question. Finally he entered a shop, where the shop owner greeted him kindly: *"Welcome, noble gentleman. Tell me, what do you want?"*

"I would like you to tell me, who I am" said Nasrudin. "Do you know who am I?" "I'm sorry, noble gentleman", answered the shop owner, "I don't know who you are."

"Well, when I entered your shop, how did you know it was me, not someone else?" wondered Nasrudin.

These words will cause laughter, but it will cause a special kind of laughter in people who had a Direct Experience of Truth to the question *Who am I?* on Gnostic Intensive.

The ancient Greek mythological story of Narcissus also points to the Direct Experience of Who am I. Narcissus was the very beautiful son of Cephissus, the river god, and the nymph Liriope. It had been prophesied that he would have a very long life if he never saw his face. Narcissus was so beautiful that many fell in love with him, but with his icy cold heart, he never returned this love to anybody. One of them was a nymph whose name was Echo. She died because her love had been left unfulfilled, and what was left of her was only her voice (echo). Once, while Narcissus was drinking in a well, he saw his image, and was left enchanted, falling in love with himself.

Sigmund Freud interpreted this myth illustrating people who love only themselves, thus incapable of loving any other being. This interpretation is correct, but only at a certain level, at the level where we invest emotional energy. As many other myths, this one is multi-layered and we are much more interested in its Spiritual interpretation. A man is truly unable to love others until, through enlightenment, he discovers who he is and such experience is usually very deep. Then a person experiences one of the strongest feelings, which is love for his/her True I and after that is able to return love to others. The revelation of oneness in oneself brings great peace and rest at the center of our being. But it also opens up an opportunity and an impulse to live and express that revelation in the world of duality.

Looking from a historical perspective, in the frame of Spiritual Technology, the Gnostic Intensive was the first method leading from **duality to Unity,** a method to transcend duality, a technique to get a gradual experience of Unity. Some people think mistakenly that the goal of an Intensive and other methods of spiritual technology is to reach emptiness, or more precisely a **dynamic emptiness.** Such emptiness is not the goal but a means to reach the state of Oneness. A Gnostic Intensive just attains that – a state of void, which is used as a path to attain Oneness.

Even if it has the great importance in raising the level of consciousness of many people and even if it served as the basis for their further development, the Gnostic Intensive lost its dominant role, which it had for a long time, and we are rapidly approaching the moment of it final disappearance from the Spiritual stage. I said previously that it lasts only 3 or 4 dyads. The last one which I led in Zagreb (in June 2005) lasted only 3 dyads and all except one participant had a Direct Experience of Truth, some of them more than one. Moreover, everyday the number of people that know who they are, even without participating in an Intensive is greater and greater. The same applies to the other questions, what is life and what is another. There are more and more people that quickly answer those questions. This is a consequence of changes in the Collective consciousness of humanity, which many of us are conscious of. It is sometimes called the phenomenon of the hundredth monkey. When this happens, the critical mass (in this case when a certain number of people get the Direct Experience of Truth), there is a quantum leap and everyone will experience such a state as a normal state of consciousness, not something which one must struggle to reach.

It led me to the creation of an IGI or Individual Gnostic Intensive (in June 2005).

Individual Gnostic Intensive (IGI)

Back some time ago, since its beginning, it was not possible to get Direct Experience or Gnosis in individual work. A group was necessary to develop a great amount of energy and in which participants gave emotional support to one another. Other conditions were the presence of the Master (Intensive Leader) and his assistants, respecting the rules of the Intensive and some other things. Due to the creation of the IGI, now it is possible to get such Direct Experience in individual work with a Processor. Applying this unbelievably simple and rapid method, we are able in minutes to empty the consciousness of a Client and enable him/her to attain Gnosis on the fundamental questions, *Who am I? What is Life? What is Another?* and many other as well. Now we can help a Client attain a Direct Experience in one short session and make the first decisive step in his Spiritual development and therapeutic processing, and then continue applying other systems.

The essence of the IGI is in the application of an Alternating method and a short confrontation with elements, where there is an emotional charge. Such extremely quick and efficient method sent the classic Intensive back into history. Whoever experiences this method that is "as quick as lightning", will never more spend his time with the old and outgrown methodology. People which tried this method had an enthusiastic reaction. Slavoljub Stojanovic (slavce@beotel.yu) posted on the spiritual technology group his experience:

> *I post for the first time on this group list. I have been lurking for the long time, because my English is not very good. Three days ago I had a session with Zivorad. He applied his new method of getting enlightenment. I should*

say that for long period I participated on many "classic" Gnostic Intensives. Many of them: 3-days, 7-days and several 14-days Intensives. Those were precious experiences, but hard and very strenuous. I participated on the first Intensive when Zivorad introduced new alternative technique 5 or 6 ago. When he announced discovery of an even quicker method I was very curious. I did not choose classic questions: Who am I? What am I? What is life? and What is another? Because I had more then one Enlightenment on them. I chose Zen koans which people believe is very difficult to get Enlightenment on: **"What was your original face before your mother was born?"** In Zen they usually spend month and month of zazen meditation until they "get it". I was extremely surprised, better say shocked! My mind field was soon completely empty, void, and then I had that direct experience of truth. In only 12 minutes I "got it". I had a tremendous catharsis, tears of joy, amazement. I was paralyzed with surprise. How is it possible??? Is there an end to shortening the time in spiritual work? It seems there is no! After I calmed down Zivorad brought me some Zen manual and gave me to read a part of it. There was a description of an experience of some Zen monk. It was almost the copy of my experience. And that young man spent months and months of long meditations to get it. Tomorrow I will have another session with Zivorad. I will work on the koan ""What is God?" I know something great is waiting for me. I feel gratitude for the whole world.*

There are some conditions for the successful application of this method. The Processor, which is here in a role as the Master of Intensive, must have some experience in leading the classic Intensive, or at least must have some experience being an Assistant to a Master. The reason is that this technique, as well as the classic Intensive technique, does not give one the Direct Experience of Truth. It just creates emptiness in the consciousness of a Client. True, emptiness is most favorable state for attaining Gnostic experience, but the Processor must know how to pull that experience out from the Client.

Sometimes it is not necessary; Direct Experience is evident by itself. In other situations the Processor must know how to do it. For the first koan, *who am I?* it is not so difficult, but for other koans the ground becomes a bit slippery.

That is the reason why one needs at least one day training to learn how to do the Master's job. Otherwise, the Processor will be prone to mistakes and to accept as the Direct Experience of Truth something else.

Excalibur

Excalibur was the first system I developed after many years practicing the Gnostic Intensive. It was based on the Formula of discreation of unwanted states and creation of new desirable states. Many changes happened in that system, probably because I used it often in processing others as well as in self-processing. After a short time, I created a perfected system, which I called **New Excalibur,** which had a more simple Formula of discreation. It was not the end of the perfecting. After several years I had **Integral Excalibur,** which as its name suggests, embraced problems and the creation of a new reality.

The greatest value of Excalibur is the practical procedure called **First method** or **Method-1,** for the dissolution of hard and chronic problems. Its origin marks the turning point in my work. Until that moment people used to have many mystical experiences, some of them deep, dramatic and universal, but they did not have an instrument to control their lives. When some Intensive participants complained about their bad emotional states, they would get the merciless answer: *Do you want the Truth? Then don't complain!* Method-1 was such an instrument. It enabled people to help themselves in everyday life. Of course, a human being is not able to control his/her life completely, but this method enabled one to do it in a great measure. From that moment the mystical path, which I and some other people walked was transformed in Spiritual technology.

In the so called **final process** of Excalibur, the participant discreates step-by-step by means of a definite sequence, contents of his/her consciousness, as if peeling off layers of an onion, until he/she gets to the end phenomenon – the state of empty consciousness, which is in its essence a mystical experience. Many people are surprised with this phenomenon, some of them deeply shaken. But the emptiness experienced in Excalibur, no matter how unusual and fascinating it is, is not THE direct experience. In it we have a subject, which is a human being that experiences emptiness, emptiness as an object, and the indirect experience of experiencing emptiness. True, in such empty consciousness some rare individuals sometimes got the Direct Experience of Truth. But there are just a few exceptions and such experience is not the primal goal of Excalibur. The goal is putting under control our own subjective universe, or in other words, the phenomena of everyday life.

Excalibur-2

Excalibur-2 is a separate system, in which the human being experiences a similar state as in **Integral Excalibur.** This other method uses the technique and the attitude of **acceptance** of all contents of consciousness without any resistance. The primal goal of Excalibur-2 is the gradual discreation or "peeling off" of the constituent elements of a certain problem, so that the entire problem finally disappears in emptiness. This method contributes also to the state of Oneness, because it eliminates mental masses, which create a problem step-by-step: body sensations, emotions and mental components as thoughts, convictions, beliefs, identities etc.

There are several sources from which I developed Excalibur-2:

1. The so called **non-resistance** from Buddhism. 2600 years ago Buddha taught us that resisting an unpleasant experience causes its persistence. So, today we have a widely used axiom: **Resistance brings persistence.**

2. In the main Buddhist schools we find a teaching about **sheer** (clear) **attention.** It is undivided awareness about that what happens inside and outside of us. It is directed toward facts, which are coming to us through the 5 senses and mind, **without any reaction to them in speech, behavior and thoughts, judging or analyzing.**

3. **Pratyahara** or separating of consciousness, from raja yoga.

4. **Self-remembrance in Gurdjieff's system**

5. **Ron Hubbard's teaching about confrontation.** What you are able to confront, is able to vanish.

The Formula of discreation of unpleasant experiences in Excalibur-2 is **ACCEPTANCE!** You should accept without any resistance any and all unpleasant experiences and then they will have a strong tendency to vanish. It's just opposite to what we have been taught from early childhood, in school, from different authorities and from many systems of so called "positive thought". They teach that we must avoid negative thoughts and emotions. But **if we avoid them, they will reappear sooner or later.** The reason for this is that our resistance to negative thought or emotion causes them to persist in your life.

With our readiness to accept, here comes our responsibility. And with our responsibility, comes our ability to change unwanted states in our life. So I use a few exercises to raise our level of responsibility, which means our ability to change the things in our life.

We ask a participant to look around a room and find something which he/she likes and **accept** them. For example, a window. If he likes it, then it's the first thing. Then he should take another look around that room and find another thing, which is acceptable for him, which is OK for him. For example, a chair. If that chair is acceptable for him, that's the second thing. He should do this three more times, so that at the end of exercise he has 5 things, which are acceptable for him in the room, because he likes them.

Now, he should take a little bit more of responsibility for things that are present. He must look around the room and accept, without any resistance, 20 things in the room.

What is the difference between the first exercise and this second one? In the first exercise he chose 5 things that he liked and accepted them.

In the second exercise, he looks around and simply accepts them as they are no matter if he likes them or not. He just accepts them without any resistance!

In the first exercise he was choosing things that he liked. In the second exercise he is making a decision to accept thing!! It's a higher level of responsibility! And the Client continues doing more and more complex exercises and taking on himself more responsibility before he starts with the process that discreates the components of a problem. The final stage remains a void where problem use to be.

Aspectics

In **Aspectics,** which is a very efficient method of integrating split off experiences, the procedure is quite different compared to the two previous systems, but the result is the same: Integration of separated parts into the wholeness of a being. For example, when a person feels anger towards a partner (we treat it as one of his/her aspects), it points out to an evident polarity. On one side there is the person and on the other side exists his/her aspect, which is anger. That negative state disturbs the person; therefore he/she wants to free him/herself from it. Before the person finds out an efficient method to free oneself, the person is resisting it and fighting against it. Just because of it that, the unwanted state persists. In Aspectics the procedure is just the opposite. One should let the aspect express itself through goals. Goals, which the aspect has for the person, will gradually integrate as you go up the chain of higher and higher goals.

The theoretical basis of this method is Hindu orthodox philosophy regarding the creation of the manifested universe from the Universal Source, or Brahma; and retreating that manifested universe back to the very same source, in endless cycles, which repeat themselves endlessly. The same teaching says that we are witnesses of the returning phase to the Universal source. Thus, everything existing in this universe has the same final and highest goal – the return to Brahma, Absolute Void or, using the language of modern physics, to quantum vacuum. Everything that exists wants to return to the realization of the final and highest goal – therefore, even **our shortcomings, weaknesses and split off aspects want the same,** no matter how strange it seems to be. I proved this theoretical hypothesis in the practice of Aspectics. Our hangups, having the the form of unwanted aspects, push us up towards the highest goal, but we cannot see it at the beginning because our perception is limited. But we are able to see it by climbing up the chain of higher and higher goals, until the Highest Goal appears in the field of our consciousness. When a person merges with it in his/her imagination, the whole goal structure collapses, disappears and with it disappears the aspect, which is the problem we started the process from.

But, in order for the problem to be totally handled, it must be embraced holistically, which means it is necessary to see if there are so-called **oppositions,** which is any other hidden aspect that opposes the solution to the problem. Such aspect is evidently the polar opposite to the solution of the problem and if we don't handle it as well, the problem will reappear. Only when we integrate it, will the problem be almost permanently resolved (I'm saying "almost" because in this universe nothing is totally permanent).

One of the reasons temporary results exist in so many therapeutic systems is the omission to remove the opposition! This simply means that all roots of the problem have not been removed, and it has not been solved completely because of that opposition, which is an undiscovered polarity that tends to recreate the initial problem again.

Entities Processing

In therapy and Spiritual development work, there is one specific area, which we call Entity Processing. Its goal is the liberation of man from invisible influences, which he experiences as separate from his true, deepest identity, his "I". The word Entity comes from Latin "esse" which means to exist, existence, therefore that Entity is a thing or phenomenon, which has a definite individual existence in reality or in human mind and is endowed with a separate consciousness. From this follows this definition: An entity is everything that has an individual consciousness and existence. Peter Smith is an Entity, his physical body is an Entity as well as his astral body, and England could be an Entity, even your headache or your allergy. A problem could be an Entity, feeling that someone prevents us to attain our goals, feeling of inferiority etc.

What is important in the process, is that a man may experience an Entity as something separate from him, and this means there is an experience of duality. In Entity processing we attain the reintegration of the split off part. In some cases an Entity is not our separate part, but it is independent and in such case, we let it go out of our psychological field and let it continue its evolution independently.

If an Entity is very big then divide it into smaller parts, yielding smaller Entities, making the process easier. The main thing is – an Entity may be felt existing as an individual phenomenon or as a thing. So we can look at it as the whole or a part, depending on what we want to attain.

If you look at an Entity as some kind of absolute definite unit, you will make a lot of mistakes, get disappointed and be less successful in practical work. To avoid this, realize that words are not the real thing or phenomenon. Also, realize that you can believe whatever you want and it will become reality for you. The basic element in Entity processing, as well as in Aspectics, is that you should treat a certain thing or phenomenon as a separate, individual being having a consciousness. As a matter of fact, it is quite unimportant whether invisible beings exist or not. **If during the process you treat them as if they have a level of consciousness with whom you are able to communicate, they will behave toward you as if accepting your communication and such relationship will give good results in processing.**

We meet beliefs in the existence of Entities for the first time in animistic societies. **Animism** believes that all forms of existence are occupied by different spirits. Not only live beings, but also the air, mountains, rivers, trees, winds, earthquakes, rain and lightning. The main way to resolve problems in such societies, is to sacrifice something dear to such Entities to render them merciful.

From the beginning of the established religions, there has been the belief in the influence of evil forces and unclear spirits. The most frequent way of handling them was exorcism in which a specially trained priest sets the possessed person free. About 25% of all Christ's healing in the Bible consists of exorcisms that cast out evil spirits from possessed people. It was typical in the Jewish popular religion, in Galilee particularly, to attribute mental and physical disorders to unclean spirits. *"And when Jesus saw that a crowd came running together, he rebuked the unclean spirit, saying to it, 'You dumb and deaf spirit, I command you, come out of him, and never enter him again.' And after crying out and convulsing him terribly, it came out, and the boy was like a corpse; so that most of them said, 'He is dead.' But Jesus took him by the hand and lifted him up, and he arose."* Mark 9:25-26

Valentin, in year 300 a.d. wrote: *"Many spirits dwell in human body, not allowing it to become clean; they misuse their host using their harmful desires which they want to realize at any price. Human heart suffers as much as human body: because in it they dig wormholes which they fill with their dirt..."*

Giovanni Filoramo in the Middle Age text **"Gnosticism"** wrote: *"IN every body there is the whole hierarchy of demons, which turn it into a miniature hell."*

To understand what an Entity could be, take a simple example from everyday life such as a jingle that "enters your head" and circles inside it day and night. Nothing is able to drive it away or replace it. Also everyday language points to them. People often say *"In that situation I wasn't myself"*, *"I don't understand what is happening to me, something caught me"*, *"He is not the man I used to know"* etc. Such statements point out to Entities entering the psychic field of a human being, or to an already existing Entity that starts to wake up and become active.

In 17th and 18th century the most famous scientist in Europe, Emmanuel Swedenborg, described his visions of hell and paradise and his relationship with Spiritual intelligences. His description is very detailed. All of them can be treated as Entities.

Teachings on Entities got a new input in 18th century with the advent of spiritism, which spread from United States to the entire world. At the same time, such beliefs appeared in Western occultism and magic. Eliphas Levi, in his book **"Transcendental Magic",** gave a detailed description of rituals that handle Spiritual Entities and even gave his readers the designs and instructions to make the so-called Paracelsus' trident to kill "larvas" or bad Entities in the aura. Thirty years ago, in my book **"Hermetic Symbols"** I presented that design together with rituals for its consecration.

Recently, work with Entities entered the so-called official psychology. Rollo May in his paper **"Psychotherapy and the Daemonic"**: *"You take in the daemonic which would possess you if you didn't. The one way to get over daemonic possession is to possess it, by frankly confronting it, coming to terms with it, integrating it into the self-system. The process yields several benefits. It strengthens the self because it brings in which has been left out. It overcomes the "split" which has consisted of the paralyzing ambivalence in the self. And it renders the person more "human" by breaking down the self-righteousness and aloof detachment that are the usual defenses of the human being who denies the daemonic.*

The statement of a well known yoga teacher points out to making a positive Entity help us during meditation: *"... These meditation exercises help to develop visualization and to enable you the deeper level of concentration. When you work for a longer period the same kind of meditation, you will understand that your success steadily grows because that way you create an Elemental (thought form) of meditation. This happens unconsciously, because working the same meditation repeatedly you constantly are creating the Entity, live being, which gets more life and power with every new exercise. That means the creation of Entity which is able to be your good friend or nasty enemy! Therefore be careful of thoughts and emotions coming up to you as you meditate. That Entity should express love and positive power, not to be filled with thoughts and emotions of everyday life..."*

Not only can one expel Entities out of the psychological field of a person, one can also create it with intention and consciously. Then they influence their own creator. A very interesting experiment was performed in 1973 by the group of Canadian psychologists. They created an Entity and with intention gave him the name Philip. It proved that with energy, imagination and will power, is was possible to create such an Entity and that after some time it became independent from its creators and started to express many new characteristics and even new memories.

Although Entity processing here described could seem new and surprising, it is not. We can find similar processes in modern shamanism, Transactional Analyses and Psychosynthesis. But it was developed farthest in the scientological teachings of R. Hubbard and after his death, some independent researchers made valuable contributions.

The quintessence of Entity processing is the negotiation with something, which has a certain level of consciousness. All beings in this universe are basically good (see the text on Aspectics). Whever the appearance, if we penetrate deep enough into it, we will find positive purposes, because the highest goal for everything and everyone is the Highest Goal, or return to Oneness. Every so often Entities want just to be heard when their host ignores them for most of his/her life. As children become mischievous when we don't pay attention to their needs, our Entities raise their heads, start to rebel and seem to express hostility. Entity processing is directed both to removing unwanted states and to respect what we process. We don't want only to remove unwanted situations, we want Entities to continue working, but it should be in the optimal way. When we have a machine that does a good job, but also makes unwanted consequences, like air pollution, we don't want to destroy the machine but to repair it. This doesn't mean that every effect is desirable. That is the reason we do the process in the first place. When we process them, first of all we listen to them, behave kindly with them and confirm their importance and their value, and their behavior changes. They integrate into us, or even if they remain a bit separate, they become allied, or they leave us and start some higher and more valuable game in which they continue their Spiritual evolution in a much better way.

This was a minimal theoretical introduction. In practice, the Processor should know it to apply Entity processing to help the Client (or himself, if he does self-processing). In some cases, other methods are more appropriate. If someone has chronic stomach pain, which is almost the same every time; the person should go to see a doctor. But if that pain activates in a special circumstances, then it would be logical to conclude that the pain is some kind of communication trying to give us a message. In such situation it would be good to apply either Aspectics or Entity processing.

Efficient Entity processing means sticking to some rules:

1. **An Entity should be separated from the rest of the person.** That means that the Client should exteriorize the qualities that we will address as a separate individual. In other words, the Client should accept the Entity and label it. That way the Client will create a certain distance between himself and the Entity. It is necessary to put a label on the entity we are working with. It is much easier to observe something that we have a name for. The name should not be negative, but positive or at least neutral, because it is not easy to find out positive intentions for someone that has been baptized with an evil name. For us it is enough to call the Entity HE, SHE, or IT. We should give to the Entity the right to exist as it is.

2. **We do not have to consider the Entity as a person**, we do not have to give it a human form. All we need is to give it a separate existence to be able to communicate.

3. **At the very beginning we should give the Entity characteristics of this universe:** the location where it exists and where it is active from, its dimensions, shape, weight, content, energy, color, strength on the scale of 0-10, age. The Entity could have any shape: as a specific person, a dwarf, a ball of light, a metal ball, a cloud, demon or some deity etc. The easiest is if it is located in the body and if we have somebody sensations and emotions connected with it.

4. **It is important not to mix logic in this kind of work.** To separate and to identify an Entity it is necessary

to observe it and not use logic that says what it should be. It seems intellectual people are the only ones that have problems in this kind of work. But they have problems in all spheres of activities where feelings are important. You should be willing to imagine an Identity and after that you can start applying the technique. This work seems to be the product of imagination.

5. **We address an Entity directly as any other Client we have.** It has no physical body, but it has a consciousness. Our words are less important than our thoughts, because entities are accustomed to communicate with us telepathically. The answers the Entity will give us rarely come in the form of a voice. Usually they will be feelings, emotions, body sensations or just indefinite impressions. If your Client has the impression that he is talking to himself, just encourage him to go on that way. Entities are most often parts or aspects the person's personality. Even when the Client says *"it seems to me I'm imagining all this"*; encourage to continue, because Entities mainly use the energy of their host.

As we advance in Entity processing, gradually higher levels will be involved. In the first phase the Entity wants something and tries to tell us what it wants by acting out. Latter on we may discover that certain Entities are just executors, performers of goals and intentions of some higher Entities, which are some kind of **controllers.** Again, even higher levels can get involved, but it would be too premature to speak now about such work. It is the subject of my next book, which I am working on now. I hope it will available in the near future.

As I said, we process Entities the same way as we process Clients, which have bodies. Individual Entities or groups of them act in unpleasant ways because they are in a state of confusion, they don't know WHO they are or WHERE they are. So, with the process we help them eliminate that confusion. We get this by means of questions, which are part of the Entity handling procedure: What is their attitude toward matter, energy, space, time, what is their function, when did they take it, what is the goal they want to attain etc.

I divide all Entities into 3 main groups:

1. Entities that are separate parts of our own being (other aspects).

2. Entities that are creations of other people. They come from outside and enter out body or aura.

3. Entities that are mainly independent and self-conscious beings, which could be either well intentioned or with evil intentions: Spiritual guides, angels, artistic muses…or so called "fleas" and "psychic leaches", then controllers or dominators, which influence us, usually from distant, and dead people that are still bound to Earth etc.

Entities that come from outside do it in situations when the host's defense is weakened like during sickness, traumas (most often), anesthesia, when a person is under drugs or when one is under the influence of strong negative emotions: sadness, hatred, desire for revenge etc.

During the Entities handling workshop, we primarily work with Entities that separated from us in the past. Then with foreign Entities like "fleas" and finally with Controllers.

Entities Work Procedure

If a client has experience working with aspects of the personality, he/she can do this process at once. If such experience is missing, one should first do the first 4 exercises described in my book Aspectics".

This is how the process goes.

1. Tell the client: **"Pay attention to your unwanted aspect/Entity."**

2. **"Where is it located? If it is in your body, in which part of your body?"**

3. **"Define its characteristics: What is its shape? How big is it? What is its weight? What is its color? What kind of material it is made from? How old is it? What is its strength on a scale from 0 to 10?"**

4. **"Shall I call it 'he', 'she' or 'it'?**

5. Tell the client to ask the Entity (him, her, or it): *"What is your attitude toward matter?"*

Usually as an answer you will get some description in one or few words. Always give the Entity an acknowledgement, saying: *"Thank you!"*

6. Tell the client to ask the entity (him, her, or it): *"What is your attitude towards energy?"* Thank the entity.

7. Tell the client to ask the entity: *"What is your attitude towards space?"* Thank the entity

Return to Oneness

8. Tell the client to ask the entity: **"*What is your attitude towards time?*" Thank the entity.**

9. Tell the client to ask the entity: **"*What is your attitude towards life?*" Thank the entity.**

10. Tell the client to ask the entity: **"*What is your attitude toward forms shapes?*" Thank the entity.**

11. Tell the client to ask the entity: **"*What is your attitude towards thought?*" Thank the entity.**

12. Tell the client to ask the entity: **"*How do you maintain your position in space?*" Thank the entity and then tell him (her, it) "*I would like to indicate that this* (what the entity told you) *is the way you maintain your position in space*".**

If the Entity tells you: **"I don't maintain a position in the space"**, or **"I can't maintain a position in the space"** or something similar, ask the entity: **"*When you used to maintain a position in space, how did you do it?*" Thank the entity.**

13. Tell the client to ask the entity: **"*How do you maintain your position in time?*"** Thank the entity for the answer and say: **"*I would like to indicate that this* (what the entity replied) *is the way you maintain your position in time.*"**

14. Tell the client to ask the entity: **"*What is your function?*" Thank the entity.**

15. Tell the client to ask: **"*When did you take on that function for the first time?*" Thank the entity.**

Now start to ask two pairs of questions alternatively. Once you take off the charge from one pair of questions, continue working with the other pair until it is also empty of charge.

16. Tell your client: **"Ask the entity to tell you one difference between you and him/ her / it and report to me what answer you get."**

17. Tell your client: **"Ask the entity to tell you one similarity between you and him / her / it and report to me what answer you get."**

18. Tell your client: **"Now YOU** (the name of your client) **tell me one difference between you and the entity."**

19. Tell your client: **"Now YOU** (name of your client) **tell one similarity between you and the entity."**

Thus the process goes this way:

Difference? (An answer from the Entity)

Similarity? (An answer from the Entity)

Difference? (An answer from the Client)

Similarity? (An answer from the Client)

During the work you will sooner or later receive an answer from the client that he is not able to report any difference between him /her and the Entity, or that they are the same, or that they fused together, etc.

If you repeat the process 5-6 times and the Entity still persists separate, without weakening and vanishing, we continue with the process in a new way. We ask the client to address the Entity with the following words: ***"I want*** *you to know that you, as a Conscious Being, have two fundamental rights in this universe:*

1. *"You have the right to self-determinism, that is, you and only you have the right to decide for yourself."*

2. *"Up till now you have played this game with me with a lot of success. But you have the right to stop this game and to go away to where you want and when you want and to start a new, more valuable game as you want. You can find a new body, you can find a new host or you can go back to the Void where you came from."*

Wait for few seconds and then ask the client: **"Has the Entity left?"**

At this point most Entities go away. If that does not happen, you should tell the Client to ask an Entity:

"Point at the Being you are separate from!"

If even now the Entity does not go away, you ask it:

"Tell me WHO you are!"

It should answer **"I am me"**, or **"I am I"**, or **"I am myself"** or tell you some definite personal name.

If it does not answer that way, but tells you WHAT IT IS, for example "A power of light" or "Angel", or "Enemy", ask it:

"Who were you before you became an Angel / Enemy / A power of light?"

If you want the Entity to leave, you must get a definite answer to the question **"Who you are?"**

If the Entity still does not leave, there are two more possibilities:

First possibility:

The client can negotiate with an Entity on a new game: to help the client in the realization of more valuable goals for the client, and for the Entity, of their common goals. At this point Processors who have mastered Aspectics could apply it efficiently to this purpose.

Second possibility:

If the Entity does not leave when you tell him about the two rights of all conscious beings and after you asked the Entity to point to the Being it was separate from and after you asked it to "Tell me who you are", that means that the Entity has a higher **Controller,** which controls the Entity we started the process with. Therefore we ask the Entity:

"Tell me who controls you? Give me a connection with the Being which dominates you, your Controller!"

The connection is realized fairly easily and it does not matter whether the Controller is a few meters away from us or is in some far-off galaxy. With a Controller the process is usually shorter. You just praise it for a well done job in that game and afterwards you tell it the **two rights of a Conscious Being** and ask it to point to the Being it has been separate from. This should cause it to leave.

Filling the Empty Space

The human mind can't tolerate vacuum; it has a strong tendency to fill it. If it was a foreign Entity (flea) which has been eliminated, the void should be filled with light. Tell the client to imagine a blazing sun above his head and let light enter them through their head and first fill the space where the Entity was located and then the entire body.

If the Entity was a split-off aspect of the client, this process is not needed, because it has already been reintegrated within the client.

Craig Herink, psychotherapist from Louisville, USA, sent the following report on our discussion list: *"I have been working with a mother and daughter (age 9) on the aftereffects of an abusive relationship between the mother and the daughter's father. Mom has felt chronically fatigued, anxious and "unable to get my life going". The daughter is extremely intelligent, intuitive, sensitive and psychic, indigo kid...with difficulty falling asleep and sleeping through night since infancy. Recently mom recalled a particularly traumatic event in the marriage when the daughter was 7 months old...there was a fight at 3 AM between her and the father that involved pushing and shoving, the father grabbing the infant girl, and them mom finally rescuing the child and leaving the home. She reported that intuitively she suspected something was still unresolved about that night. I talk to her about Entities and we scheduled a session with both her and her daughter for yesterday.*

After talking with a girl about what we were going to do... she said that she knew there was "bad energy" that was "stuck to me" and didn't know how to get it to go away.

The Process:

I asked both to let themselves connect with whatever they might experience about the night there was a fight and they had to leave home.

Mom quickly located and described an entity as a dark, tingling, heavy mass down both arms, across her chest and up into her throat. Daughter sat directly next to mom, she reported exactly the same experience. Both said entity was very, very old... over 1000 years. Intensity was 9 on a 1-10 scale.

I asked if I could call it a "he", "she" or "it". Mom quickly reported the response was: "I am Me".

At this point I passed the steps on energy, space, time, etc...and asked: "What is your function?" Response: "To be Me."

I moved directly to the Two Fundamental Rights statements. After a few moments Mom reported a shift...she reported seeing the entity going back the house where the fight had occurred, but not totally leaving her body...daughter said she could tell that it was not happy yet. Mom reported there was somewhere other then the house it wanted to go, but it did not know where.

I asked: "Point out to the being you were separated from!"

Mom pointed with right hand above her shoulder. Intuitively I decided to read the Two Fundamental Rights statements again. At that point both mom and daughter reported another shift. Daughter said it was getting happy. Mom reported seeing a picture of an ancient woman, the same image she had seen in a dream and had later discovered her sister had the very same image in a dream as well Daughter reported the "bad energy" was leaving her arms and chest. She said it was very happy. Mom had a dramatic shift – tear down her cheeks, indicated she saw the entity going to the woman in her and her sister's dream.

Mom and daughter both said all the "bad" in their bodies had left. They filled the empty space with light. At the end the daughter made a most wonderful comment. She said: "It was like E.T. (the movie Extraterrestrial)."E.T. goes home!" It went home.

Narrating this experience leaves me great humility and reverence towards this work and what we can do to serve our fellow humans and all consciousness."

Expansion of the Being as Light

Ask your client to make on his 1st Eye-point the **kasha mudra combination**, that is his middle fingertip and thumb-tip connected. Then, with his eyes closed let him imagine above his head a source of shining light, as some small sun. Then let him imagine the light penetrating his body, filling it completely.

Tell him to inhale and exhale, spreading light by breathing until it is about 1 meter around his body. Then tell him:

Imagine that light, which is the quintessence of you, spreading in front of you into infinity!...

Imagine that light which is you spreading behind you into infinity...

To the left into infinity...

To the right into infinity...

Above you into infinity...

Under you into infinity...

Now imagine that light which is you spreading around you into infinity in all directions AT THE SAME TIME! In front and behind, left and right, upwards and downwards into infinity at the same time! After 15-20 seconds ask him:

Tell me, how big are you now? Do you have any limits? and after that: **Take a look to the places where the Creators of that unwanted part of your life used to be and tell me, what is the happening with them? What kind of energy, messages, words, thoughts and emotions are coming NOW from ...(first Creator) ?**

That Creator should be empty of charge, or from him should come very neutral or positive messages, energies, words or emotions. Or he does not exist any more.

Ask again: **Does anything limit you in space? Do you have any limits?**

Then: **Out of that endless space, where you are a clean Spiritual Being, put your attention onto your body which sits in this room, here on the chair. It is the I you are every day, or the "Small I". Tell me, how big is it?**

Now ask about similarities and differences concerning the following domains of activity:

Is there any difference of you as Endless Being of Light and you in everyday life?

Is there any difference of you as Endless Being of Light and your emotional partner and your family?

Is there any difference of you as Endless Being of Light and the group which you belong to?

Is there any difference of you as Endless Being of Light and the whole of humanity?

Is there any difference of you as Endless Being of Light and the whole live universe?

Is there any difference of you as Endless Being of Light and the whole physical universe, from the tiniest atom to the biggest galaxies?

Is there any difference of you as Endless Being of Light and GOD as you imagine GOD to be?

Finally, ask him: **"Tell me, who created all your experiences?"**

Holographic Life Repair

Every human being has got pleasant and unpleasant parts of its own life. Even if man does not like unpleasant experiences they also have unquestionable values. We learn from them. But when unpleasant experiences start to influence us in a bad way, rendering us passive and unable, we should remove all negative charge from them and set us free.

The overall amount of unwanted or negative experiences, which influence our emotional states and behavior, can be called the **unwanted part of our life.**

In the **holographic process,** and especially in the **Holographic Life Repair** we remove emotional charge from the unwanted part of our life using the hologram metaphor. To help you understand it, I will briefly explain something about holograms, using scientific research regarding memory.

In the fifties of the last century, the Penfield theory on memory was widespread. Its main characteristic was the belief that memory is inside the brain and the basis of memory were traces in the brain called engrams. Penfield came to his theory experimenting with the human brain open. What should be clear is that the brain itself is completely insensitive to pain. If an experimenter renders the skin and bones in a head insensible using anesthesia, it is possible to make different painless operations on the open brain. During one of these operations, Penfield stimulated the temporal parts of the brain with electrical current and the patient got very vivid images from early childhood. Penfield's conclusion was that inside the brain reside countless memories, and that in it is recorded everything we experienced: from people's faces we meet on the street, to the little insect a man saw as a boy.

A strange fact is that many medical doctors, psychologists and psychiatrists still accept Penfield's theory although later research did not prove it. It was contested by researches carried out by Karl Lashley and many other scientists. They were not able to find traces or engrams of memory in the brain. What is most important, repeating Penfield's experiment with the electrical stimulations of the same part of brain; researchers did not get the same memories. Also, they got the same memories stimulating different parts of the brain, what was the evident proof was that memory was not located in definite areas of the brain tissue.

Lashley trained rats to do complicated activities in a labyrinth and after he would remove parts of their brains with surgical methods. He wanted to see in which parts of the brain resided their memory and learned abilities. When he removed large parts of their brains they became clumsy and sluggish in carrying out the learned activities, but it was impossible to delete the memory of the learned activity removing parts of the brain. The same applied to the visual function. One could remove 98% of the brain tissues responsible for seeing and still the animal was able to see. The same results he had with people. There are individuals that live with huge parts of the brain removed and do not experience the loss of specific memories.

One of Lashley's associates was Karl Pribram. He came to the conclusion that memory was not situated in specific parts of the brain, but was spread around the brain as a whole. In 1960, the ***"Scientific American"*** magazine published a detailed description of the so-called hologram photograph or hologram. That article deeply impressed Pribram because the hologram made it possible to understand his research on memory. To be able to understand this we should say a bit more on about the hologram.

A Hologram has two main characteristics: It is a three-dimensional photo and the entire hologram exists in all of its parts. Many alternative disciplines and teachings accepted the hologram as extremely valuable in the illustrations of their models of reality. For example, it is a good representation of the "Hermes law": microcosmos is equal to the macrocosmos or in other words, as above so below. From this, many other conclusions were made: the entire Universe is connected by one universal mind. Everything we do is recorded in that universal mind and our subconscious is able to draw from it.

People applied the hologram principles long time before it was discovered. For example, Marcel Proust in his novel

"Remembrance of Things Past" describes his experience from early childhood, where just a simple cake he used to eat, was able to revive other very detailed memories from his childhood. The principle of the hologram can be found in American Hopi Indians. They wear vials with strong smells around their waist. Whenever they have some important experience they open the vial and inhale the fragrance. Later on in life, inhaling and smelling that fragrance will allow reliving the entire experience connected to it.

Something similar happens in hologram processing. If I ask a person who created his inferiority feeling, he could say, my father. My father used to tell me constantly I was good for nothing. But if we start from the father, as one part of the hologram of inferiority, we will see that the hologram is a complex whole, having more then one creator or source, that the father did not create his inferiority alone, but that there are more sources of such feeling.

To solve a problem we must externalize it. That means the Client imagines a hologram outside himself. That hologram represents the problem or unwanted state, which the person wants to remove. We ask from him to tell us what messages, feelings, energies and thoughts flow from the source of the problem (there is more then one source) towards hologram and create it; and what messages, feelings, energies and thoughts flow from the hologram back to sources of that problem.

Because opposite forces are confronted at the same moment, what happens is that they collapse. Such process of annihilation of two opposite states are called collapsing anchors. A person enters simultaneously into two opposite body-mind states, we post anchors for both states and then we stimulate both of those states at the same time. Doing this, the two states will be dispersed and will annihilate each other. Basically, we direct the nervous system and consciousness to enter simultaneously into two different opposite states. As result, the mental-emotional energy is dispersed and what is left on the stage is only I, pure and cleared. For a short period, the Client will only feel himself, whole and integrated, because the energies that prevented such integration are eliminated.

A short description of the Holographic process and Holographic Life Repair follows.

Before beginning, ask the client to do several identification exercises with other human beings, groups, places or times.

After these exercises, pay attention to the two points, which are very important in this process:

1. You externalize the client's problem and

2. You confront opposing goals.

The process goes like this.

Shortly explain to the Client what a hologram is. The main point is that a **hologram is a 3-dimensional image, created from more than one source or Creator.**

Ask the client to identify a problematic Aspect of himself. He should then choose a hologram to represent this problem. Ask the client to give the hologram **a name or label**, and then to give to it some characteristics (used then in the wave collapse method): Ask the client the hologram's shape, dimensions, colors, weight, age, strength on the scale from 0 to 10.

Then ask the client to imagine in front of him/her the hologram representing his problem, for example a feeling of inferiority. People mostly imagine a ball, a football or a balloon. Then ask him for the Creators or Sources of that hologram. For every Creator he gives you, ask him to identify with that Creator, to look at the hologram from the Creator's position and, AS THAT CREATOR, answer your question: **"What kind of energies, messages, thoughts or emotions are flowing from that Creator toward the hologram, create it, support it or contribute to it?"**

Write down the answer. Then you ask him to change the point of view, to go into the hologram, identify with it and from the center of the hologram to answer your question: **"What kind of energy, words, thoughts and feelings are flowing from the hologram back to that Creator?"**

You repeat the process with all Creators he gives you in turn.

When he has finished you start asking him questions from the following list (otherwise he will surely miss some very important Creators/Sources).

Don't forget to ask him to change the position every time, to identify with every source, and then to change position and to identify with the hologram and to tell you what is coming back from the hologram to the source.

"Do some negative energies, messages, thoughts or emotions come from some Image/ picture from your past, creating this hologram, contributing to it or supporting it?"

If the answer is "**YES**" ask him to identify with that **Image picture** and then ask him:

"What kinds of energies, messages, thoughts or emotions are flowing from that Image picture <u>toward the hologram</u>**, creating it, supporting it or contributing to it?"**

Write down the answer.

Then ask him to change the point of view, to go into the hologram, identify with it and from the center of the hologram to answer the question:

"What kind of energies, messages, thoughts and emotions are flowing <u>from the hologram</u> **back to that Image picture?"**

Do some negative energies, messages, thoughts or emotions come from some Place from your past, creating this hologram, contributing to it or supporting it?

If the answer is "**YES**" ask him to identify with that Place and then ask him:

"What kind of energies, messages, thoughts or emotions are flowing from that Place <u>toward the hologram</u>**, creating it, supporting it or contributing to it?"**

Write down the answer.

Then ask him to change the point of view, to go into the hologram, identify with it and from the center of the hologram to answer the question:

"What kind of energies, messages, thoughts and emotions are flowing from the hologram back to that Place?"

"Do some negative energies, messages, thoughts or emotions come from some Trauma in your life from your past, creating this hologram, contributing to it or supporting it?"

If the answer is "**YES**" ask him to identify with that **Trauma in his life** and then ask him:

"What kind of energies, messages, thoughts or emotions are flowing from that Trauma in your life toward the hologram, creating it, supporting it or contributing to it?"

Write down the answer.

Then ask him to change the point of view, to go into the hologram, identify with it and from the center of the hologram to answer the question:

"What kind of energies, messages, thoughts and emotions are flowing from the hologram back to that Trauma in your life?"

Do some negative energies, messages, thoughts or emotions come from some **Particular period of time from your past**, creating this hologram, contributing to it or supporting it?

If the answer is "**YES**" ask him to identify with that **Particular period of time from his past** and then ask him:

"What kind of energies, messages, thoughts or emotions are flowing from that Particular period of time

from your life <u>toward the hologram</u>, creating it, supporting it or contributing to it?"

Write down the answer.

Then ask him to change the point of view, to go into the hologram, identify with it and from the center of the hologram to answer the question:

"What kind of energies, messages, thoughts and emotions are flowing <u>from the hologram</u> back to that Particular period of time from your life?"

Do some negative energies, messages, thoughts or emotions come from some Particular part of your future, creating this hologram, contributing to it or supporting it?

If the answer is **"YES"** ask him to identify with that Particular part of his future and then ask him:

"What kind of energies, messages, thoughts or emotions are flowing from that part of your future <u>toward the hologram</u>, creating it, supporting it or contributing to it?"

Write down the answer.

Then ask him to change the point of view, to go into the hologram, identify with it and from the center of the hologram to answer the question:

"What kind of energies, messages, thoughts and emotions are flowing <u>from the hologram</u> back to that Part of your future"

Do some negative energies, messages, thoughts or emotions come from some **Part of your horoscope (astrological sign)** from your past, creating this hologram, contributing to it or supporting it?

If the answer is "**YES**" ask him to identify with that Part of his horoscope (astrological sign) and then ask him:

"**What kind of energies, messages, thoughts or emotions are flowing from that Part of your horoscope (astrological sign)** toward the hologram**, creating it, supporting it or contributing to it?**"

Write down the answer.

Then ask him to change the point of view, to go into the hologram, identify with it and from the center of the hologram to answer the question:

"**What kind of energies, messages, thoughts and emotions are flowing** from the hologram **back to that Part of your horoscope (astrological sign)?**

Do some negative energies, messages, thoughts or emotions come from some Identity **you sometimes use** from your past, creating this hologram, contributing to it or supporting it?

If the answer is "**YES**" ask him to identify with that Identity he sometimes use and then ask him:

"**What kind of energies, messages, thoughts or emotions are flowing from that Identity you sometimes use** toward the hologram**, creating it, supporting it or contributing to it?**"

Write down the answer.

Then ask him to change the point of view, to go into the hologram, identify with it and from the center of the hologram to answer the question:

"What kind of energies, messages, thoughts and emotions are flowing from the hologram **back to that Identity you sometimes use?"**

Do some negative energies, messages, thoughts or emotions come from some **suffering which you experienced** from your past, creating this hologram, contributing to it or supporting it?

If the answer is **"YES"** ask him to identify with that Suffering he experienced and then ask him:

"What kind of energies, messages, thoughts or emotions are flowing from that Suffering you experienced toward the hologram, **creating it, supporting it or contributing to it?"**

Write down the answer.

Then ask him to change the point of view, to go into the hologram, identify with it and from the center of the hologram to answer the question:

"What kind of energies, messages, thoughts and emotions are flowing from the hologram **back to that Suffering which you experienced?"**

Do some negative energies, messages, thoughts or emotions come from some Special group of people, beings or entities from your past, creating this hologram, contributing to it or supporting it?

If the answer is "**YES**" ask him to identify with that Special group of people, beings or entities and then ask him:

"**What kind of energies, messages, thoughts or emotions are flowing from that** Special group of people, beings or entities toward the hologram, **creating it, supporting it or contributing to it?**"

Write down the answer.

Then ask him to change the point of view, to go into the hologram, identify with it and from the center of the hologram to answer the question:

"**What kind of energies, messages, thoughts and emotions are flowing** from the hologram **back to that Special group of people, beings or entities?**"

Write down the answer.

Do some negative energies, messages, thoughts or emotions come from some **Part of your body** from your past, creating this hologram, contributing to it or supporting it?

If the answer is "**YES**" ask him to identify with that Part of his body and then ask him:

"**What kinds of energies, messages, thoughts or emotions are flowing from that** Part of your body toward the hologram, **creating it, supporting it or contributing to it?**"

Write down the answer.

Then ask him to change the point of view, to go into the hologram, identify with it and from the center of the hologram to answer the question:

"**What kind of energies, messages, thoughts and emotions are flowing** <u>from the hologram</u> **back to that Part of your body?"**

Then ask the Client: **Are there some other Creators or Sources which we have not covered?**

If the answer is **YES,** add those Creators to the list and do the same process with them.

Now, read back to him all Creators (Sources) he gave to you, the flows that go from them to the hologram and back and ask him to do the following:

"Enter into the center of hologram. When I say: One, two, three! You imagine all energies, messages, emotions and thoughts coming from all Creators toward you and AT THE SAME TIME all messages and energies going out from you back to Creators. One, two, three! Do it now!"

Then tell him very quickly:

"To you, from you! To you, from you! To you, from you!! Z-z-z-z-z-z-z !!!"

Then tell him: **"Go back to yourself, feel yourself and tell me.... who you are?"**

He will almost always say: "I am me" or his own name.

Then ask him: "What happened with your problem and the hologram?"

If you did it as it should be done, there will not be any. If there is something left, it means that there some Creators left untouched, but now he will find them very easily. Then continue the process with the Expansion of Being as Light.

Deep PEAT

The large part of my book *"**PEAT and Neutralization of Primordial Polarities**"* is devoted to the description of the Deep Peat process. Interested people should pay attention to it. But PEAT (Prime Energy Activation and Transcendence) is a live system in constant change and perfection, thus I will describe some new methodological procedure, which I recently developed (I'm writing this in 2005). I can't cover completely all elements, which I cover in the Advanced Peat workshop, but what I give here will make the PEAT process quicker and easier and will help you be more successful with so-called "hard Clients". I will also try to explain some previously known elements, which I did not pay much attention to in my previous book. For example, participants often ask, why is it important to inhale deeply when we experience a content on the chain and so on.

Deep inhaling is the quickest way for contacting deeper thoughts and emotions. People that breathe shallow don't get into full interaction with their mental and especially emotional processes. Rigid persons, which have a personality built mainly on a mechanism of repression, do not breathe deeply because they unconsciously know that such activity will bring them into contact with their deep emotions. Breathing through the left nostril for a few moments activates the right hemisphere in our brain (emotional one) and facilitates this contact. I will give you these indications as we go through text.

In all variants of Deep Peat we primarily tend towards the integration of polarities. Every individual process, if it is done correctly, brings about a gradual liberation of the Being from the dual forces it is exposed to in this life. They continue influencing us, because we live in a dual universe. But as the Sixth Patriarch of Zen, Hui-Neng points out (see later on), when we neutralize (integrate) our basic polarities, we are freed from our extreme behavior and feelings. In any kind of situation we find ourselves we activate an adequate polarity, which represents the optimal behavior in that situation.

Integration or neutralization of the opposite polarities which create a problem is the most valuable end of the process. This is the only way we can entirely embrace an experience and solve the problem close to for good. Therefore we strive to integration whenever it is possible. Unfortunately the majority of other systems lack such knowledge and the operational ability tied to it. Their practitioners are unable to penetrate to the deepest roots of problems, and remain on the surface, catching only half the problem, because they exclusively tend to the desired component.

The basic axiom of Deep Peat is this: We live in dual or two-pole universe. During Deep Peat there always, always exists the polarization of a content! It is nothing new, polarization exists in all forms of life, but in therapeutic and Spiritual processes people tend to overlook it. It is sometimes visible, but most often it is invisible and one should make it become visible with appropriate questions. We do it discovering the polarity, which the Client overlooked and failed to disclose and that is always present. The reason why a Client does not notice the polar opposite to the content he is concentrated on, is because in life and especially during Deep Peat, we are strongly attracted to the one of the two polarities and are not conscious of the opposite one, with which he/she is indissolubly tied to and **without which the opposite cannot exist.** Asking appropriate questions, we bring the other polarity (pole) to consciousness, which means we see the other half of the experience. It is a holistic process, because we involve the entire experience (both connected polarities) not just half of it. We can do it both with positive and negative polarities.

I will point out the typical situations in which we uncover opposing polarities, but one can find other similar possibilities.

Nothing or Nothingness

Many inexperienced Processors are confronted with a seemingly unsolvable problem when their Client tells them *"there is nothing"* or *"I experience nothing."* Previously I tried many different ways to make clients experience "something" in that "nothing", usually without success. It was one of the rare occasions in which the Processor had to stop the Peat process and continue it some other time. Finally in a lucky situation, I found the solution during a process. In the middle of a process, a Client bogged down. There was "nothing" in his consciousness. In the moment of inspiration I asked the Client: *"You feel nothing...Do you feel that nothing inside of you, outside of you or inside and outside simultaneously?"*

He said he felt that **nothing** outside of himself. It pointed to the polarity. I asked him to experience himself in that moment, then to experience **nothing** or **nothingness,** then to experience himself and nothingness at the same time, to inhale, exhale and to report what was happening to his "I" and nothingness. He said the **nothing** was rising up, over-flooding him, then the two of them merged and at the end there was no difference between "I" and nothingness, they became One. Primes of that person were **"I" and Nothingness** and I found about a dozen people with such Primes.

Later on I started to differentiate between **pleasant nothing** and unpleasant **nothing.** This is important because a pleasant nothing, when it persists on three points is a **Pleroma** state and it is the end of the process. In such case a Processor does not indicate the Primes to his Client because they did not show up.

Sudden Turn of States in Consciousness and in Body

Pay attention to a sudden turn over of one state to its polar opposite! That element is important for efficient processing. When a sudden turn from one state to its opposite takes place, we always ask, is there a part of the previous state left? For example, after feeling upset and tense, a Client reports his state **peace.** The question that always follows is: *"Now you feel peace...Is part of the previous tension and your being upset still there?"* If the answer is "yes", the Processor asks the Client to experience first one polarity, then another, then both simultaneously, because evidently there is polarization.

Looking for the Opposite State

Another approach is to look for the opposite state: *"You feel peace...What state is opposite to peace for you?"* What follows is the same procedure as in previous example.

We can also ask: *"Now you feel peace...What is the state you would not like to feel at all?"* What follows is the same procedure as in the previous example.

Creating Consciousness of Polarization

What follows are some new contributions to Peat processing. We use the words a Client tells us, describing his state, to create a new consciousness of the polarity in him.

To his/her statement *"I feel isolated"*, the question follows: *"Isolated from who?...* or *Isolated from what?"* or a similar question: *"Concerning whom do you feel isolated from?"* We use the same principle when a Client says something like *"I feel lonely."* The question follows: *"Concerning whom do you feel lonely?"*

Generally speaking, whenever a Client reports a negative state, we can provoke the consciousness of polarization with the question: *"What do you want to feel instead of it?"* We direct him/her to feel that state completely, then to feel both simultaneously the existing negative state and the desired positive state.

Sometimes we use given descriptions as a basis for comparison. For example, when a Client says *"I am a failure"*, what follows should be *"You are a failure when you compare yourself with whom?"*

Space location or a location in the body always means the existence of some other position:

"In front of me is some wall," is followed with *"And what is behind you?"*

"Left hand side of my body is heavy (...painful, warm...) is followed with *"And how is your right hand side?"*

"The upper part of my body is ..." is followed with *"And what sensations do you feel in your lower part?"*

A Processor should be careful not to stimulate a Client into so-called "swimming" with his questions about polarization. "Swimming" is the act of remaining on the surface of consciousness, not going down deeper and deeper into the layers of mind. In such situations, an efficient Peat process changes into a friendly talk. But the Client did it hundreds of times in his life and he did not come to any positive result. For example, in one moment a Client gets the image of his father followed by an emotion of sadness. An inexperienced Processor will ask *"And what about your father?"* Doing this, the Processor leads his/her Client to stop doing Deep Peat and to start confiding things.

Symbols of the Deeper Contents

When, during Deep Peat, vague symbols or some indefinite contents **persist a bit longer**, the processor should ask what do they represent, what they stand for? For example, in two or three consecutive contents the client speaks about what happens with the upper part or lower part of his body. The processor should then ask: *"Does the upper part of your body represent something for you?"* or *"What does the upper part of your body symbolize for you... What does the lower part of your body symbolize for you?"* The Processor could vary this question, as *"What does the upper part mean for you..?"* etc.

We proceed the same way with two colours persisting in consciousness: *"Are these colors just contents of consciousness as *such, or do they represent something?"* or *"What does the red represent for you...and what does the green represent for you?"*

The most frequent polarization appearing in processing is between the left and right parts of the body. Usually a client reports a feeling of his body being cut down the middle. Also we find frequent polarization between the head and the body. Usually those two poles represent **the mind and the body** or **physical (material) world and spiritual world.**

The Container and its Content

Actually we can always create the consciousness of polarisation in a client using his "I" as one polarity (and any kind of state, situation or object which he gives) and the content of his body or his mind as the other polarity. For example, if a client says the he feels a fear, what follows is the question: *"Are you that fear, or do you just feel that fear?"* When he answers that he is not the fear, but he feels the fear, what follows is: *"Experience yourself. Then feel the fear. And now feel yourself and the fear at the same time. Inhale, exhale, and tell me..."*

As you see, it is pretty simple. Two polarities always exist as the two halves of the same whole. What is needed is to demonstrate the other polarity.

In the human being there is innate tendency for wholeness, which conventional psychology calls **gestalt,** but until recently scientists did not pay attention to that element. From the practical side what is most important is that now we have **the method** for realization of the whole experience instead of long and tiresome processes which were only partially successful.

This anecdote comes from the natural propensity of humans to have entire and whole experiences. Two students used to share the same room. One was tidy and orderly, studied diligently, used to go to bed early, and did all things which diligent students do. The other was the complete opposite. He was untidy, spent his time having good times and came back to their room late at night when his diligent colleague was already sleeping and commonly woke him up with his inconsiderate behaviour. He would undress with a lot of noise and at the end he would throw one shoe in one corner of the room and other shoe in the other corner. They had many arguments about their different behavior and finally they made a compromise. The noisy student can come in late at night, but he must be silent. The next night he came late again, but he undressed himself carefully. When he took off his first shoe, he automatically threw it in the corner. Then he remembered their deal, took off other shoe carefully and put it down at the bedside. He lay down and tried to fall asleep. After a couple of minutes his calm friend shouted aloud from his bed, *"For God's sake, throw that other shoe so I can fall asleep."*

The Duplication of the Decision of Defeat

Sometimes during Deep Peat processing a negative decision which the client made in times long passed comes to the surface. It certainly influences the process. For example, a Client says: *"I can't go on. I surrender!"* In such situations we apply the procedure of repeating that decision, duplicate it, and remove it (see more about duplication at the other part of this book). We ask the Client to bring himself completely into that state of mind and to repeat the same assertion a few times: ***"I can't*** *go on, I surrender!...I can't go on, I surrender!...I can't go on, I surrender!"* or something similar. Such repetition, fully bringing himself into the feeling, will cause the duplication and vanishing of that decision. The vacuum that appears in its place will suck a new content into itself, which we then continue processing.

Pleroma and the Neutralization of Polarities

Pleroma is a gnostic term meaning fullness,"grace" and "the mercy of God". In space and time pleromatic states were the first manifestations of Oneness in the manifested universe. Pleroma states are closest to oneness and therefore they have characteristics people often attribute to the highest: peace, cosmic peace, light, golden light, I AM, love, universal love, cosmic love, unconditional love, OK-ness and similar.

I said more than once that the Deep Peat process could end two different ways: integration (neutralization) of polarities and with the pleroma state. I also said that integration of polarities gives most permanent results. Therefore when a client ends the process with a pleroma state, the processor should try to attain the integration of polarities with appropriate questions:

"Now you feel that positive (pleasant) state... what state is opposite to this one?" or,

"Now that you feel that good state... what would you not like to feel at all?"

Sometimes the client will express an undesirable state and the processor should then start a new process with two new polarities: the positive state which the client feels in that moment and the state he would not like to experience. If the client is deeply immersed in a pleroma state, he can tell the processor that no other thoughts are coming to him or there is no interest in anything else. In such situation you should end the process and you apply the **Procedure of Expansion** (See it later in this book).

However, the pleroma state per se has definite value. First, it could signify the end of the process. Second, many people have far-reaching and valuable experiences through it. I will quote examples which Peat trainer Carol Saito sent to me (letter from February 5, 2005).

I wish to share with you a great experience I had working with Peat! Recently I had some very thrilling experiences with PEAT practice, working with the elderly! Some time ago, I met a few people who had read Peat and wanted to do some Peat processes. To my surprise the first client I had was age 78, the second was 69, the third 71, and so on; all still working hard on their spiritual evolution. The main issues I was asked to process were coping with body aging and ailments caused by "mechanical" problems rather than psychological ones.

What remained to work on as psychological and emotional aspects, were guilt feelings regarding how things should have been done or said differently to children, friends, and also parents who had passed away many years before. The majority of them were in overall good spirits, had a good life, did not have big money or emotional problems. Yet they felt Peat could help them prepare themselves better for the years they had left to live and, why not, be more prepared to "die" and, believe me, it really did! I noticed that experiencing the pleroma state was very beneficial for all of them. All defined this state as very different to what they had experienced in the past with "normal" meditation techniques, and described it as a real physical feeling! There was a general feeling of cosmic communion with the spirit of the universe, and a redefinition of time, space, life and death.

This was all new material for me, as we are so used to seeing elderly as individuals who have often renounced life and are just waiting to pass away, among the boredom of feeding pigeons in the city gardens and some transitory emotions and satisfactions mainly tied to their grandchildren. What I saw here was something very different. I actually saw in them life in its entirety as I had never seen before, and new dimensions of understanding. So what I did, was look around myself, hungry for information, and retrieved some interesting information regarding the theory of gerotranscendence, which suggests that human aging, the very process of living into old age, is characterized by a general potential towards gerotranscendence. Simply put, gerotranscendence is a shift in meta perspective, from a materialistic and rational view of the world to a more cosmic and transcendent one, normally accompanied by an increase in life satisfaction.

So what is the most precious thing Peat did for these people? Experiencing pleroma states and consequently working with them once the corridors of new dimensions had flung open, proved that in most of these people, the fear of death had disappeared and they had suddenly a new comprehension of life and death. Many of them had realized that the pieces of life's jigsaw puzzle form a whole and experienced for the first time the difference between one's self and one's role.

The most touching moment? The day one of my clients told me after ending a Peat process and opening his eyes after experiencing pleroma; "I deeply acknowledged myself for the first time and actually experienced it physically! Now I know what it means to die and where I will go when it happens... Now I know I mustn't fear death... because it simply means moving on!"

Months later...The memory of what they experienced is still there and has never changed. Peat contributed in making them become spiritually awakened individuals.

Circular Processing

*For a detailed explanation please see Chapter 16 ("Holistic Processing in PEAT") from my book **"PEAT and the Neutralization of Primordial Polarities"**. Here I will present some additions to that text.*

Sometimes people ask, is it possible to neutralize (integrate) primes, that is, primordial polarities from meta-position, which means identifying with another person and doing the Deep Peat process from other person's position ?

There are two ways to do the process from other points of view:

1. Surrogate processing and

2. Circular processing, or doing the process from more then one points of view.

In **surrogate processing** we do a process for a client, a friend, a relative or any other being we want to help to (even home pets, plants, flowers etc). The processor identifies with the client, feels as he feels that the client is experiencing (it is his subjective estimation) as if he is that subject. Sometimes we attain a surprising result with this method. Whatever happens, it is the processor's experience, but the consequences manifest in the client. For example, a child has a high fever and you do the surrogate process for it. Suppose you enter the pleroma state or you attain integration of some polarities. As a consequence of that process the fever diminishes or vanishes completely, but it is the experience of the person **which is conscious of that process**, which means yours, the processor's !

In circular processing **the client assumes** different points of view toward the same problem and does processing from each of them. **Here an axiom from the holistic approach is valid:** in order to solve a problem completely and permanently, a person has to solve it from all points of view relevant to the problem! This approach is very valuable for obtaining a permanent result. An old Chinese proverb says, *"Only with other's eyes you are able to see your own defects."*

Suppose you have a bad relationship with your father. You process and clear the first position ("I-position"), but after some time the problem comes back to you. To have a complete and integrated process, you must process all relevant points of view (see in more detail in the PEAT Manual). Relevant points of view are points you connected with the problem on which there is an emotional charge. Suppose that working from your father's point of view you finished the process with an integration of some pair of polarities. Suppose further that your father has no any experience with the processing, so that these polarities are his first integrated (neutralized) polarities. The question arises: are these polarities your father's primordial polarities? They are not, of course. If you did not experience neutralization of your primes, they are your primes. You simply neutralized (integrated) them on your father's position (meta position) using your father as the vehicle of the process. It happens very, very rarely and uncommonly. If you integrated your primes previously, those are just two other polarities of yours. The result of such happening will manifest on the first position; that means, in you. It may manifest on the father's position as well in a change of your father's behaviour. Don't forget that you have created that point of view (father's). Subjectively the father usually has quite a different opinion and feeling about himself than what you think about him. Again one can ask, which person is conscious of that process? It is you, of course, although consequences of the process could manifest in the other's point of view, i.e. father's. By the way, all those points of view are yours!

Once, in the Advanced PEAT processors training, one participant insisted that, doing circular processing, he integrated the primes of his wife. They had some problems concerning the divorce and he did the process from her point of view. The man said their pet dog also suffered because of their arguments. Therefore he did a process from dog's point of view as well and he came to a pleroma state. Then I asked him: *"what would have happened if you attained integration of primes as you were doing the process from the dog's point of view? Do you think, then, they would be the primordial polarities of the dog?"* He just laughed and said, *"Now I understand."*

When your client asks you the same question; can he do surrogate and circular processing not only on individuals, but also on groups of people, animals and plants, ask him if they experience integration of primordial polarities? In this period of our spiritual evolution they cannot. Perhaps they will be able in the future. But he himself can experience it from their positions.

On the Importance of Exact Verbalization of Primes

One of the important responsibilities of the processor in Deep Peat is to indicate to his client the client's primes. It is the processor's job during the Deep Peat process to bring his client to the integration of primes. At the moment of integration of primes the client is usually disoriented and the processor asks himself, what happened with him? In a great majority of cases it is evident which are the client's primes and there is no problem with their verbalization.

Problems could appear if the processor indicates the client's primes inaccurately stated. Man is a communicative being, expressing in symbols strongly burdened with emotion He has a strong intention to express that state exactly. If he gets his primes wrongly verbalized, the damage is not major because primes are integrated, but until their verbalization is correct, the client feels a mild dissatisfaction or agitation.

The processor should never insist that the verbalization he indicates to the client is the only possible one. He does not give them as a factual statement, but as an indication. As soon as he indicates them he should ask his client: *"Take a look at your life and tell me, does it make sense that these are your primordial polarities?"* If the client hesitates with his answer 10-15 seconds, he should ask him: *"Would you state your primes differently?"*

If the client gives any other verbalization, no matter how illogical they sound, the processor should accept them. They are his primes and about their verbalization, their names, only he decides. Even when he gets wrongly indicated primes there is no great harm. A day or two later clear verbalization will break into client's consciousness.

Primordial polarities of personal codes are first polarities; first plus and minus, first Yang and Yin which the being creates after it decided to drop from unity with oneness and enter this universe (reality). Before primes only oneness existed and they represented the first step toward the endless multitude. Actually primes have no names (freedom/slavery, creation/destruction etc.). They are only primitive Yang and Yin. But when people make them conscious and integrate their primes, they give them different names. What you call your primes depends upon your education, upbringing, cultural surroundings, personality and many other factors.

This is what J.C. from Scotland writes about his primes: *I'm Jared. I'm new to this group though I did the Peat Processor Training, DP3 and Past/Future rundown last year in Lake Garda and Livorno with Zivo and Alda. I'm a psychotherapist, energy worker, Sekhem/Reiki trainer. and live some of the time in Edinburgh, Scotland, the rest in Portland, Oregon, USA.*

I had an initial powerful catharsis with the primes followed by a deep feeling of peace. Same with the past /future rundown, though it was transitory, lasting only days. I've since worked solo Peat a great deal and anguished about my Scottish reserved genes... were they the issue? A great number of you lovely expressive Italian people in my groups had such major life-changing experiences!

Not one to give up, I've experimented with what I got as my primes. These were peace v. suffering and got an intuitive insight that this polarity was close and indeed an expression of my primes, but not exactly it. What came up for me instead was peace v. control, and when I neutralized these and the life decisions around these pillars recently, the weight of my burdens about my past, carried for years in mind and body, have literally fallen away. I don't feel I have to control life, or others, or my heart any longer, and the suffering that comes from doing so has almost dropped away. WOW! Such an incredible relief! I feel ready to serve life rather than demanding it serve me, and I have so much gratitude about what I saw as problems in my life.

I should mention that such situation rarely happens. Primordial polarities are usually evident and their verbalization forces itself upon us. The idea that one should find exact verbalization of primes is neither original nor new. A Chinese proverb from the ages says, *"The beginning of the wisdom is to call things by their right names."*

Judith Daniel, experienced PEAT Trainer writes On the Nature of Primordial Polarities: *I have a few thoughts on the polarities question, which has been very interesting. When we speak from the world of content, which is where we live most of the time, we talk about things being good and bad. In this discussion Bruce* (another member of the discussion group) *is talking about a polarity being called good or bad. Do we "need" this polarity to keep ourselves from being "bad", or to keep us motivated to do "good"?*

*Once we experience and explore the world that opens to us when we neutralise polarities, we have some lasting knowledge that these terms refer to illusory concepts. Remember when you neutralised your primes? There **is** no good or bad. To me, that was an experience of truth, and even though I cannot maintain* *an ongoing experience of that state at this point, I choose to remember as much as I can that all my perceptions of polarities are non-realities that separate me from experiencing acceptance and who I really am.*

If we recognise that there is not good and bad, will we be behaving "badly" and not care about our behavior? I think not. In the absence of polarities like good and bad, there is peace or emptiness, and from that experience there is no resistance and no reason to want to hurt any other being. Our behaviour will come from a choice, and our intention would be to recreate peace. We might give up an obsessive need to help others, and surrender them to their own choices. We might choose to behave in a way that others would call "bad" but whatever, we would recognise it as simply our behaviour in that moment, and accept responsibility for it as our choice. There would be no spiritual punishment to fear.

We all make value judgements every day, from what to eat to whom to vote for. If our intention has integrity, then this is the best we can do. It seems to me that all the great avatars have said something like, "The only sin is ignorance," as in "they know not what they do," People do what they think is good, but we are often ignorant of the highest good for ourselves and others.

So we do cause suffering, and from that we learn. Recently I lost my temper about an issue and behaved in a way I later regretted. I lost my sense of the illusory nature of good and bad, and allowed myself to be swept into a perception of judgement and blame. Good and bad seemed very real to me in that moment. I thought I was "right" in some absolute way, and another person was wrong. Although I would not hope to repeat the experience, the experience helped me to see more clearly that I was out of touch with the Truth about the other person and myself.

A List of Primordial Polarities

Very often new Peat processors ask, which primes (or Primordial Polarities or personal codes) are possible? Is the list endless or is it limited to a definite number? Our experience shows so far that it is practically impossible to exhaust all possible primes because their verbalization depends on individual history of a human being and his social surroundings. Actually your primordial polarities do not have any real names (freedom/bondage, I/ non-I etc.). They are first Yang and Yin, the first polarities, the first positive and negative, the first plus and minus, the first two energetic pillars that you created when decided to fall out of the state of oneness and enter this universe. Before primes there was One, and primes were the first step to many. When they uncover and integrate primes, people interpret them using different names. How you are going to interpret your primes depends upon your upbringing, your cultural background, your personality and other things.

Anyway, for better orientation, I present here a list of Primes, but I must stress it is not final because other processors with whom I am not in contact have found others. Here Primes are given without any specific order. I did not take into account the time they appeared in processing nor alphabetic sequence.

I emphasize that primes are not ordinary dichotomies. For example, they can never be "left" and "right". They always have a noticeable value for the observer and for oneself. They have a touch of destiny.

I repeat here: if during a process some ordinary dichotomies appear in the body or consciousness of a client, the processor must make them more clear with adequate questions and lead the client to their exact verbalization.

A list of Primes

Freedom and Oppression
Love and Aggressiveness
Consciousness and Instincts
Greatness and Nothingness
I and Emptiness
Visibility and Invisibility
Victory and Defeat
Satisfaction and Dissatisfaction
I and No-I
I and Another
I and Others
I am and I am not
Existence and Non-existence
Light and Darkness
Good and Bad
Oneness and Duality
Emotions and Reason
Passion and Spirituality
Love and Freedom
Love and Pain
Love and Loss
Love and Power
Freedom and No-Freedom
Freedom and Slavery

Freedom and Responsibility
Active and Passive
Conscious and Unconscious
Limited Consciousness and Unlimited Consciousness
Material and Consciousness
Material and Spiritual
Endlessly small and Endlessly big
Power and Powerlessness
Fear and Peace
Fear and Love
Security and Insecurity
Expansion and Contraction
Creating and Destroying
Sadness and Joy
All and Nothing
Earthly and Alien
This World and Other World
Material Universe and Spiritual Universe
Inner World and Outer World
Entering Experience and Going out of Experience
Divine and Material
Consciousness and Body
Inside and Outside
Something and No-thing
True and Untrue
Dependence and Independence
Knowledge and Ignorance
Advancement and Retreat
Strength and Weakness
Inside and Outside
Good I and Bad I
Happiness and Sadness

Control and Freedom
Knowledge and Ignorance
Being and Creating
Acceptance and Rejection
I and Nothingness
Love and Rejection
Togetherness and Separation
Moving and Stopping
Learning and Knowledge
Happiness and Sorrow
I and Everything
Relaxation and Tension
Peace and Control
Perfection and Imperfection

Fundamental Polarities

Some of our predecessors have invested a lot of effort searching for fundamental polarities. Some contemporary thinkers are doing the same. The main effort was paved to find a few key polarities so that one would be able to reduce all other polarities layered upon them. Their common belief was that such discovery would make shorter the process of their integration and realization of Spiritual freedom.

Famous Eastern philosopher Nagarjuna, in his work **"Mulamadhyamikakarika"** reduced all polarities to 4 pairs of them:

Finite and Infinite
Becoming and Disappearing
Localisation and Nonlocalisation
Part and whole

Paul Brunton, eminent expert on Yoga, declares that 3 fundamental polarities are **Attraction, Repulsion and Rest.** The third element, Being at Rest, is evidently a third element, reconciliation of two opposites. In his notebook he writes:

*These three ideas are so fundamental that they will always reappear. They are built into the universe and therefore into man himself. These three cosmic forces -- **Attraction, Repulsion, and Rest** -- constitute the triune manifestation of the Universe. You will find them in every department of existence.*

Geoffrey Filbert, eminent ex-scientologist, who is still active in California, exposed his complete version of Independent Scientology in his book *Excalibur Revisited*. Most people, he said, are implanted with 3 pairs of polarities:

Good and Bad
Love and Hatred
Survive and Succumb

Lester Levinsson. the creator of Sedona system, came to the conclusion of only four pairs of polarities existing:

Desire to control others and Desire to be controled by others
Desire for safety/survival and Desire for Death
Desire for separating from others and Desire for Unity
Desire for approval of others/desire for love and Desire to approve others/desire to love others

Edward Francolini, a well known therapist, claims **love** and **fear to** be basic polarities. He believes that from them all other polarities of human beings originate.

All these eminent thinkers came to those fundamental polarities based on their philosophical speculations or spiritual practice. Using Spiritual Technology on pairs of polarities, which those thinkers consider fundamental, practitioners can come to valuable results. In the chapter **Inner Power of Words** I point out that polarities, fundamental and essential for the whole human race are "**good**" and "**bad**". I found them in the very beginning of the Bible and the practice of processing justified such my attitude.

DP2 (Deep PEAT Second Level)

I developed this method after Deep PEAT. I use it in 3 situations:

1. When a person is not able to do successfully classic Deep PEAT (whatever reason).

2. When working with Clients having tendency toward depression.

3. With extremely intellectual clients. Such people have difficulty separating thoughts from emotions. Instead of feeling their problems, they report their thoughts about them. DP2 forces them to separate thoughts from emotions. Such people usually understand the difference between those two kinds of consciousness contents the first time.

The Practice of DP2

We start with a specific problem and we ask the client to tell us alternatively an emotion (and a body sensation) then the thought (and mental image) which follows it. We accept if the client gives us just one of two contents (for example, only emotion). In other words, if he gives us only a thought and omits a mental image, or if he gives only an emotion and omits body sensation.

In the beginning of the process the client usually gives us very unpleasant, heavy and painful contents. In one moment, during the process, a change happens. Clients start to report emotionally neutral contents, then positive or apparently optimistic contents. If the polarization of contents happens, so that in the consciousness there are two clear polarities, the processor passes from that activity to the classic Deep PEAT process. That is the reason why every processor should first master Deep PEAT to be able to apply DP2 processing.

Another possible situation occurs when a client reports a few consecutive positive contents (usually 3). If the Processor asks him what happened to the problem, the client would answer that it disappeared, seems to be far away, stupid, and similar adjectives. That is the end of the process, because the problem has been solved.

In some rare cases the client reports the polarization of contents, and if we continue with the DP2 method there is a sudden integration of those contents. The client is surprised, because both contents disappear from his consciousness. Then the processor asks the **test question,** which is of crucial importance for clearing the perplexity of whether the integration of polarities has occurred: **"Could you feel (experience) them separately?"** Usually, for a short time the client is not able to evoke them in his consciousness because they disappeared. If they appear, they come together, because they are inseparably merged into oneness.

If the client is not able to feel or experience them separately and they are first polarities that have been integrated, the procesor could remind the client of his Primordial Polarities. The processor could also accept this as integration if the client says something like, "they are one, but if I want to experience separately I am able to, I need some effort to do that," etc., but all charge has vanished if he is not able to experience them separately.

Here is an example of a DP2 process I led recently. It lasted only 8 minutes which is more an exception than a rule. The client's job was to present some data in public and he had a problem with it.

Starting problem: **In front of cameras or a group of people I feel and behave as a child.**

Thought: That is the sign of immaturity.
Emotion: I feel that's bullshit.
Thought: I have a real problem.
Emotion: Embarassment.
Thought: I need help.
Emotion: Feeling of urgency.
Thought: Where can I find it?
Emotion: Joy and feeling of activity.
Thought: I will succeed.
Emotion: The feeling of determination.
Thought: Nothing can stop me.

At this point the process was finished, because all three consecutive contents were evidently positive and opposite the state the client experienced at the beginning. The problem vanished.

DP3 (Deep PEAT Third Level)

DP3 is the third level of Deep PEAT. The name comes from the fact that the second level of PEAT was an alternative exchange of thoughts and emotions and this is the third level.

The value of this method comes from the intention of consciously attaining neutralization of a *chosen* pair of polarities. With classic Deep PEAT it was not possible; neutralization depended on chance.

With DP3, however, we are not able to get neutralization of primes, because we don't know if polarities neutralized with DP3 are primes or not. For this task we must apply Deep PEAT.

Theoretical Foundations of DP3 Method

To correctly understand the foundation of this method it is necessary to review some data I presented earlier.

In one moment, out of Oneness or the void the being starts with a decision (**alpha**) to create something or to have some kind of experience. For example, *"I want to experience* love*."* If the being realizes that decision, the decision vanishes back into the void from whence it came. Remember that **there is nothing stranger that desire. When we see it realized, it does not exist anymore.**

Troubles begin when the human being, in his intention to attain something, gets defeated. In the moment of defeat the person makes a **decision of defeat,** which we call **beta,** for example *" love brings humiliation"* or *"love is dangerous"* or *"I should avoid beautiful women"* etc. But be careful, this decision of defeat cannot and does not remove previous positive decisions from existence, because the decision is a part of Atman stuff. It exists outside of the physical universe of matter, energy, space and time until the being himself discreates it. Therefore these two decisions exist, one opposite the other, making life an unpleasant seesaw. That mechanism resembles the bifurcation of creek water when it comes to a big rock. The negative energy or charge, which is created in the individual during the defeat, separates these into confronted decisions until the conflict is eliminated. Of course, in many past lifetimes we have had countless numbers of similar traumas, and the charge accumulating between two separate ideas grew progressively. For the majority of people in this lifetime, it resembles a huge black hole full of poisonous serpents. That charge prevents us from seeing polarities as they really are – as two halves of the same whole. Therefore the majority of people are not able to accept that having and not having make one whole, as it makes health and sickness, love and hate etc..

Happily enough for us, because polarities are two halves of the same whole, which are temporary separated by force (trauma, defeat, whatever...), they permanently tend to reunite, and when we discharge the charge that separates them they automatically fuse and become one again. After processing their integration we are, as conscious beings, able to express either one or the other polarity based upon the existing situation. We can say that with such a pair of polarities we have our job mostly done.

How can we remove that harmful energetic charge which separates polarities? Many methods of meditation and many spiritual disciplines help to attain it, for brief or extended periods. To be immodest, I can state that no method does it more quickly, easier, or more efficiently than my DP3 method. What I am going to tell you explains why DP3 is faster and more efficient than any other known method so far.

Studying many systems, methods and techniques of self-development and therapy, I found out that their creators emphasize some elements, considering them to be the main cause of disturbances. I had a kind of revelation when I realized that in the whole history of humanity **no one found in the body or consciousness of the human being anything but 4 elements:** mental image, emotion, body sensation and thought. All other elements which famous thinkers speak about, like prejudices, beliefs, convictions and many others are just combinations of these 4 elements.

Even though a decision seems to be a separate element, it is a clear thought.

These 4 elements make up the negative energetic charge existing between all numberless polarities. When we remove them, and DP3 does it the most simply, polarities unite, duality vanishes, and what is left in the consciousness is just the experience of oneness. That miraculous procedure consists simply of confronting these 4 elements. When we experience them AS THEY ARE, they vanish into the void, and what is left is just the human being with a whole, undivided experience.

What follows are essential instructions for the application of these methods. If one does not follow these instructions, one can expect reappearance of the problem; in other words, either short lasting integration or the complete failure of the process.

Essential Conditions for the Successful DP3 Process

1. The Client should try to be **associated into experience**, at least in the beginning of the process. Later on, during the process, it will be impossible, because during the process the image picture is vanishing, gets smaller, or fades into the distance, etc. (See **states of association and disassociation** in the PEAT Manual).

2. We always **work with emotions**, therefore we ask the client to **feel** the state or the situation.

3. It is necessary for the client **not to resist the negative polarity**, or unpleasant elements, which appear during the process. He must feel them completely and accept them no matter how unpleasant they are. Resistance brings persistence! (Working with an inexperienced beginner, it is advisable to do a couple of exercises of acceptance before DP3).

4. **It is necessary for the client to confront and tell the processor all 4 elements of his experience:** <u>mental image, emotion, body sensation and thought</u>. **We repeat this demand to the end of the process, but we warn the client that these elements will start to disappear** during the process and at the end there will be only the void.

Important Details of DP3 and the Preparation of the Client

DP3 begins with finding polarities to work with. It is not as simple as it might seem, but it is important, because upon precise identification of polarities depends the success of the session.

When the client relates an unwanted state, we ask him to tell us the opposite desired polarity, and then start DP3 with these two polarities. If the client has difficulty finding the opposite desired polarity for the process, we help him by asking one of the following questions:

1. **For you, what is the opposite of that state** (we point to his problem)?

2. **For you, what is the most beautiful and most desirable state?**

3. **For you, what is the most beautiful and most desirable situation?**

Let him describe it briefly, then begin DP3 with that state (thing, situation) and the negative polarity he started from.

Next you should ask the client what **goal** he wants to attain as the end result of the session. This way the client will create a so-called **goal structure** and he will direct his energy to flow toward that goal. It is good to ask the client to imagine himself in the future being able to manifest both polarities at his own will.

The two most important elements for success of this method are described in the section: Principles of Spiritual technology. They are:

1. Taking just one drop of water from the whole ocean and
2. Stopping time.

I will explain them once more individually. For example, your problem is starting many activities without finishing them. **One drop of water from the whole ocean** means you will not process many of such experiences, but only one of them. Moreover, from that experience you must choose just one brief moment when that experience was at its peak. When, with processing, we discreate or remove just that narrow peak moment of the chosen experience, all such experiences will vanish (as a matter of fact, all such experiences of which you are conscious). The more narrow that part of the experience, the better generalization of all such experiences. It is a strange fact that so many researchers did not notice this fact, but the great poet William Blake expressed it with his famous verse:

To see a world in a grain of sand,

And a Heaven in a Wild Flower.

Hold Infinity in a palm of your hand

And Eternity in a hour.

The second principle, **stopping time,** is tightly connected to the first one. In that chosen, narrow moment there must not be any movement. It is the fixed moment, as one snapshot photo from the movie, in which time has been frozen and stopped. Such approach supports even Albert Einstein's

Without movement nothing can exist. When in our imagination we stop any movement in some experience, it has the tendency to vanish.

You should do the same thing with the second polarity. That means, and I repeat, you will choose one narrow moment representing that polarity and during the process you will hold it "frozen", which means without any movement.

As I said at the beginning of the process, the client should do his best to be associated in his experience. That means he sees everything but himself in that experience. He should **feel himself** in the middle of it. During the process there will surely be a change in his experiential position – he will gradually become progressively more dissociated, because the image of that experience will retreat from him, become smaller, and finally vanish.

We do the process using **emotions,** therefore the command is **"feel!"**

We instruct the client to accept all elements of the experience **without any resistance,** especially negative or unpleasant elements. **Any and every resistance, any incomplete acceptance, brings about persistence of separated polarities and impossibility of their integration!** Pay attention to the fact that inexperienced people have a natural tendency to resist unpleasant contents. Only that which one is able to confront, can one control or eliminate. One old story tells us about it. On the sea shore there was a village constantly attacked and devastated by a sea monster. In many years it robbed them and devoured fishermen, their women and children. One day villagers heard about a mighty magician who is able to disperse any evil just staring at it with his powerful gaze.

They called him to help them and he accepted. He climbed on a high rock at the sea shore and waited for the monster to appear. When the monster surfaced, the magician directed his powerful gaze and watched it without retreating and the monster vanished forever.

We should ask the client to avoid long descriptions, associations, and comparisons with previous experiences etc.. We ask him to report all 4 elements the best he can, which can appear in consciousness and body. But we should emphasize as well that during the process, elements will start to fade and vanish, so that at the end of the process there are none left.

At the conclusion of the process it would be a mistake to ask the client all 4 elements and insist on them. Such approach would move him to recreate elements which already have vanished. Therefore, we give him this instruction: *"Feel yourself in that experience and tell me what is left of it."*

Instructions

In the beginning of the process the Client should state the FAM: *"Even though I did not integrate polarities X and Y* (should name both polarities), *I accept and love myself, my body and personality and the fact that I did not integrate polarities X and Y."*

Then give alternative commands to the client:

"**Feel**...(positive polarity) **and tell me which elements come up in your consciousness and in your body: image, emotion, body sensation and thought.**"

"Feel ...(negative polarity) and tell me which elements come up in your consciousness and in your body: image, emotion, body sensation and thought."

How the Integration is Attained

The integration usually happens very quickly, in 10-30 minutes, even less. When one gets more experience with this method one should not be surprised if the process is over in a few minutes. If we ask the client what happened at the end of the process, he will give us one of 4 possible answers:

1. Polarities vanished and what is left is just emptiness. Polarities have integrated into the person. This result happens most frequently.

2. Polarities vanish and the client says that "there is only me". It is also a frequently seen result.

3. Polarities visually merge into each other.

4. Polarities vanish, but the client has got a **deep insight** about his problem, which is followed with good indicators like laughter, tears etc. If this happens, the processor should ask him: *"Would you like to say something? Do you have some thought about your problem?"* That way the client sometimes can uncover his decision of defeat, which was in the core of the problem.

Any combination of these four endings could also occur.

Stabilization

At the end it is advisable to put a couple of questions (to an inexperienced client):

1. **What happened with those polarities?**

2. **In the future, will you be able to manifest one of those two polarities at your own will?**

The specific kinds of answers are unimportant. The main thing is to ask.

The Opposition

It is necessary to ask the client if some opposition exists **inside of him** or **outside of him?**

This is necessary because the opposition is an remaining charge, of which the client, until that moment, was not conscious, and now he confronts it. Some problems have more than one chain of deeper contents, so it is possible that one of them activated. In DP3 we don't see an opposition very often. If there is opposition, then we apply DP3 to two new polarities. It is important to know this procedure exactly:

The first polarity is the experience or feeling that **two previous polarities are integrated.**

The second polarity is that which makes the opposition (mental image, emotion, body sensation, thought, or their combinations).

Now, working with the opposition the alternative commands are:

"Feel that you have integrated ...(names of starting polarities)" and then

"Feel ...(the opposition).

Now do another DP3 process until you get the new integration. And repeat checking for the opposition.

Forgiving

At the end of the process the client should do the forgiving exercise (see PEAT manual), if the client has a need for that. Experienced clients usually don't feel such need.

Circular Processing

If the problem, which we processed, was a relationship with someone or a group, it is necessary to do the circular processing. As we already learned, circular processing is processing from other points of view. Suppose the client has a bad relationship with his brother Peter. The client will do DP3 with two terminals: "I" and "Peter". The first phase is the normal DP3 process between "I" and "Peter". When it is over, we start the second phase. The client should identify with his brother Peter. He puts two fingers at the chest point, and stirring his feelings the best he is able to, says: **"I am not** (...his name), **I am Peter."** Then as Peter he does DP3 again on two terminals, one is he (Peter) and other is his old "I", until all charge dissipates and vanishes. Such procedure is very efficient even with a very strong charge.

If the client's attention is drawn to some polarities visible at the other being's position, he should also do the integration with the other's points of view. We should handle all relevant points of view and this means **all charged positions** if we want permanent results.

Mistakes in the Application of DP3

In the application of this method mistakes can prolong the process and even abort it. The most often encountered is **resistance** to the negative polarity. In the beginning of the practice of DP3 I had a very long lasting session with a woman client. I discovered she had an attitude of non-acceptance of the negative polarity. She did integration of the polarities "giving & receiving" and thought she was doing fine with resistance to "receiving", but she felt disgust and strong resistance to receiving anything from others. That was the reason for the prolonged session. The resistance gets activated often when one polarity is evidently negative, like **love & hate**, or **power & powerlessness** etc.

To avoid such mistakes, we should emphasize to the client to not resist polarities, especially negative ones, but to accept them as a part of life as completely as he is able to and not resist individual negative elements of the polarity.

If the client is caught in negative emotions and creates them incessantly, do not let him identify with the positive polarity, because he will gradually invest negative elements in the positive pole, and thus he will create **two negative terminals.** He should stay with the feeling that he is neither one of them, he is just experiencing both. When you work with an extremely negative client (hard problems etc.) do not take him as a terminal. You should take two other persons, one as the positive terminal and the other as the negative terminal (but not himself) and then do DP3 on them.

The Practice of the DP3 Method

I divided polarities suitable for application with DP3 into two groups. The first group contains polarities concerning practical problems of everyday life: removing unwanted emotional and psychological states, interpersonal conflicts, creation of desired identities etc. Their integration will change the life of an average person a great deal. For example, asking favors from others and offering favors to others are polarities we encounter often in everyday life. The other group of polarities we can call **"philosophical problems"** which create easier understandings of our situations in life, the world, and relationships, which exist between phenomena of life. Although I call them "philosophical", their integration brings about more balanced behaviour of an individual in daily life.

Now I should point out to you the breadth and scope of some polarities. I emphasize this because some very broad polarities are impossible to embrace with just one process. Let us take for example **happiness & unhappiness.** They are very nearly all-embracing polarities and it would be naive to expect to integrate them completely in one narrow process. Such wide polarities we call **"umbrella polarities"** because they embrace many individual, narrow polarities. Examples are Power & Powerlessness, Good & Bad, Subject & Object, God & Manifest World etc. Such polarities consist of many components and we should handle all of them, one after another. For example, one person lacks the power to express his opinion in front of other people, but at the same time he has a great power in realization of his duties. This means that different kinds of power and powerlessness exist. Such a person should integrate the power and the powerlessness of expressing his own opinion. Therefore we should choose adequate examples for the application of DP3 process.

The importance of breadth of the scope of polarities is evident in the practical work. Once, while working with my experimental group, I noticed the following situation. During the process, a woman approached integration of "Giving and Receiving". I stood close to her and her partner observing the process, because integration of those two polarities had, for me, subjectively, far-reaching implications; they were giving and receiving of material goods, mainly money. When the subject attained integration, I said to her: *"Very good. You will never more have any difficulties with money."* As I said that, she gave me a surprised look. About two months later, she explained to me what happened. Her main problem was her inability to give and receive love and emotions in general. In love she had to be either master or a slave. After the integration she was free to give and receice love, she was free of her old compulsive game of "master and slave." What I want to stress is this: there are different kinds of giving and receiving. One should integrate both components of pairs of polarities, where there is a problem, and be very cautious about projecting your subjective interpretations upon the client.

All complex polarities ("umbrella polarities"), which have more components, should be separated with respect to those components and subject them to individual processes. In the example of Giving and Receiving you should do processes on Giving and Receiving material goods, Giving and Receiving of love, of gratitude, of praises etc.

DP3 has extensive potentials for these applications. It is practically impossible to see the limits of its application.

Here I will describe the areas with which I experimented principally.

DP3 and Soul Retrieval

In the last twenty years we have been witnesses of a revival of shamanism, probably the oldest religion in the world. It has become widely popular because it is simultaneously a therapeutic system and a system for human integration.

Soul retrieval is a body of shamanistic techniques, which has attracted the attention of practitioners. It became very popular through the activities of the famous contemporary shaman, Michael Harner. His disciple Sandra Ingerman published an entire book devoted completely to that shamanic practice (Sandra Ingerman: ***Soul Retrieval: Mending the Fragmented Self through Shamanic Practice***").

Soul retrieval for the integration of personality is very simple. The loss of some of its components in the human being causes physical and mental disturbances and "dis-eases". The most frequent causes of loss, or fragmentation, of "soul parts" are situations of great stress, fear, perceived great dangers, repetitive trauma, physical shock, and serious illnesses. They overpower the persona and the individual splits off a part of itself for the sake of survival, as a lizard might separate its tail to survive. Consequences of such happenings are fragmented and split-off "*I*"'s. One of its parts is temporarily lost; thus the being is less capable in many activities of everyday life.

When we try to help such a person, with any process, there are always many problems and their success is often short lived. Why? Simply because the person does not participate as a whole in the process. One of his parts is absent, split

Return to Oneness

off. Processors speak about such clients as "difficult cases". They succeed only partially. During processing, the processor frequently feels that something is missing in his client.

Take a simple example. If a child feels unloved by his strict and severe father, who often judges and punishes him, he will feel injured and inferior. In the presence of such a father he will feel shame, fear, sadness and muscular rigidity. There could be only one response, splitting of the personality; or there could be the sequence of smaller painful incidents. Because of its limited abilities the child will not know how to behave to avoid the father's abusive and crude behavior. The child cannot leave the father. He sees the only solution is to hide that part of himself that the father criticizes. That is the way the lost or separated part is created. From the child's subjective consciousness the split-off part is invisible and non-existent. The life energy of that part will be covered and deadened with the negative charge created by negative experiences. When the child grows up he will have a lessened capacity of his life energy, he will not confront life challenges as a whole, integrated being, but partially, with only part of his being; that one which is left after the trauma. Many human beings go through life with a small percentage of their essential Life Force available.

One indication that a part is lost may be the feeling that a person does not want to, or cannot speak about, some areas of his own life. It is his secret, or it is too personal to expose or share. This person may feel a strong sense of separation with others. The percentage of Life Force that the person loses determines how dysfunctional the person may become. All kinds of psychological disturbances, including confusion, fear, anxiety, anger, depression, learning disabilities, procrastination, or feelings of being overwhelmed, are some of the disturbances that these people commonly encounter when lost parts are present in the body-mind system.

The consequence of losing a part is a sense of a lack of completeness and may lead to the search for wholeness. A constant feeling of not being worthy or good enough will be present. If you are unconscious about the sense of separation and wholeness, you may feel intense craving and neediness. In this case there is a bottomless black hole that needs to be filled with sex, alcohol or drugs, money, success, power, or recognition. To be complete, the person strains to accomplish these things, only to discover afterwards that the black hole is still there.

But lost parts of personality are easily recoverable and the process is quicker than one may think. One session may represent a big difference for the physical and emotional well-being of the person who was suffered a loss. There are many versions of Soul Retrieval. In my book *"Aspectics"* (translated into English and Italian) I described its simple version and many people obtained excellent results using it. Individuals processed after that achieved better results, because through such processing they were more whole and integrated. The most important thing in all versions of this technique is finding the split off and lost part, negotiating with it to come back to its proprietor and reintegration with him. Once the split off part re-enters the client's body (and his energetic body as well!) it will reintegrate and start to function normally.

Some followers of the West African *Ifa Cult* point out the possibility of intentional creation of "split off parts of a soul", as a practice in the cults of black magic and in the process of channelling angels. They claim that an experienced magician is able to create, at will, out of his energetic field, an entity or a "thought form", and to send it to perform tasks for him.

What has DP3 to do with soul retrieval? Soul retrieval is one of many of its valuable possibilities for application. DP3 makes that classic shamanistic procedure much quicker and simpler. Working with fragmented personalities I found out that DP3 is exceptionally applicable in place of Soul Retrieval. A couple of sessions of DP3 will bring about significant and noticeable changes in the emotional life of a person. The process is mild, rapid and efficient. It allows a reconnection with person's split off and lost parts in 10-20 minutes, on average, and results are relatively permanent. It is evident that we can apply new procedures of Spiritual Technology to many old methods.

In Soul Retrieval we apply DP3 to these polarities:

1. "I" in this, present moment of time and

2. Split-off parts of a person (which continues living its life in some period of past time)

In my book *"Aspectics"* I described in detail the whole procedure, so I will not repeat it here.

Application of DP3 on Eight Life Dynamisms

The basic and most fundamental drive and tendency of every living being is survival. At first sight this does not appear as something new, because it has long been spoken of in science as the instinct of self-preservation, but the news is the existence of life mechanisms through which man survives. Different people point to different numbers of these dynamisms. To me, the most acceptable number seems to be eight of them.

First dynamism and most narrow, is self-survival. Biologists would say, the instinct for self-preservation. It is survival as the individual, as "I".

Second dynamism is survival through the family or the emotional partner. Sometimes this dynamism is stronger than the first, for some people the life of their partners and children is more important than their own.

Third dynamism is survival through a group the person identifies with: religious, national, professional etc. For some people the well being of the group they belong to is more important then their personal well being. Commonly people sacrifice themselves for their nation or their religion.

Fourth dynamism is the drive to survive through the whole of humanity. There are examples of people sacrificing themselves for the well being and advancement of humanity.

Fifth dynamism is the tendency to survive as the member of the whole living universe, as one of the endless numbers of sentient beings.

Sixth dynamism is survival through the whole physical universe.

Seventh dynamism is survival as a spiritual being.

Eighth dynamism is survival through God or eternity.

Again, we can ask, where is the place of DP3 concerning these eight dynamisms? Some people are separated from these dynamisms; in other words these dynamisms are not well integrated into them. For example, some people have a better attitude toward animals (the fifth dynamism) than toward human beings. Many feel themselves being completely separated from their higher "I" or from God. Applying the DP3 method it's possible to realize a relatively complete integration of all eight dynamisms.

The Procedure of Integration of Life Dynamisms

At the **first dynamism** a person is mainly integrated. If the person is not, the best way to attain it is to achieve Gnosis, or Direct Experience of Truth, on the question (koan) *"Who am I?"* The quickest way to get it is with the Gnostic Intensive.

Second Dynamism: The person should apply DP3 on two terminals or polarities: "I" and one's emotional partner, or "I" and one's family. The integration usually happens pretty quickly.

Third Dynamism: In the integration of this dynamism, polarities for application of DP3 are "I" and some group the person belongs to. It could be the group of his friends, the company the person works for, his national or religious group etc.

Fourth Dynamism: In this activity polarities are "I" and the whole of humanity, humanity as the person imagines it to be.

Fifth dynamism: Polarities are "I" and the whole sentient world, as the person imagines it to be. Here come animals, plants, and pets; in brief, all living beings.

Sixth dynamism: In the integration of sixth dynamism polarities are "I" and the physical universe: ground, stones, rivers, oceans, rocks, planets, galaxies...

Seventh dynamism: In the process of the integration of the seventh dynamism, polarities are "I" and one's True Being, as the person imagines it to be. Usually a person imagines his True Being as better and higher then his everyday "I"

Eighth dynamism: In this case we apply DP3 on polarities of "I" and God, the way the person conceives God.

These processes should be done until there is merging, into **one**, of both polarities. The processes do not last long and they are good for the integration of personality.

PAST/FUTURE RUNDOWN

Let's start with clarifications.

The Past/Future Rundown is the application of the DP3 process on time.

Past/Future Rundown (PFR) empties the charge from past and future. Many people, as a result, have a clear realization that past and future really don't exist. They are just illusions that they have created in the mind. All traditional spiritual paths teach us just that; there is only the present. PFR doesn't solve your present time problems! Not at all! For the solution of present time problems you have many different methods and techniques and before PFR you are taught DP3. The majority of people are trained first in Deep PEAT processing in the same workshop, so they should be able to apply it. If you feel inferior in the present, you will continue to feel inferior until you discreate your inferiority feelings in present time. If you have fears in present time, you will continue to have them until you handle them. This principle applies to all present time problems. You will not be burdened with your past memories, nor will you anticipate and fear future problems (which don't exist, as a matter of fact).

I must stress one important consideration. One may delete only the charge from problems, traumas, and unwanted memories of which you are conscious or able to remember. That is the reason I ask, at the end of the PFR; "take a good look at your whole past, your who-o-o-o-le past, scan through it, and tell me; is there any charge on it, or is it empty?"

It may be obvious that one cannot delete a charge of which he is not conscious because at that moment it is unimaginably huge. You see, we have a nearly endless number of past lifetimes behind us. Meher Baba says nearly 900,000 past lifetimes. Is it true? I don't know. I certainly couldn't count them, but I know there are many. Other researchers in this field say there were 31 different universes before this one physical universe. You can delete only charges of which you are conscious and only charge that you are able to confront at this moment. If you would be exposed to more than you are able to cope with, you would be instantaneously burned out emotionally and spiritually. As a matter of fact, at the deepest level, you are GOD, and there is unimaginable charge around that truth.

Moreover, if you would delete all charge there is, you would have no karma left and you would finish your evolution in this universe; you would become a perfect being, a perfect teacher, call it what you wish. If you wouldn't like to become a perfect teacher and remain on this planet, you would leave it. In everyday language, you would die.

So, if you get some previously dark and invisible charge at this stage, do DP3 or Deep PEAT, or any other method to eliminate it. That's the real spiritual development!

Some people complained about unpleasant reactions after PFR. Let me be clear. In my first announcement about the discovery of this rundown I wrote, "This is not for everyone!"

I repeat it once more: it is not for everyone. My practical application of PFR shows that the more experience one has, the more benefits from the rundown. It is not some cheap trick to tell you, *"You haven't got benefits. Sorry. That means you are not spiritually and psychologically developed. It's your fault."* No, it's a fact. To check it out, look at reports written by experienced people, such as devotees having many years of Zen practice; people who tried many different disciplines such as Qabalah, yoga, exercises of concentration and meditation, Gnostic Intensive, Excalibur and similar. They have had enormous benefits. Usually they are astonished at the far-reaching effects and speed of the process. Often it is real love for the process! Many of them want to go on with this and similar processes and ask to be trained as Trainers for Spiritual Tech at any price.

SPACE RUNDOWN
(Elimination of emotional charge from the space)

This process is the application of DP3 process on Space, one of the four components of the physical universe. During this process what happens is "the breaking down of the space". After we finish the process, we apply so called stabilization. We ask the Client these four questions:

1. Is there any difference in space between here and there?
2. What do you feel, are you now here or there, or you are at the both places at the same time?
3. Do you need some effort to transfer yourself from here there?
4. How far from this place is the place which you call there?

If the process is successful, the space stops existing for the Client. Usually he feels himself omnipresent, for him there is no difference between the place where he is physically and the farthest point in space. Such effect is not permanent, of course. After only a few minutes the Client feels the space as before, but he has quite a clear impression what kind of result he can expect in the future Spiritual development.

Carol Saito, PEAT Trainer, posted on our discussion list her experience with the Space Rundown:

"I would like to share something that happened after my Space Rundown. At first I thought nothing particular had happened, although something very special had actually taken place. I have always been afraid to travel. When I was a child, I had no choice, back and forth from Italy, Hawaii, and the States etc. Then I grew up, and as soon as I was able to decide for myself, I decided not to travel anymore. I stopped. As years went by my summer vacations were always nearer to home. The problem wasn't only taking a plane, but also a train or even a car! The fact of moving just terrorized me and I never understood why. Even my job turned out to be a job I could handle from

home, a good job, but that allowed me to stop traveling around, even for professional training!

With PEAT I was able to overcome this phobia and with my Past/Future Rundown I was able to start thinking of traveling again, having also removed charge from past events... And I started moving around, yes, maybe just taking short trips, but for me a big achievement! The turn for me was with space rundown! Actually two great things happened to me! The first is that since then I started traveling on a monthly basis for courses and work, I thought they were simple external circumstances, but then I stopped to think and realized I've been receiving proposals in these last months I had never received before. It was like magic, all of a sudden, people from other cities started calling and asking me to go for courses, PEAT sessions, events etc...And I have a full schedule for the next three-six months that will even take me in foreign countries! No more space...no more need to worry for traveling. :o))"

The second thing was something even more subtle. I don't see through walls, but ever since my space rundown, when I or someone else is looking for an object he/she lost, I have a sudden flash, a sudden thought! I actually see the object and where it actually is. At first I didn't realize this, and thought it was luck or good memory.

However, when I sat down to think about this, I realized I wasn't reading the person's mind, I wasn't guessing, because I never tried to guess, it was something that happened hic et nunc, without having to think about anything nor concentrate to try to find it! I just saw it in *my mind, as if there were no walls, no distance between the object and me, no space..."*

Carol sent to me another letter, thinking that it would be too much to send directly to the list. I am sure it is also a good contribution for all of us and that there will not be any bad consequences from making it public. I consulted Carol before putting it in this book. Here it is:

"Dear Zivo,

I just wrote in the list to share my experience after Space Rundown.

What I would like to share with you is something I didn't want to write in the list because I thought it would be better to share this with you!

In the second part of my story, I talk about the fact that I locate objects because space seems to have vanished... but at the same time something more has happened!

This is the last sentence I wrote...'I just saw it in my mind, as if there were no walls, no distance between the object and me, and no space!!!'

To say it all, what actually happened is that there was yes, no space, but at the same time... no matter and no time. They seemed to have vanished too! All at the same time!

After having understood this I realized after space, also time and matter do not exist either! If I saw objects that were lost in time (who knows when) and saw them in an nonmaterial state, actually saw through matter, so time and matter must have vanished too.

I realized these are just states that I need, to be able to confront myself with the everyday world and the everyday life, but now to me it is quite clear how I actually play my game! It's been a few weeks that I'm having a hard time to settle down, not because of the enthusiasm...but because in a material world, living like this is becoming difficult.

I do realize it's a game, a wonderful game, and I feel as I've never felt before... free as an eagle soaring in the skies....could it be that matter and time rundown could come spontaneously after a space rundown?? Did it ever happen to anyone else in your working group?? Could it be that I went through a spontaneous rundown process?? If there is no space anymore, could I have actually been there with you to do this process....maybe actually with you???

I know this sounds weird, it still sounds weird to me too...please believe me...I didn't lose my mind... :o))

I would really appreciate to have your feedback!!!"

Patrick Downey, a Professor at an Italian University recently sent me the description of his experiences and the experiences of his girl friend, Denise. With modesty, typical for him, he presents his experience of discreating the space as a beginner's experience.

It could be interesting for list members to read this first hand experience:

"Dear Zivo,

I've been experimenting with DP3, as you suggested, and generally with fairly 'personal' polarities (e.g. anxiety-peace, duty-freedom etc.). This evening, working solo,

I tried to discreate space by applying the process to the polarities here-there, and the result was surprising, although not very easy to put into words. Here are some immediate observations:

Immediately after the process, a feeling of not being entirely present in the usual way, together with a feeling of being very present; this feeling was a little unpleasant to begin with but now (a couple of hours later) I've got used to it. A slight difficulty in 'placing' things, which are not in my immediate vicinity: 'here' seems to be a sort of bubble around me, and I can't spontaneously picture 'where' things are outside this bubble;

Space does not seem to have the absolute quality about it that it had before: when I look at things, space seems to form around them only to facilitate my perception of them, as it were, but does not have any compelling reality of its own. In fact, qualities like color, line, texture, seem to take on a much greater importance in visual perception.

Just thought I'd let you know what even an inexperienced person can do with DP3. It's is an incredible method! Is there any limit to its application??"

Other Applications of the DP3 Method

DP3 is a rapid and efficient method. It is hard to believe that at the present time there is a process equal to it with regard to efficiency. It is possible to get exceptionally important results in personality development inr a short period of time.

It will be useful if you integrate the following polarities:

1. Responsibility – Irresponsibility

2. My will – Another's will

3. Capability (to do something) – Incapability

4. Enthusiasm – Lethargy

5. Anxiety – Tranquility

6. Yielding to others – Imposition of one's own idea

7. Decision to do something – Postponing doing it

8. I must be right – I don't have to be right

9. Others are right – I'm right

10. I must – I will

11. I want to smoke – I don't want to smoke

12. Approaching the goal – Retreating from the goal

13. Tolerance – Intolerance

14. "I" - My spouse

15. "I" - My boss

16. "I" - the person I separated

17. Man – Woman

18. My father - My mother

19. "I" - My child

20. Ability to be creative - Inability to be creative

The following is suggested to people who want to attain deep changes in their personalities. These processes seem to demand a lot of time, but if you compare time spent on them and the benefits it becomes clear that it is a good investment.

Make a list of 17 unwanted aspects, identities or situations (later on you can add other lists) and apply DP3 to them:

1. Individuals who influenced you negatively and whose influences still persist.

2. Incidents which negatively influenced you, whose influences still persist.

3. Did your parents negatively influence you and that influence still persists?

4. Some acts harmful to yourself whose influence persists.

5. Did some scenes negatively influence you?

6. Is there an incident where you saw one person influence another person negatively and the influence of that incident still persists?

7. Do you feel there are invisible factors which influence you negatively?

8. Is there any aspect or characteristic which prevents you from expressing yourself freely?

9. Any person which sometime ago used to control you.

10. Any person which you wanted to be like (including heroes from literature, movies, TV as well as real life).

11. Any person whose body parts you wanted to possess.

12. Any person whom you wanted to be.

13. Any person you miss now.

14. Any compulsive desire or aspect which persists.

15. Any experience you postpone.

16. Everything you feel you use to justify yourself.

17. Every spiritual, occult or gnostic experience which is still separate from you, which is not well integrated in yourself (mystical experience, void, God, enlightenment).

Let us take a look at how to apply DP3 in these situations say from the first list: individuals who influenced you negatively and whose influence still persists. For example, your elder brother influenced you negatively in your childhood and that negative influence is still persisting (parents and relatives compared you often and he always "was better").

> **The general principle is this: when you have a person, element, state or situation which you want to eliminate, find the opposite person, element, state or situation. Out of both situations you choose the briefest possible moment, which represents them both, and apply DP3 to them until there is complete integration.**

From your past choose one typical situation when you felt your elder brother was better than you. Choose a very narrow moment from that situation lasting only 1-2 seconds and stay with it in the process. That means do not go a few seconds before nor a few seconds after that narrow moment.

Then choose the opposite polarity: A situation when you were better than your brother and your parents or relatives said you were better than your brother; or your brother himself said you are better than him (in any kind of activity). Again choose one short moment of that incident and use it during the DP3 process.

The process goes like this. Feel yourself in the »negative« situation and give all 4 elements (image, emotion, body sensation and thought). Then remember yourself in the »positive« situation and give all 4 elements etc. until all elements vanish and in their places there is just emptiness. Or (another possibility) the negative situation will merge with the positive and they will become one, so that we have a transcendent situation which is above and beyond both the positive and negative situations.

Let us take another example, integrating **giving and receiving.** There are people who are not able to give something to others. It seems strange but there are also people who are not able to receive anything from others. If people from both groups force themselves to do what they avoid, they feel strong guilt, regret, revulsion, and similar negative emotions. We can say that both groups are "strongly polarized" between the polarities of giving and receiving.

When such persons integrate polarities of giving and receiving, they become able to give and to receive, depending on the situation. Such persons are not forced from inside to **give or receive unconsciously and compulsively. Such persons are able to give and receive consciously and freely. They can do it, but do not have to.**

Therefore, the fundamental thing in integration of polarities is **freedom**: freedom to be something, freedom to do something and freedom to have something. On one side we have compulsion and unconsciousness, on the other, freedom and consciousness.

From the point of view of spiritual evolution, when we integrate the most important polarities of the universe, we come to a crossroads from which two possible paths lead. Like Buddha and his followers, we can start a crusade for the liberation of all sentient beings on the planet, or leave the planet and start higher and more challenging games in other realities. No wonder all of us wants to get to that crossroad as soon as possible.

Some Observations on the DP3 Process

The principle of alternative technique upon which I built most of my systems, starting with the Gnostic Intensive and through the latest, Inner Magic of Words, was hanging in the air for a couple of decades. As I have said before, in 1977 I found in some printed material the following sentence of L. Ron Hubbard: *"When you want to create an efficient process, don't forget that we live in dual universe."* I felt like I had received a strong punch to my solar plexus. In those words there was some gem which I was unable, in that moment, to extract from a mass of hypotheses. Many times afterward my thoughts went back to it, until I finally succeeded in applying it to the Alternative Technique. The time for all processes was shortened up to ten times.

Now, after developing DP3 I can understand why Ron Hubbard was unable to attain similar results. In his "practical philosophy" there was always the urge to bring a man to a causative point. Man should always have been "the cause", never "the effect". Tending to such results he created just half-efficient processes of "powers". But cause and effect are just two sides of the same coin. As Geoffrey Filbert rightly pointed out in his book *"Excalibur Revisited",* the practitioner should do that process until he experiences not only the source, but also the consequence.

But Filbert also stopped at the verge of discovery. A man should become conscious that he is the source and that he is not the source. Not one experience after the other, but actually simultaneously, which means through integration of the states SOURCE and NOT-SOURCE. It is strange how we are not able to see the simplest relationships and solutions, but first we try to resolve problems in more complicated ways.

Hui-Neng's Platform Sutra

Existence of polarities is the source of both suffering and positive experiences. If we were not sad from time to time, we would not know what joy is. Through search and understanding of polarities and through their integration it becomes possible to reach to the state of spiritual transcendence, to experience both opposing sides as two sides of the same whole. This way one can set himself free from the influence of one polarity by introducing the other, which is in conjunction with it and then may realize their integration.

Hui-neng, the Sixth Patriarch of Zen, understood the complex field of polarities better than the huge majority of people in his time and of our time as well. In his opinion, enlightenment is the realization, which gives meaning to one's life, and at the same time it is the discovery and understanding of one's true nature. Responding to questions of his disciples on how to discover one's own true nature, Hui-neng used to give a very simple answer: work on neutralization of chosen pairs of polarities and you will understand the world and your situation in it on a very balanced way. Here is the translation of his own words:

> *"He who knows how to use these thirty-six pairs realizes the all-pervading principle which goes through the teaching of all Sutras. Whether he is 'coming in' or 'going out', he is able to avoid the two extremes."*

Hui-neng's process primarily removes delusions born from the polar opposites. Therefore we can understand it as the process of collapsing polar structures and removing delusions.

Further, owing to polarities incarnated in our speech, to collapse polar structure means to supersede spoken language and go beyond language into immediate experience. Removal of delusions and neutralizing polarities happens completely because all polarities are mutually connected and interwoven. Therefore, the destruction the world picture built on them facilitates deep enlightenment. When the polar structure is destroyed and a man is liberated from illusions, he is able to step out of the world of constructs and to stop being tied to them. Then the man is free to choose. He can stay in his thought constructs or to leave them behind.

To be able to live such liberated way of life, one should neutralize/integrate the main pairs of opposites:

Heaven and earth
Sun and moon

Light and darkness
Positive element and negative element
Fire and water
Speech and dharma
Affirmation and negation
Matter and no-matter
Form and formlessness
Matter and emptiness
Movement and rest
Clean and dirty
Ordinary people and sages
Ignorant people and wise people
Old and young
Big and little
Long and short
Good and Bad
Vain and enlightened
Disturbed and calm
Honest man and swindler
Full and empty
Flat and steep
Body and mind
Permanent and transient
Merciful and cruel
Happy and angry
Generous and miserly
Advancing and retreating
Exsisting and nonexisting

Everything changes in time, Spiritual practice as well. If practitioners of DP3 try to work with Hui-neng's Platform Sutra polarities, they will see that they already have integrated some of them. That means between such polarities there is no charge. Therefore a person can experience them without being compulsively bound to one or the other. It is easy to accept, because Middle Age Chinese people had a lot of charge on some natural phenomena and entities such as sun and moon, which are empty of charge for most contemporary people.

Hui-neng gave us a clear clue. The liberation from the iron tongs of polar opposites is through superseding them via their integration or neutralization. All one needs is to find polarities which for one are burdened with charge. Some from my practice I give here, so choose those which are significant for you.

Love and fear
Love and freedom
Love and pain
Love and power
Love and loneliness
Big and small
Light and dark
Good and bad
Man and woman
Limited and unlimited
"I" and "no-I"
Visible and invisible
Manifested world and unmanifested world
Appearing and disappearing
Movement and immovebility
Matter and energy
Matter and emptiness
Existence and nonexistence
Point and three dimensional object
Point and space

Whole and part
Inner world and outter world
Permanency and transiency
Present moment and eternity
Present and past
Present and future
Beginning and end
Finally and eternally
Advancing and retreating
Win and loss
Oppulence and poverty
Giving and receiving
"I" and life
"I" and other beings
Oneness with others and isolation
Joy and sadness
Life and death
Peace and unrest
Cause and consequence
Domination and submisiveness
Attraction and repulsion
Creation and destruction
Expanding and shrinking
Freedom and destiny (karma)
All and nothing
Coagulation and dissolution
Sound and silence
Coming and going
Forgeting something and remembering something
Victory and defeat
Satisfaction and dissatisfaction
I am and I am not

Oneness and duality
Emotions and reason
Passion and spirituality
Freedom and no-freedom
Freedom and slavery
Active and passive
Conscious and unconscious
Limited consciousness and unlimited consciousness
Consciousness and materiality
Material and spiritual
Endlessly small and endlessly big
Peace and fear
Love and fear
Safe and unsafe
All and nothing
Earthly and unearthly
This world and other world
Material universe and spiritual universe
Entering into experience and going out of it
Body and consciousness
Something and nothing
True and untrue
Dependence and independence
Knowledge and ignorance
Strength and weakness
Good "I" and bad "I"
Something and nothing
Happiness and sadness
Control and freedom
Creation and existence
Accepting and rejecting
"I" and nothingness

Love and rejection
Moving and stopping

I give here pairs of "philosophical" polarities from my practice which you should integrate using DP3 if you want to attain balance and harmony in your thinking, feeling and behavior. Many of these polarities are personal codes or primordial polarities of some individuals, which were discovered in my sessions with processors I trained. Some of them will be empty of charge for you. You should skip those and find others that I did not give here which for you may be burdened with more or less charge.

Every pair of these basic polarities points to the world state and the state of consciousness which should be transcended. For as much as the whole world is, despite its great complexity, understandable and describable through pairs of opposites, one is able to transcend the whole existing universe integrating the opposites it is built upon. It is the explanation of enlightenment which Hui-neng and his followers gave us is a formless state of nonattachment for the outer sides of life based on the game of polarities. The process of integration and neutralization of polarities is, in essence, removing delusions about life and ourselves, which originate in illusory opposites.

Dual opposites are reflected not only in our consciousness, but also in our language. Therefore the elimination of energy-emotional burden from the consciousness means going beyond language and its constructions. It is the reason why enlightened teachers of Zen often give senseless answers to logical questions. Seeing through the unreality of polar opposites in oneself and in the world, one stops gravitating toward one of them and avoiding the other. They still exist as illusions, but one is free to experience them or to abstain from such experience. Hui-neng described such state with the following words: *"...One who knows how to integrate these pairs of opposites will be able to avoid extremes in his behavior and feelings."*

After a number of Deep PEAT and DP3 processes, the consciousness of the practitioner generates something like a hologram of wholeness. From that moment on, whenever one thinks of a thing, phenomenon or features, their polar opposites appear at once in his consciousness as its Siamese twin. One half magnetically attracts the other into the whole, into a so-called "gestalt". Before processing, polarities were sharply separated and seemingly irreconcilable. What created that split between them was the energetic charge that prevented two halves of one whole reconnecting. Now, after that negative, repulsive energy is eliminated, reconnection happens spontaneously, automatically, and it is impossible to thwart it.

In practice it looks like this. Someone tells you some rough or insulting statement, or a foreigner insults your country, and in the same moment you remember a situation when you did the same or some similar thing. As soon as emotional protest of such behavior begins to appear in your memory, you begin to recall similar things members of your nation or you personally did or said. That is the main advantage of the Alternative Technique of psychological and spiritual work – it embraces the whole experience, which has its positive and negative, active and passive, components. Most other techniques and methods involve just a half an experience, because they try to embrace and realize only its positive half.

FINGERTIP TECHNIQUE

I discovered this technique "spontaneously" in September 2003, in the PEAT Processor Training workshop in Verona, Italy. One participant was not able to do Deep PEAT, because she was unable to concentrate on the process. Such statements usually point to great charge created by some trauma blocking the attention. In that moment I suddenly got the idea that it was necessary to "break time and space", because her trauma happened seemingly in the past, and as a matter of fact, past and future don't exist. Only **NOW** exists.

In the very beginning of the process the mental image of the traumatic incidents started to dissipate. At the same time, negative emotions started to vanish. The process lasted less then 5 minutes and the trauma vanished, however, it took longer with other people and I needed to repeat the process. I had been perfecting it for some time and after few months I came to the final version. In workshops I led in Canada, the USA, and Italy, individuals with a long experience of many other systems were surprised with its simplicity, rapidness and efficiency. As a method for removing traumas, the Fingertip Method is unequalled, at least at this moment.

This whole procedure is described in the **PEAT workbook,** compiled by Joel DiGirolamo, but I included it in its entirety because of its efficiency. Watching an application of the fingertip method, many psychotherapists and psychiatrists are not able to understand the mechanism of its operation. The essence is in the interruption of time and space, and in confronting a trauma, gradually, bit by bit. Owing to the difficulty of humans in confronting very unpleasant experiences, we lead the client to it gradually. The application uses elements from other methods. First, we ask the client to estimate, based on his subjective impression (objective estimation is not important), when the trauma happened, not only how many years, but also how many months, days, hours and minutes. Then we ask for other modalities of the traumatic experience: dimensions, colors, whether they see it as a movie or a snapshot, and other descriptives. Every one of these requests is designed to lead the client to confronting the trauma. At the end, we help the client break the space/time continuum by merging the space where the trauma occurred, with the space in present time, where the client is working the process.

In the great majority of cases the trauma vanishes in only one "round". If the client resists the trauma (because it is unpleasant or painful), some part of it could be left at the end of the process. All that is necessary is to repeat the process, which lasts again only a couple of minutes. Some traumas require circular processing with the fingertip method.

This method has great potential for further development. Based on it, it may possible to develop a whole new system of Spiritual Technology, and at this time I'm doing experiments to further develop this approach. Other processors are also doing the similar things. Joel DiGirolamo, a PEAT processor, sent our discussion list the following report: *"Some of my friends used the fingertip technique to discreate their image of God. This was the result: They would disperse the original image, and that way they were able to enter into a deeper relationship with God, as they imagined it. They all felt such experience was useful for their Spiritual development."*

We use the fingertip method for removing a traumatic memory or an emotionally charged event for which the client can identify a peak moment.

Instruct the client:

1. **Choose an event or trauma.** Think of the worst moment.

2. I am going to **have you stand up and turn around a few times** and then **I'm going to ask you a few questions** about the trauma. This will only take a few minutes.

3. **Close your eyes. Keep them closed and place the image of the trauma in your mind.**

4. **Turn the client around** two or three times.

5. **Remember the peak moment** of the event. Go to it and **feel** it.

6. **Point the index finger of your dominant hand** to where the event is, to the image or picture of the incident. The tip of your finger should be in the middle of the image.

Ask the client:

1. Is the image **panoramic or framed**?

2. Is the image **black & white or in color**?

3. Is the image **moving or fixed**?

4. What **kind of material** does it consist of? Is it **gaseous, fluid or solid**?

5. Is the image **3 dimensional or 2 dimensional like a photo**?

6. Are there any **sounds**?

7. How many **years ago** did the incident happen?

8. __ years ago and **how many months** ago?

9. __ years, __ months and **how many days**?

10. __ years, __ months, __ days and **how many hours**?

11. __ years, __ months, __ days, __ hours and **how many minutes**?

12. Estimate and tell me the distance from the tip of your finger, which is in the middle of the image, to the **ceiling** in **this** room.

13. Estimate and tell me the distance from the tip of your finger, which is in the middle of the image, to the **floor** in **this** room.

14. Estimate and tell me the distance from the tip of your finger, which is in the middle of the image, to the **right wall** in **this** room.

15. Estimate and tell me the distance from the tip of your finger, which is in the middle of the image, to the **left wall** in **this** room.

16. Estimate and tell me the distance from the tip of your finger, which is in the middle of the image, to the **wall in front of you.**

17. Estimate and tell me the distance from the tip of your finger, which is in the middle of the image, to the **wall behind you**.

18. Tell the client to **open his eyes**.

19. Ask, "**What happened to the trauma? Is it still there?**"

If **anything remains** go back to step 3 with the remainder of the event.

When everything is gone, **fill the client with light**, then **fill the space of the event with light**.

It is fine to touch the client's finger to remind the client where he is.

The fingertip technique could be used in the Deep Peat process, as a helping procedure, when there are some difficulties in PEAT processing. There are two possibilities for that:

1. A Client may have encountered some kind of a block or barrier between two polarities, which prevents their uniting. Use the Fingertip method to disperse that block, then merging of the polarities happen quickly.

2. During the session a client encounters a trauma which is so strong that it is difficult for him to continue with the session. The processor can disperse it using this method and go on processing.

3. Sometimes, during the Deep Peat process or DP3, the client is not able to bring the process to an end because of persistent body sensations which prevent it. For example a headache, strong pressure in the throat or

solar plexus, etc. In such situations we stop the process we started and we apply the Little Magical Method (LMM) to remove such obstacles. After we complete it, we continue with the main process. We can apply LMM in many other situations for removing unpleasant body sensations. Its efficiency usually causes great surprise for clients. That is the reason for its name.

LITTLE MAGICAL METHOD

The basic mechanism of this method is the collapse of a wave to a particle, which we can easily manipulate. In the LMM we give a body sensation characteristics which actually it doesn't have, and that way we enable the client to confront the unwanted state successfully. Every such confrontation eliminates a portion of energy from that unwanted body sensation, so it gets smaller and smaller, becomes weaker and at the end it vanishes thus we can go continue the basic process undisturbed.

We ask the client to describe the unwanted state, but we do not let him do it arbitrarily, but follow a definite sequence of questions. *Instruct the client:*

Put your intention on the body sensation.
Tell me the exact location of it.
If it had weight, how heavy would it be?
How big is it?
What is its shape?
What is its color?
What is its temperature?
What is its age?
How deep is it in your body?
Is it inside or outside your body?

Estimate the intensity on a scale from 0 to 10, how strong is it?

You repeat the same sequence of questions a couple of times. If the client follows instructions, which means he isn't resisting, the body sensations should vanish quickly and in 2-3 rounds of the same questions it disappears completely. What do you suspect diminishes the qualities of the body sensation as the dimensions become smaller, the colour becomes progressively more pale, it comes closer to the surface of the body, etc.?

The processor can also ask for additional characteristics of the body sensation, for example, what is the level of consciousness of it or how intelligent is it?

Some inexperienced clients are confused with these kinds of questions, so they are not able to answer at once. In such situations we should help them: *"You say that pressure in your head has no color...OK, if it has no color, give it a color"*, or *"If it had a color, what would it be?"*

Be careful; every kind of persistence of body sensation evidently means that the client is resisting that sensation. If after 2-3 repetitions of the sequence of questions there is no lessening of dimensions and strength, add the following.

"In that body sensation there must be some movement, otherwise it would not exist. Every cessation of movement brings about the vanishing of the body sensation. Therefore, observe carefully that body sensation and tell me, what kind of movement of energy is there in it?" (You can show him possible movements with your hand: vertically circular, horizontally circular, oblique movement, alternatively contracting and expanding etc.)

When the client answers what kind of movement he notices, tell him: *"Now, as you feel that movement of energy in your body sensation, imagine making an effort to direct the movement of energy in the opposite direction. Be careful! Simultaneously imagine both of those opposite energetic movements!"*

After the client does this, the body sensation nearly always vanishes and we are able to continue with the basic process. If even after that the body sensation persists, then it is a so called **indicator of the Great Space** and one should do the procedure for entering the Great Space (see my book ***"PEAT and Neutralization of Primordial Polarities"*).**

14

IDENTITIES

Identities are a very important field of Spiritual Technology. Using them we fall into trouble; using them we also realize our goals and states of satisfaction. By processing identities we are able to resolve many unwanted situations and to create desired states. There are many different definitions of identity. In my opinion the best is this one:

Identity is a temporary personality or role that we take on to be able to realize a goal. Identity consists of the **point of view plus the goal one wants to attain**.

In different situations we identify with identities that are appropriate for the situations. Man creates his identities, they are his creations and through them he accomplishes his relationship with the outer world and with himself. We can compare them with a kind of cloth garment that we put on in different situations. During cold weather the warm and thick cloth is adequate, but if you want to swim across the river in it, you will drown. A normal, well-integrated person easily changes the identities to fit a variety of situations. For example; when a man, whose professional occupation is a medical doctor, enters his office he automatically takes on the identity of a doctor. When he finishes his job and sits in his car to go home, he enters the identity of a driver – he respects traffic sighs, he is careful in driving etc. When entering his home he encounters his wife- he enters the identity of a husband, and if his children address him he immediately enters the identity of a father. The transition from one identity to the other happens in unnoticeable and quick leaps.

A well-integrated person has an unlimited number of identities. In the majority of them he/she enters and goes out without thinking, easy and automatically. Taking on identities is nothing bad by itself. Moreover, it is unavoidable, without them we would not be able to function in the world. The only problem with identities happens when we get stuck in one of them. The trouble with them is that they are limitations and when we get stuck in some of them we are necessarily limited. The Human Being in its deepest nature is limitless, but the identities it takes on are limitations. If a man is blocked in some identity, he becomes limited in a very unpleasant and sometimes painful way. Whereas a normal person changes identities without a problem, a neurotic person is more rigid in his behavior and usually is firmly attached to only a few identities. The extreme case is that of a psychotic person, who is often firmly attached to only one identity and it is very difficult to pull that person out of it. Some people say that in every madhouse there are a few Napoleons.

Even so called "normal people" are often firmly bound to certain particular identities more so than to others. They usually identify with them very much. For them such identities are dominant. For example, there are people "frozen" into the identity of an honest person and for them is almost impossible to do anything dishonest. It is their dominant identity. They are highly identified with an honest person and they think that the honest person is their True Being. Others trying to be always witty make jokes in every situation. They would tell you – "It is me, I've always been that way". If they force themselves to behave differently, the decision cannot hold for long and after a short period their dominant identity takes over the main role again.

However, no matter how strong an identity is, the human being is not that identity. It is the Spiritual Being that has many identities, but it is not one of them, as it is not different parts of its cloth. Typical identities and most often encountered identities are professional, roles of the family (father, mother, son, grandson etc.), sexual, religious and national belongings.

Identity consists of two elements: **Point of view and the Goal we want to attain.** In everyday life identities do useful functions for us, mainly automatically. We cannot live without them. When they are not under control, but enslave the person, as it happens in loosing one's temper or in dependencies like alcoholism and drug addiction, then they become cruel masters instead of good servants. Every day we can hear people saying, *"I don't know why I behave that way"* or *"Something inside me is stronger than myself"* etc. They are good servants, but bad masters.

For optimal behavior in different situations we need to integrate our main identities, especially those that could cause problems for us and maybe even prevent our creating desired identities. At the base of inadequate and non-efficient behavior we can always find identities, because through them such behavior appears. In the formula "be-do-have" identities find their place in the first state of existence, in "to be". If in therapy or Spiritual work we try to remove one's problem by handling his bad behavior, by affecting the "do" state, we can attain good results, but they are usually not lasting. The problem will come back because the identity, which is the cause of such behavior, is not reached. What is reached is only the behavior that is the consequence, not the cause. To have permanent results we must handle not only the symptoms, but also the identity, because it is the source of the consequences.

Working with Identities

To be able to resolve the problem of unwanted identities, or to be able to create a desired identity, we must imagine them as clearly as possible. With visualization, we should make it three-dimensional, that is, present it as if real, in 3D space. We imagine the identity as something belonging to us, as we would do with our car, bicycle or a piece of furniture. We should also create a clear feeling that we are not that identity, but it is something which we created and which belongs to us.

Elimination of Identities

I developed two methods for elimination of unwanted identities so far. The first is Fingertip method, and the second one is the application of DP3 on unwanted identities. The second method actually does not consists of elimination, but of neutralization or integration of two opposing identities, so much so that we are able to express any one of them in an adequate situation. Such approach is superior to first one because it involves both sides.

Fingertip Method

I described this method in detail in the section of discreation of traumas, so study it there in details. Here we apply it when we need to quickly remove some unwanted identity, or to eliminate all negative charge from it. The procedure is the same, as when we discreate painful traumas from the past, only in this case we should first create an unwanted identity in our thoughts and feelings. I will repeat because it is important: You should imagine the undesirable identity as real as you are able to, yet with the full consciousness that it is not you, but it is something belonging to you. Let us see how it goes. Suppose a Client complains about his sudden attacks of rage and aggressiveness. Evidently it is an identity that he does not control.

1. Say to the Client: *"In your thoughts go to the situation when you used to be in that identity, when you felt and behaved that way. Tell me YES or nod your head when you are in such state."* When he does this, you go on:

2. *"In your imagination, watch that identity of yours and describe it to me in full detail. Tell me all of its characteristics as you would describe a person you know well: How do you appear when you are in that identity, how do you behave, what do you feel, how do you speak etc."*

You should encourage the Client until he creates a clear image of that identity of his, and it is his image in the situation where he expresses that identity. For example, the Client should create the image of himself in the aggressive state: How he looks, moves, make gestures, speaks etc. as if he is watching another person who is acting aggressively.

3. Now apply the Fingertip Method to that unwanted identity: Let the Client close his eyes, turn him 2-3 times around his axis and then ask him: *"Now, where do you see*

that identity? Using the dominant hand, put the tip of the index finger (forefinger) in the middle of that image..."

Then continue with the Fingertip method until the identity vanishes (see Fingertip method in detail). If, after the application, its image picture remains, it must be pale, without any charge on it, like a pale, faded photo.

4. When this happens, ask the Client to fill with light the place where that identity was previously.

That is all!

Application of DP3 to Unwanted Identities

I'm afraid I will become boring to you repeating that not one thing or phenomenon in this universe can exist without its opposites. When we remove the negative component of the experience, we have removed only one half of it. We usually hope that which is left is only its positive half. However, one side cannot exist without the other, because it is the other side of it. It is like stretching a rubber band. When we stretch the upper part of the rubber band, the lower part is also being stretched. Likewise, after a very short period the negative side appears again on the stage of life, because the positive one pulls it into manifestation. Therefore, I repeat, the most efficient action is integration (neutralization) of both sides. It gives the most permanent results.

We will apply DP3 on an unwanted identity so that we can integrate with the opposite, positive identity. For example, if a person suffers because of his aggressiveness, we should ask the person to remember situations when he expressed the opposite identity – calmness, self-control etc. Then apply

Return to Oneness

DP3 on these two identities. All Clients may not feel the same identities as opposites. One person could say that opposite to aggressiveness is the tolerant identity, another could say it is a calm identity, and a third might say that it is the identity of love for others. You should accept whatever response the Client gives you. If he hesitates, help him by giving him a couple of examples.

The Client should see, with as many details as possible, three-dimensionally, first one then the other polar identities. The process usually goes something like this:

"Feel your identity (tell him which one) and tell me all 4 elements: image, emotions, body sensations and thought."

"Feel your identity (tell him the other identity) and again, give me all four elements: image, emotions, body sensations and thought."

The elements of both identities will gradually disappear, until only emptiness remains. Sometimes, rarely, they visually merge with each other into one. The DP3 procedure goes further, much like the basic Deep PEAT process. When the process is finished, ask the Client:

5. *"Who controls the situation now, you or your unwanted identity?"*

6. *"Will you in the future be able to manifest both these identities at your own will?"*

I emphasize one important element. You do not have to take your positive identity as a polar opposite to the negative one. You can also take a person who is for you an excellent example of that positive identity. You can choose a person from literature, movie star, TV, from anywhere, in the situation where that person expresses that identity. Moreover, you can create an identity in your imagination, but be certain to make it very realistic to yourself.

The Creation of Positive Identities using DP3

The creation of new, desired identities goes quickly and efficiently with DP3. I called that procedure the Indiana Jones method. I started to apply it after an engineer from Slovenia came to visit me in Belgrade to be processed. The two polarities for integration he chose were himself and Indiana Jones, a well-known hero from American adventures movies. He achieved integration pretty quickly and at the end he felt extremely well. After a month I got an e-mail from him in which he wrote: *"It's incredible, but I still have the same feeling as the last session with you – when I want I feel as Indiana Jones. I miss the adequate words to express that feeling. I wonder, what would have happened if I chose Superman as other polarity? Now I feel much better, I'm more concentrated then before, I know what I want and I have much stronger feeling of love for other people."*

It is difficult to say for how long such an identity will persist, because nothing in the human being or in this universe is eternal, but if that identity becomes weaker, it is possible to easily recreate it in a couple of minutes.

Created identities are stronger and more stable when they embrace many characteristics that go with them. In essence, they consist of clusters of personality characteristics and features. Thus the process of creating persistent identities goes this way: Every characteristic that is a part of the identity should be integrated with the opposite, unwanted one. That way we will make relatively long lasting identities, for example, an identity of a happy person, a person that attracts to self a good life, a self-realizing person etc. Pay attention to this: If you do not integrate features that are opposite of the desired ones, they will sooner or later overturn the newly created identity. I describe the procedure in detail in the next section "The Money Game and How to Play It".

This is also interesting: It is possible to integrate any state or characteristic that you have in this world and yourself as the Great Space (void, quantum vacuum etc). The reason is that all features and states are polarities in their relationship with the Void or All-Source.

The procedure is very simple. First identify your unwanted polarity. Then perform the Holographic Expansion of Being. Then identify with Great Space or Void, paying attention to your everyday "I". Then integrate that state, which represents one polarity, and yourself as Great Space, taking it as the other polarity.

15

THE MONEY GAME AND HOW TO PLAY IT

The human being has many problems and Spiritual development is nothing else but resolving them. In contemporary society the majority of people state that their problems involve power (position in the society), emotional relationship and money (properties). In my workshops, when I ask participants what problem they would like to work with, the first thing they insist on is money. However, problems connected with money are multilayered and complex. They must be embraced from many sides and every one of their components must be processed.

People usually have wrong notions and ideas about money. They groundlessly believe that the possession of money will create desired inner states – positive states of consciousness and feelings. The truth is evidently just the opposite – states of consciousness (states of unconsciousness as well) decide about inflow of money and about the capacity to receive it, possess it and direct it. As always, in the relationship between the inner world and the outer world, the inner world is the cause and the outer world is the consequence. The money is no exception to that rule.

Great differences exist in how people get money and use it. There are people unable to make significant sums of money; there are people able to do that, but they spend it quickly and uncontrollably; there are people that are able to earn money in one period of their lives and in other periods are not able to. There are many reasons for such happenings, but some common reasons are noticeable. For example, a person makes enough money, then squanders it unreasonably for a short period and such behavior repeats again and again. We are able to understand it if we know that the person has a strong feeling of guilt. Squandering money and suffering because of the behavior are an unconscious mechanism to alleviate the painful feeling of guilt.

Other reasons are also possible. Let me give you an example from my practice. A few years ago I processed one lady with memento method for remembering and integration of past lives (it was before I developed PEAT and DP3). We revived a frequently met situation: In a previous lifetime she was financially relatively well off. In one moment she was robbed and killed. At the moment of death she made the decision, which for that situation was quite logical: *"If I have money, I will be killed! I will get rid of the money and I will live!"* That fear evidently persisted in this life. As soon as the lady made some money (consciously she wanted that very much and tried to do it all the time), she would feel insecure and endangered and quickly would spend it. Now, we have DP3 and the basic process for this unwanted state of hers would be the integration of the feeling of insecurity when she has money and security when she has money until the integration happens.

Fundamental problems and negative states of one's personality, which can create the problems with money, should be resolved with Deep PEAT, and specific problems should be handled with DP3.

Identities and Acquiring Money

Money is neither good nor bad. It is a kind of concentrated energy that we use as a means for exchanging of goods and service. As with everything else, it is a good servant, but a cruel master. The good news is this- a man is able, by creating good identities and using the abilities that come from them, to earn a decent sum of money. Simply put, this means he can attract to himself concentrated energy, for the realization of the valuable goals of his True Being, not his Ego.

Your attitude toward money reflects your relationship toward energy, other beings, yourself and your attitude toward giving and receiving which is one of the cosmic laws. If you want to have a spontaneous and efficient relationship with money, you must first of all set yourself free from inner conflicts and bad identities (see later in this section). **Our unconscious negative beliefs are like mine fields** of conflicting ideas, beliefs, desires and polar opposites **in all the spheres of life** and especially in three of them and again, they are: **power, love** (emotional relationship) and **money**.

Very often, on the conscious level of existence, man can consciously desire money, but his unconscious, hidden negative beliefs can be insurmountable difficulties to get it without a lot of big problems. The solution of money problems begins with uncovering any guilt feelings and negative beliefs that money is something bad, negative, immoral etc.

A good starting position is to clarify why do you want money? People usually say money gives safety and confidence. What does that mean? It means that actually, **people want the feeling of safety, not money**. The money is just the means to get a feeling of safety. Often people want money so as to be loved by others, to have love in their life. That means **some people want love, not money.**

Because **money is one of the fundamental components of contemporary life, it demands the holistic approach and resolution.**

That means we must involve all components concerning money, not only the making of money. The **essential components concerning money are polarities** and all of the important polarities should be integrated so that one can express them in an appropriate manner in any given situation.

Elements which laymen often miss are **identities** through which we realize our interactions with our surroundings and thus realize our goals. In "**The Money Game**" identities have an essential role. I wrote about them in my book <u>Integral Excalibur</u> (available in English soon), but here I will point out the most important elements.

A person should be able automatically to take certain identities if the person wants to, then easy and naturally resolve problems with material properties, especially money. For example, to ask without hesitation favors from others and to offer them as well, to be open to using the favorable conditions, to feel and believe that he/she deserves a good and pleasant life, to look at money making as a game in which he/she participates with pleasure etc. Unfortunately, many people try to resolve money problems without having the adequate identities. It should be clear to you: **First, you must change your identities to change the situation in the outer world, and to experience a changed situation with money.**

This is one unbreakable rule: In the formula "**Be - Do - Have**" the following axioms concern identities:

Positive identities bring about **positive doing** and give **positive results.**

Average identities bring about **average doing** and give **average results.**

Negative identities bring about **unsuccessful doing** and give **negative results.**

The trouble with the majority of participants in workshops focused to teach life success and money-making, is in their attempt to make success or positive results result from negative identities. They try to swim over a wide river dressed in a heavy winter coat. Creating adequate identities is what they need to be able to swim well in the "money river". Fortunately, with instruments such as Deep PEAT and DP3, now it is possible.

Previously I said there are permanent identities that are expressed automatically in appropriate situations. Such identities are created from clusters of personality features and characteristics. One should create such identities using the DP3 method. Perhaps you want to create the identity of a successful person that you will automatically assume when the situation requires it. I will give you an example of such an identity, but it is something changeable, you can add any characteristic you like. At the left hand side are characteristics you lack, which you want to create as permanent and on the right hand side are the negative features that can ruin your desired identity.

Identity of a Successful Person - Using DP3

1. I have clear goals in my life - I don't know what I want

2. I use every good opportunity - I misuse good opportunities very often

3. Every fruitful idea I transform into action at once - I hesitate to take action

4. I take initiative - I'm not able to start the ball rolling

5. I insist on my rights - I'm not able to fight for my rights

6. I persist at the realization of my goals - I abstain from my goals very often

7. I make money with ease - For me it's hard to make money

8. I deserve the best of everything - I feel I should be satisfied with a minimum

Applying DP3 you could integrate all these identities and thereby create within you a **successful person identity**. You should do it this way, taking for example the first pair of polarities: *"I have clear goals in my life"* and *"I don't know what I want"*. You should find **any situation** in your life when you had a clear goal and isolate one short moment from that state, the peak moment of it, lasting only 1-2 seconds. Then remember one situation from your life when you did not know what your goals were and again choose from that situation just a short, peak moment, lasting only 1-2 seconds. Then apply DP3 on these two polarities until they integrate. After some time you should integrate another pair of polarities, *"I use every good opportunity"* and *"I misuse good opportunities very often"*. Go on with such work, without forcing it, writing down in your diary about processing until you integrate all 8 pairs of polarities. You can add other polarities that you think this identity consists of.

Because of its importance I will repeat once more: **It is necessary to create in yourself positive identities**, consisting of clusters of desired abilities and characteristics. They will automatically bring about your **positive activities** and without special effort you will attain **positive results**. True, some people attain good results without good identities. They are able to do it for short periods and with great strain. To be able to confront situations which are above their identities they take sedatives, drink a couple of glasses of alcohol, light cigarettes in stressful situations, react with high blood pressure etc. One can avoid all such means. Good identities switch on and act automatically just as bad identities do. So, it is best to create appropriate identities and not have to worry about the results.

After the creation of **positive identities**, which together form the solid base **for attaining deep positive changes in life**, you should use DP3 to integrate the following list of polarity pairs. Then the flow of material goods, primarily money, comes without difficulties:

1. Success in making money - Failure in making money

2. Giving - Receiving of money (material goods)

3. Asking money - Offering money

4. Win - Loss

5. Making money - Spending money

6. Making money - Saving money

7. Getting Money - Losing money

8. Having money and Not having money

9. Feeling good when you have money - Feeling bad when you do not have money

10. Good feeling when you have money - Feeling guilty when you do not have it

11. Squandering money - Stinginess with money

12. Feeling inferior when you have no money - Feeling superior when you have it

13. Feeling powerful when you have money - Feeling powerless when don't.

14. **Money - Love**

15. **Money - Spirituality**

The last two pairs of polarities I wrote in bold letters, because they are extremely important in this area. When money and love integrate and we remove all charge between them, then the money will have the same attractive power for you as love has and it will arouse in you the same strong and noble emotions. Many people, especially New Age people, have problems with money because they are burdened with a deep, core belief that it is impossible to be Spiritual and at the same time have money or that they must strain to get it. If they come to a financially bountiful situation, they feel guilty. As their ideal they often model people they believe are very spiritual, who seemingly do not pay much attention to money. But if one knows the situation behind the screen, one can get quite a different picture. One example of modesty was Mahatma Gandhi, a brave man, ready to sacrifice himself. Many people associate him with conscious poverty and a simple life. This is widely known. Lesser known is the comment of a rich Hindu man, who supported Gandhi during long periods of his fight for the liberation of India: *"It cost me a real fortune to enable Gandhi to live his poor way of life."*

Bohemians, painters, poets and authors often have a reputation of not caring much for money. They sometimes ignore it or openly despise it. In this sphere there exist also happenings behind the scene. One example involves William Faulkner, the famous American author, who had the reputation of being an alcoholic and ragamuffin. The man was indifferent toward money. However, people who knew him well described his behavior in how he classified the postal letters he received in great numbers. Faulkner would cut an envelope with knife, turned it upside down and shake it strongly a couple of times. If a check or money note fell out, he would read the letter. Otherwise he would throw it into the trash basket.

In solving money problems circular processing is extremely important. Money has no soul, but there is the impression that it has. Every person who wants to realize a decent inflow of money should do the following process! Assuming you know how to do regular and circular processing, as taught and practiced in PEAT workshops, one should go deeply into his relationship with money. If it is not positive, process to remove all existing charge from it. Afterward, the person should process to all relevant positions, all positions with emotional charge. There are usually people from the person's surrounding (for example, his relatives and close friends) who are adding to the charge around money. What are the attitudes of his relatives concerning his relationship with money? Does his brother think that he does not deserve to live better? Are some of his friends resisting the idea of his increased income? Is someone jealous of his new money making ability? And so on. All the relevant positions should be cleared using circular processing.

The last position, but extraordinarily important, is the position of money itself. In this process the person should identify with money as a conscious being. Then, as if he was Money, take a look back to his old "I" to see and feel what Money thinks and feels toward the person. That means, what is Money's attitude toward the person? Does Money feel that the person does not deserve it? Does Money like the person, or dislike him? Does Money reject him? Perhaps Money wants to punish him, because that person said many times that money is unimportant? If there is any negative reaction from the standpoint of Money (which means there is a charge), processing on that must be done.

It is possible that after some time you will discover other polarities inside of yourself that need to be integrated. Some polarities that you previously put on paper will be without charge and no longer need to be processed. What is the end result of these processes? The experience of many people teaches us that money will stop being a problem! That does not mean you will automatically become rich, neither does it mean you will become a hermit indifferent toward money. It means exactly as I said - money will not be a problem for you anymore! Money will come and go, as naturally and spontaneously as breathing. In everyday life it will come to you when you need it and on the other side (remember the other polarity!) it means that you will feel a very strong need to help someone with money when you have it.

16

THE DYNAMICS OF POLARITIES

Polarities are dynamic categories. They are not forever given and unchangeable. They are simultaneously forces of attraction and repulsion, depending on what the polarity is. There must always exist another force to which they react - attracting to or repulsing from it. They cannot exist without the opposing polarity.

All objects, phenomena or entities in the physical universe persist in their own shape because of the forces of inner balance that hold their parts together. The same applies for the human being. For polarization to occur, inner or outer force is necessary. In the human being the inner force is the decision (or desire) to make some change happen which differs from the existing state. The outer force is usually judged as disturbing, unpleasant and painful. We usually call it traumatic.

When splitting, dividing or the polarization of the previous whole into two polarities, the attracting force inside the structure comes into a state of stress, because the poles are separated by force. For separation to happen it is necessary to invest some force. After the polarization, which means separation, each of the two separated parts enters into its own new inner balance and lives as an individual entity for some time. Now two entities exist, each one with balanced polarities. How can we connect them again into one? In the relationship between physical objects and phenomena we use physical energy. For example, if we want to merge two pieces of metal we apply thermal energy. They start to melt, their inner balance is disturbed and they can become one. After thermal energy stops acting, polarized energies neutralize each other and they again make a unified structure.

In psychological, emotional and psycho energetic relationships, two terminals were created with the splitting of a person by traumatic force (so that two terminals came into existence. Example: I and my painful memory). There is also an illusory balance. A man continues his existence, so in him there is the trauma with all its consequences, which sometimes are active and sometimes are inactive. They are separated by charge, like an energetic wall, which exists between them. Applying an outside force, for example, a therapist practicing this technique, the energetic wall between them vanishes. The attracting force between them is still active and when that energetic wall disappears, they automatically merge into one.

After separating the whole of the person into two, the person experiences himself separately from the rest of the world. That fundamental separation is the source of human suffering, because it creates irreconcilable polarities of life, such as good and bad and the resulting tension between them.

On the mental and emotional level ideas and feelings about who we are, what is life and what is a human being strengthen the original separation. It is the artificial barrier through which we experience reality. The separation from our painful experience creates our fear, anger or numbness. The situation gets even worse if we don't accept the thoughts and emotions following this experience, but repress them into unconsciousness. After some time they start to manifest in the body and nervous system, creating disturbances and illnesses. Many physical illnesses are unconscious attempts of the organism to restore its own wholeness. Sending to us clear and painful messages, our organism tries to attract our attention to that part of our body where our suppressed emotions and thoughts are accumulated. That way it tries to force us to notice them, to free them and to recover our wholeness.

Unity is at the beginning and at the end of our individual path and the developing of the whole cosmos. Between these two extremes, during endless eons, we experience the illusion of duality. It is an illusion, but we must pass through it to get experiences and finally to return to Oneness. During our journey our path leads us to experience uniting with other beings, the world and the All-Source. Our life is quickly changed, because we no longer feel separated from the rest of the world. We are not a separate ball of threads, but parts of a vastly woven rug. **"We are all One" is not an empty religious idea, but the deepest experience of Truth."**

17

THE EVOLUTION OF PROCESSING

Processing, like everything else, has an evolution. Thus you should expect changes in the processes after some time. In the first period of application of Deep PEAT and DP3, the emotions and body sensations dominate. After a significant number of processes the emotions and body sensations are present less and less in the sessions and when they are present their intensity is weaker. Processes mainly are reduced to thoughts and images. Further processing brings about the domination of thoughts. An inexperienced practitioner could get the wrong idea that his processing has lost its power, or that he is making some mistake. The truth is this: the client has eliminated a lot of mental and physical content. The content consists of four well known elements. For the majority of people emotions and body sensations vanish first, then pictures, and all that is left are thoughts. If you experience that, there is no reason to worry. It means you are working well.

The practitioner will get more and more ability for seeing both sides in every situation. If in a situation the behavior of a person starts to irritate him, instead of criticism and judging the behavior, the memory of his own similar behavior will powerfully come to him, and then thoughts of positive characteristics of that person will dawn in his mind. People are often surprised with such events, but it is normal, because after a number of integrations of opposite polarities the practitioner will see in everything both sides simultaneously, not just one isolated and split off from the other.

Judith Daniel, PEAT Trainer, in her letter to me in 2004 describes her experience. I quote it because it is typical:

"...I am writing about an experience I am having that I am not worried about, but I am wondering what it means.

I have been using PEAT for myself and with clients pretty regularly. Recently, as in the last month, I feel that I am having trouble using PEAT for myself. I sit down to do DP with a polarity in mind that I want to work with, but I am having trouble feeling any distinctions in the two polarities. I am thinking of past times in which I experienced each of the poles, but as I focus on them they feel the same in my body and emotions. Sometimes there will be slightly different thoughts that go with them, but they do not seem like real thoughts, but like a role, not things I truly believe. Any distinctions seem very subtle or not existing at all. So there seems nothing to pendulate back and forth between. I do not know if the polarities are already neutralized, or if I am resisting somehow.

I have experienced this with everything I have tried to do DP with in the last month, things like money-no money and all the money polarities you suggested in your email, and beliefs about myself, like I am good, I am bad.

I also have had the experience when I am trying to choose a polarity to work on, of seeing that all the polarities are the same. They seemed each to be really one big polarity, just this and that, or really this and this, because they were the same. Just a way of breaking things but so we can talk about them. I could not figure out how to work on these. So I just stopped.

I would appreciate it if you had any suggestion for me about this. I am feeling fine most all the time, but not having any of the kinds of experiences that Carol has talked about on the list. I want to continue this work, and am trying to find my way as to how to do that.

Using PEAT in my practice has given me a wonderful tool, especially for those clients who present with spiritual goals. They love it and especially like that they can do it on their own."

It is evidently a universal process. Well known Sufi Hazrat Inayat Khan said:

"Mind clearing means that comprehensions which block mind as good and bad, right and wrong, win and loss, pleasure and pain must be removed through seeing their opposites. Then man is able to see the enemy in his friend and friend in enemy. When a man is able to see nectar in the poison and poison in the nectar, that is the moment when life and death become one as well. Then opposites are not opposites."

18

LEVELS OF CONSCIOUSNESS AND PROCESSING

Better efficiency is the common striving of all systems of psychotherapeutic, psychological and Spiritual processing. Our desire to create quicker, easier and simpler methods and systems is quite logical. Many different elements determine the efficiency. One, commonly less known, is the level of consciousness from which the person is performing.

That idea comes from traditional systems of Perennial Philosophy, but it is every now and then "rediscovered". In essence it is the datum from the practice: The higher the level of consciousness we are doing the processing from, the more efficient the process we are applying.

Qabbalah speaks openly about it. On its basic model of the cosmos and the human being, the Tree of Life, there are 10 Sephirots (Sephira), which primarily represent levels of consciousness. Above the highest Sephirot, Kether, the Void exists, Ain Soph Aur, or Endless Light. Everything coming into existence originates from It and, passing through 10 Sephirots, finally comes into physical manifestation, whose symbol is Sephiroth Malkuth. Therefore, the man that wants to have the most efficient structure must start from the Void or Endless Light.

Magic teaches its followers a simple rule. If you want to create a stable manifestation, you must evoke into activity a cosmic Intelligence, which governs that sphere of activity. However, when you start working with that Intelligence, we discover pretty soon that it is under the domination of some other, higher Intelligence. Therefore you must evoke that higher Intelligence and soon you discover that even higher Intelligence exists above it. So, step-by-step, climbing upwards, we approach Almighty Creator (or Endless Light) as the strongest Source and starting from It you get the most permanent results.

Speaking about the magical fight, Dion Fortune said that in such a war the magician that is acting from the higher level of consciousness always wins.

New systems of therapy, such as NLP, speak about that phenomenon as a Hierarchy of logical levels, stressing the importance of rising to the higher one. Practitioners of NLP evidently took this conclusion from Gregory Bateson, who simply said that higher levels govern the lower ones.

In systems that I created, embraced with the general term Spiritual Technology, it is possible to notice the same. For example, in Excalibur, when a practitioner applies so called First Method for the elimination of chronic problems, he discreates one element of the problem after another. Starting from the body sensations, as the roughest elements, he continues discreating emotions, mental components (beliefs, prejudices, justifications etc.) to finish finally with the starting decision or starting clear thought. When he discreates the decision, there is nothing left, just Void. In it, there is no problem, of course.

Rising to the higher levels is easiest to notice in Aspectics, because it is evident that during the Chain technique we raise to the higher levels of thought and emotion, until we enter the Void or Emptiness. We have s similar process in the Sunyata system, which is well known to the people experiencing it. It is evident in PEAT as well, even though someone can have an impression that we are moving in the opposite direction (down the chain of content instead of upwards into the Void), but that orientation is unimportant. When one enters Emptiness it is the beginning and the end of every manifestation.

How we can apply this knowledge? Knowing how to do that, we are in a better position when we create new systems or when improving old ones.

The main element in this approach is the self-reflecting ability of the human being. That means we are not staying in the same negative thought when we have one, but **we think about it.** Or if we have some negative emotion, we do not stay in it, but notice what **new emotion** we have about the **old emotion.** For example, we have an emotion of fear while in front of people. We do not stay in that fear, but we ask ourselves, *"What do we feel toward that fear of ours?"*

19

Polarization and Integration

It seems we need some explanation on the state of polarization and unity. In an emotionally hot discussion some people accuse one another of being "polarized", as if it is something bad. They expect people who neutralized their Primes not to be polarized. They hope and expect that the state of non-polarization they experienced at Primes Neutralization will be a permanent state.

It's a bit naive and an unreal attitude, because there are two fundamental possibilities for us as conscious human beings: dualistic consciousness and consciousness of unity. We live most of the time in the dualistic universe, in which we experience everything in opposites. On rare occasions we enter the state of Unity (Tao, Great Unmanifest, Oneness, Quantum Vacuum etc.). Such states can be of different depths. For example, in Zen they know about 18 levels of Unity. In Deep PEAT you always experience Unity when you experience integration of polarities and it seems it is deepest when you neutralize your Primordial Polarities. You experience it when you integrate or neutralize polarities in DP3 as well. But even after such neutralization you will be polarized every now and then as long as you live in a dualistic universe. In an old Indian poem **"Ramayana"** it is said: *"The world must suffer eternally of the pairs of opposites"*. The I Ch'ing states similarly: *"To be able to find his place in the eternity of existence, one must be able to separate as well as to unite."*

Differing from a typical religious and philosophical attitude dominating in our Western civilization, the oriental philosophy has an attitude based on a better understanding of this world and its laws. It points to the transcendence of all opposing polarities, which is to view them as inseparable sides of the same whole. But until one becomes a perfect man of wisdom, one must respect the laws of both worlds in which he lives as a Spiritual amphibian. He must have both hands, he must inhale and exhale, living he should be conscious that every day of his life is one day closer to his death. Many motivating metaphors in the form of edifying stories teach us to accept such an approach. One is really an object lesson for us. It is the story of the Man of Justice. It is the story of the Righteous Man. For many years he learned about his True I in the ashram of a wise Teacher of yoga. One day, the Teacher called him and told him:

> *"This is all which you should know. Between True I and Brahma there is no difference. All is Brahma. I am Brahma, and you are Brahma. Brahma is sun, moon and stars. Brahma is serpents and tigers, cactus and lotus. There is nothing except Brahma. Go home!"*

The Teacher's words rung true to the Righteous man and he went home satisfied. Walking through one village, he heard a noise and saw people running away in front of an angry elephant. An elephant rider, who barely sat on the elephant's back, shouted at him: *"Move away! Elephant is mad!"* For a moment the Righteous man felt a fear and wanted to run away, but in that moment he remembered the words of his Teacher and these thoughts passed through his mind: *"Everything is Brahma. Brahma is my Teacher, I am Brahma and elephant is Brahma. Brahma will not injure himself."* He calmly kneeled down on the road and started to glorify Brahma. The elephant ran over him.

By some miracle the Righteous man survived, but he became a cripple. People brought him to his village where he needed months to recover. Embittered he told everybody how his teacher deceived him and how painfully he paid for believing it. But, being the Righteous man, he started on a long journey to his Teacher. When he came before the Teacher, he accused him of being a phony. But the Teacher answered him this way: *"I told you the Truth. Everything is Brahma. Brahma is sun, moon and stars. I am Brahma, you are Brahma and elephant is Brahma. But Brahma is also that elephant rider. So, when he shouted at you to move away, why did you not obey him?"*

So, what is the difference between neutralized polarities and un-neutralized polarities? Why do we strain so much to get as many polarities neutralized as possible? The easiest clarification is this: When you neutralize two polarities you don't stop expressing them. Then in you there exists the whole, which is their essential characteristic, they are integrated into you as a whole. With such integration you are not unable to express them. On the contrary! You can explore either one of them at will. You have the equal freedom for expressing both opposites of behavior.

Let us take as an example, polarities of **individuality** & **unity with others**. For some people it is very difficult to be alone and they compulsively ask the company of other individuals or groups. On the other side, there are people unable to be relaxed and satisfied in a group. When they force themselves to contact others, they are tense and can hardly wait for the moment to retreat to aloneness. These two kinds of human beings are evidently polarized around aloneness and uniting with others. When these polarities neutralize, which means integrate, the individuality and unity with others, one becomes able to be either alone or with others, depending on the situation. Now the person does not have to be in the company of others compulsively and unconsciously. Such a person could be with others consciously and freely. Or, from the other point of view, such a person no longer tries all the time to retreat into loneliness compulsively and unconsciously, but the person can do it if the person wants to.

After the integration of polarities, every time when one of our integrated/neutralized polarities gets activated and starts to pull us on its side, we have the freedom of choice. We can let it pull us over in its direction or we can ignore it. In other words, we decide with our own free will. Until integration/neutralization of these two polarities we did not have access to that freedom of choice, we had to follow the commands of polar forces unconsciously and compulsively. Before the integration of polarities, reactions to inner conflicts could happen in three ways:

1. **Changes of moods, attitudes and feelings**, which oscillate from one to the other extreme. Such oscillations could last a long or short time. When one of the polarities pulls us strongly, we identify with it, until the swing pulls us toward the other polarity and the whole story repeats with it. K.G. Jung called that phenomenon of oscillation between polarities **enantiodromia**, which means in old Greek *"walking to opposite direction"*.

2. **Ambivalence**, in which polarities in conflict exist in you simultaneously. It is not the balanced position, of course, because the man is torn in the state of awkwardness even though he seems to be in the state of illusory calmness. It is the state of stagnation in which he is unable to take the appropriate action.

3. **Denial** is one of the most frequent ways of reaction to the opposites inside of us. It enables us to cope quickly with problems of opposites, but prevents our advancement and transformation. In such a state one most often regresses to identification with one's own socially acceptable mask.

In therapeutic practice and Spiritual work we are able, for the first time, owing to the DP3 method, to attain for a short time that which Middle Age cabalists needed years: balancing our psyche through active integration of opposing polarities into the dynamic whole.

So, **the bottom line of this work of ours is** just the old fashioned word **FREEDOM**: to **Be**, to **Do** something and to **Have** something. On one side we have compulsion and unconsciousness, on the other side freedom and consciousness. The true development means harmonious integration of all impulses, strivings, sub personalities and aspects into the whole Being. That process is the true emotional, psychological and Spiritual transformation. It is the path of getting to the Oneness of our Selfhood.

From the standpoint of spiritual evolution, when we neutralize/integrate most of the polarities of this universe, we get to the crossroad and have to choose one of two possible paths: Either like Buddha and his followers to start a crusade for liberation of all sentient beings on this planet, or to leave this planet and start higher and more challenging games in some other worlds. It's not strange that all of us want to come to that crossroad point as soon as possible.

20

Inner Magic of Words

In the beginning of this year (2005) I developed two new methods for elimination of unwanted states or problems: **"Ivana End of Words" (IEW)** and **"Verbal Reduction and Expansion" (VRE)**. I developed on completely new fundaments - on the inner power of words. In practice they proved to be exceptionally easy, elegant and rapid. It seems their potential for application in new fields is inexhaustible.

A long time ago Sigmund Freud said that words were originally magic. However, these two methods evidently show that words have never lost their original magic and may indeed, be more magical then Freud imagined. The main principle of magical belief is that words exercise power in virtue of their primeval mysterious connection with some aspect of reality.

Owing to the magic of words we are able to solve problems very easily as well as create desirable situation in their place. Written reports of Clients undergoing these methods show how we can use this magic of words in therapy as well as in Spiritual development.

Many eminent thinkers used to speak of the power of words. Such thoughts appeared in my mind many years ago when I read the three sentences in the Bible: *"In the beginning there was the Word. And the Word was in God. And God was the Word."* I had an impression of deep and hard to understand power existing in words. Those were not just religious verses;

in them there was some kind of religious revelation. It teaches us that the first sign of manifesting life was a sound that means a word. When we compare this interpretation with the Vedanta philosophy, we find that the two are identical. What attracted my attention was also the attitude which many linguists support that the word is the soul of one nation, so much so that people who lose their language vanish from history. Exponents of romanticism supported almost the same thought - the collective spirit of one nation is expressing itself through their language. Many individual thinkers hold the same opinion. Thus Moshe Fildenkrais, the well known creator of the method of body therapy bearing the same name, points out that the way members of one nation articulate words, vowels and consonants, define their mentality and the spirit understood in the widest possible way.

Some mystically oriented linguists consider that the thousands of all existing languages have one "mother language", the source of all others. The majority of them believe it was Sanskrit. Throughout the ages, Yogis and seers of India have worshipped the Word-God, or Sound-God. Around that concept is gathered all the mysticism utilizing sound or utterance. Also among the Hebraic races the great importance of the word was recognized. The sacred name, the sacred word, was always esteemed in the Jewish religion. Likewise in Islam one finds the doctrine of Ismahism which, translated, is the doctrine of the mystical word.

Followers of Yoga believe that as the primordial language exists, so the primordial word exists, which was the source all other words developed from it. That Primordial word, they believe, was **Aum** or **Om**. Many attach to it an extraordinary significance. Om as a word is a tool, an instrument and a mystery. Yogananda Paramhansa called **Om** the *"vibration of the cosmic motor"*, and Patanjali, the author of Yoga Aphorisms suggested the repeating of Om to remove the obstacles on the Path. Well known Yoga Teacher B.K.S. Iyengar, in his book The Light on Yoga, writes: *"The letter A symbolizes the wakeful state, the letter U dreaming and the letter M deep sleep without dream...The whole of this symbol represents the realization of divinity in a man."*

The deeper we dive into the mystery of human life the more we find that its deepest secret is hidden in what we call words. All occult science, all mystical practices are based upon the science of word and sound. One of the most amazing areas of therapy and creation of our subjective world comes in the form of words. The things we think and say to ourselves and the things we think and say to others carries a creative surge of power. It is truly incredible how one can become unaware of the words one uses. When we don't make the effort to use them carefully, that power can easily slip out of our grasp and act as a boomerang upon us, because our words are powerful instruments either creative or destructive. They are the energies that can either realize or destroy our dreams. They can make us and others laugh, they can make us cry. An unknown man said, *"Words can kill you, or release the life of God within you."*

The proper use of words penetrated today's incessant search for success in life and realization of our dreams. Well-known self-improvement workshop leader Tony Robbins started using only positive terms and called such use of words Transformational Vocabulary. For example, instead of using the word *"problem"* he insists on the term *"challenge"*. Robbins says, *"Instead of calling things problems I call them challenges ...*

and the truth of it is that you can take a challenge and turn it into an opportunity".

Health is another field where the power of the word started to manifest. In the health field, the term "organ language" is beginning to gain more attention. Organ language is noted, for example, when someone constantly complains about how things are a *"pain in the ass."* The person could later develop a mild to severe case of hemorrhoids. The reason for this is that the impact of words actually causes measurable biological changes in us. The experiential truth is that the words we attach to our experience become our experience. Common sense tells us not to use words that make us feel bad, but to replace them with others which give a positive or at a least neutral response. Our knowledge of polarities could help us here. Instead of *"I am lonely"* we can say *"I feel a need for company"*, instead of *"I am withdrawn and shy"* one can say *"I want to be open and easy going"*, instead of *"I'm angry"* one can say *"I want to be calm"* etc.

Many mystically oriented thinkers and writers were puzzled with the idea, how language, especially poetic, is able to induce the transcendental states of consciousness. It seems it is the power of poetic language to move the attention of the poet, and the readers of poetry, from the actual outside of objects to the inner and abstract. Some of the best known are the experiences of Allen Ginsberg, who admired the poetry of William Blake very much. He explains:

> *"So you find in Blake or any good poetry a series of vowels which if you pronounce them in proper sequence with the breathing indicated by the punctuation...you find a yogic breathing...that will get you high physiologically...*

And so I think that's what happened to me in a way with Blake."

Anne Waldman and Marilyn Web quote Ginsberg's experience of poetical higher consciousness in their book Talking Poetics. Ginsberg was only 22 years old and was reading Blake's poetry in his apartment:

"I had my eye on the page and I heard a big solid solemn earthen voice saying Ah, Sunflower, weary of time. My voice now actually...reciting first "The Sunflower", then "The Sick Rose" and then "The Little Girl Lost". At the same time, there was outside the window a sense of extraordinarily clear light...Everyday light seemed like sunlight in eternity...and then I looked further at the clouds that were passing over, and they too seemed created by some hand to be conscious signals.... I had the impression of the entire universe as poetry filled with light and intelligence and communication and signals.... Kind of like the top of my head coming off letting in the rest of the universe connected into my own brain.... There was a sense of an Eternal Father completely conscious caring about me in whom I had just awakened. I had just wakened into his brain or into his consciousness a larger consciousness than my own. Which was identical with my own consciousness but which was also the consciousness of the entire universe. So basically it was a sensation of the entire universe being completely conscious."

All human beings, by their innate nature, have access to the universal source of inspiration and creative ideas. Everyday thoughts are like a fog seen from a distance. They view life from a vantage point far removed from the ultimate source...

Inspired thoughts are like a view close-up. The view is close to the source of life because the inspired poet's awareness has temporarily expanded to a fundamental level. So the poet, inspired people and mystics see closely into the fundamental nature and that enables them to describe it vividly.

Ralph Waldo Emerson, in his essay "The Poet" points out to the poetical source of inspiration:

"It is a secret which every intellectual man quickly learns, that beyond the energy of his possessed and conscious intellect, he is capable of a new energy - as of an intellect doubled on itself by abandonment to the nature of things. That beside his privacy of power as an individual man there is a great public power on which he can draw by unlocking at all risks his human doors, and suffering the ethereal tides to roll and circulate through him; then he is caught up into the life of the Universe . . ."

In my research I found many valuable ideas and unusual data. A magical spell is believed to be a primeval text which somehow came into being side by side with animals and plants, with winds and waves, with human disease and happiness, human courage and human frailty. They are not uttered to carry ordinary information from man to man. The natives of primitive tribes might naturally expect all such words to be very mysterious and far removed from ordinary speech.

Because there is a definite mysterious connection between words and the things they stand for, if you can name it, you can control it. Throughout the Ancient Near and Far East this important principle of magic predominates: the knowledge of the name of a thing is the same as knowledge of that thing. What follows is this: By naming, one can control what is named, be they Deities, Guardian Angels or Demons and others evil intelligences, in order to exorcise and dispel them. This aspect of the sacred word is even evident in several ancient myths in which a goddess must get the secret name from a god in order to achieve her desired goal.

Some primitive people have two names. One is their everyday name, which they use in communication with their group. The other is their "true name", which they keep in secrecy. If one discovers the true name of a man, he gets the power over him and possibility to inflict pain and misfortune to him.

Members of some tribes in New Guinea use special kinds of stories, called Kuquanebu to influence nature and insure a good crop. They greatly depend on climate. Therefore, in the times of monsoons, storytellers go from village to village telling stories, believing that such stories have a very beneficial influence on the crop.

People usually come to magical thinking trying to explain things which science did not explain or when they try to control things and phenomena which science is not able to control. A good example is given by E.E. Evans-Prichard in his book <u>Witchcraft, Oracles and Magic Among Azande</u>. Members of that tribe said to him that the roof of a house fell down on a specific person because another person cast magical spells on him. They accepted "the scientific explanation" for the falling of the roof, that termites ate supporting pillars of the fallen roof, but they insisted that scientific explanation couldn't explain why the roof fell down in a definite moment, when that man was taking rest in his home. From the standpoint of the practitioner, magic explains that which science calls coincidence.

Data, which I have been collecting for a long time, accumulated some energy and in one moment there happened a quantum jump as with an electrical spark and a new revelation appeared. I was strongly impressed by the thought that nations, which lost their language, vanished from existence. It brought me to the creation of the method of **Verbal Reduction and Expansion (VRE)**. Its basic idea was my own discovery that **with the reduction and vanishing of the words with which we describe a problem that problem simultaneously vanishes**.

Many other realizations from my practice supported it. For example, if during Deep PEAT one experiences the neutralization of Primordial Polarities (Primes) and the Processor indicates incorrect labels for the Client's Primes to him, even if they are very similar to the true ones, often the Client will experience feelings of uneasiness, nervousness and dissatisfaction. It happens very often. If words had no innate power, this would not happen. But they have it, they are not just an assembly of sounds, and they are creative elements of our subjective universe.

Much research data I had to throw away, but some was very fruitful. Based on research and my experiments I created those two very rapid, simple and elegant methods. The basic and starting idea of **Verbal Reduction and Expansion (VRE)** is this: **If we put our thoughts, emotions and other elements of our psychic life into words, we start to create our reality. When we change those words in a specific way, as VRE method demands, we change our reality!**

As I already said, **Inner Magic of Words** embraces these two methods which I developed so far. I say this because this is a field with great potential, so new methods and techniques will surely be created soon.

Ivana End of Words (IEW)

My daughter Ivana sent me an e-mail from Japan, where she used to live, asking me if a variant of DP3 was the method she started to use. And she gave me the description of that method. It was similar to DP3, but it was a new contribution. The end phenomenon of that method was that a Client would become speechless, would not be able to find words for his/her problem and the problem would vanish as well. So I called this method **Ivana End of Words** (IEW).

I checked the method and I polished it. I found the explanation for its efficiency in the Bible. Practicing PEAT for almost 6 years and finding out a great number of different Primordial Polarities, I had been suspecting for a long time that there exists Primes characteristic for the whole human race. And I found them in the beginning of the Bible. They are the most fundamental polarities for the human being: Good and Bad. These two concepts are ingrained in our beliefs, values, and perspectives on life. Since time immemorial, humans have categorized things as good or bad.

Knowledge of good and evil is the source of the biggest confusion, resentment and anger that exists. We have created conflicts and wars over a belief that we were right and the other wrong. Whole cultures have been annihilated because their way of life or their beliefs were not considered "good" or "right" by those who had more power. The belief that something is good or bad has created more misery on this planet than anything else. It is quite natural if you remember that your personal Codes, your Primordial Polarities, created the worst misery for you at the individual level. **One of the important moments in your Spiritual evolution is the**

Neutralization of Primordial Polarities, using the Deep PEAT method.

The account of man's trial in the Bible is exceedingly brief and simple. It was written that "the tree of the knowledge of good and evil" had been placed "in the midst of the Garden of Eden," and of the fruit of this tree God forbade Adam to eat, threatening him with death. But the serpent, which suddenly appears in the Garden of Eden, said to Eve, *"You will not die. For God knows that when you eat of it your eyes will be opened, and you will be like God, knowing good and evil."*

The temptation did not last for long. The tempter deceived Eve as to the real consequences of eating the forbidden fruit. This led Eve first to eat, and then to induce Adam to eat as well. Their sin had immediately bad consequence. Now their eyes were opened, as the serpent had promised, "to know good and evil." Now comes a very strange happening. Speaking of himself in plural, Lord God said: *"Behold, the man has become like one of us, knowing good and evil."*

The Procedure of IEW

Begin by asking what problem the client would like to solve. Ask the client to describe his unwanted situation. Let him/her briefly elaborate on the problem. Do not accept as a problem an "objective" state, the reaction or emotion which a Client experiences about it is the problem. For example, *"I am without a job"* is not the problem, but rather how I feel about being without a job is the problem.

It is necessary to explain that there is always something good in every situation and vice versa. If a Client is not able to see the positive side in any unwanted state, then don't try to apply this method. It will not work for that person.

The Processor could elaborate about this situation a little bit. For example, he can say to the Client something like this: *"You see, even when a close relative dies, there is something good in such an unhappy experience - the person will become more independent, will stand on his own legs and take more responsibility for oneself."*

Alternate between good and bad:

"Tell me what is bad about (the problem)."

"Tell me what is good about (the problem)."

The "end phenomenon" happens usually very quickly - the Client is left speechless. He/she says, *"I can't find any more words."* Then the Processor should ask: *"What is the matter with the problem we started from? Do you still feel it as a problem?"*

There should be no problem left. The Client would say, *"No, there is no problem, or I don't feel it as a problem, or, it seems unreal to me"* etc.

If the problem changes, then start a process with the new problem. If others are involved, do circular processing from the relative points of view.

That good and bad are fundamental Primordial Polarities or Primes for the whole of humanity, I offer the proof that any other pair of polarities used with the IEW procedure will take a longer time to handle. Cause and effect may also work well, but they will take longer.

People are very often surprised with the quick and positive results of this process. Here are some reports that people sent to me. I avoid processing people by phone, but the first one that I did was Antonio Miklavc from Udine, Italy. He wrote:

> "… Magical Zivorad, as efficient as always, in a few minutes he made me find out that I am playing with my life as if it was a movie. Feeling 'I am old, years are passing and I will be dead anyway' kept me away from feeling the juice of life. This new 'No words' technique is great. And quick. No more playing around with mind, you get to the point."

Another person was Bojana, PEAT Trainer, and Practitioner of Memento. I processed her via phone as well:

> "Last night Zivorad called me on the phone and asked if I had 5 minutes. I had. He told me to sit down for we are going to try a new thing. He never processed me by phone but I was willing to try anything he invented. He asked me, if I had any problem and I said I have. In some 5 minutes my problem vanished and I stayed wordless. The thing was my fascination with death. I don't have it anymore and I am feeling fine."

My daughter Ivana, the original creator of this system, applies it fairly often. She usually gets quite different results compared with other people. Reasons for this are not very clear. Perhaps the longer practice of this method will give to other people similar results. This is one of the reports Ivana sent to me:

"Today I did this process and it went fantastic way. In last period whenever I applied it I come to the void and to the insight that this world is just illusion. Also that I have created that illusion to be able to experience those emotions belonging to it. Almost all processing around me are some light beings (or white beings) - I called them so. Very often my merging with light beings brings me to the insight that I myself am the light being. These light beings are around me, helping me to pass through those experiences, accept me whatever I'm doing and their acceptance I feel as an incredible help. I think I'm approaching the time when I will be able to communicate with them fully. It's interesting that today, instead of that usual experience, I got the complete void, but in the form of energetic net which was all involving and all penetrating. My body vanished in one moment and I was able to see around me sparkling around me and inside of me."

Verbal Reduction & Expansion (VRE)

To begin this process the processor should briefly describe the process to the client.

Then the processor asks the client to describe his unwanted situation in a couple of minutes. Ask him to briefly elaborate on the problem. Again, it is most important not to accept any "objective" state as a problem, but to focus on the reaction or emotion the client has about the problem. For example, "My mother-in-law is a bitch" is not the problem, and the process cannot handle it. The problem is the client's reaction or feeling about the mother-in-law.

Reduction

Don't discuss the starting problem. Instead elicit from the client four sentences by asking, *"Describe to me your present state (or situation), how you feel about the situation, in four short, concise sentences. Write these sentences down."*

As the client writes the sentence the processor also writes them down.
Have the client close their eyes. Read the four sentences to the client.
Then ask what images, thoughts, emotions and sensations are present. Record these elements.

Again, don't mention the starting problem. Instead say, *"Describe to me your present state (or situation, how you feel about the situation, in three short, concise sentences. Write these sentences down."*

Write the sentences down yourself.

Have the client close their eyes. Read the three sentences to the client.

Ask what images, thoughts, emotions and sensations are present. Record these elements.

Again don't mention the starting problem. *"Describe to me your present state (or situation), how you feel about the situation, in two short, concise sentences. Write these sentences down."*

Write them down yourself.

Have the client close their eyes. Read the two sentences to the client.

Ask what images, thoughts, emotions and sensations are present, if any. Record these elements.

Don't mention the starting problem. *"Describe to me your present state (or situation), how you feel about the situation, in one short, concise sentence. Write this sentence down."*

Write the sentence down yourself.

Have the client close their eyes. Read the sentence to the client.

Ask if there are any images, thoughts, emotions or sensations present. Record these elements.

Don't mention the starting problem. *"Now tell me how you feel in only one word or one concept. Write this word or concept down." Write it down yourself."*

Write the word down yourself.

Have the client close their eyes. Read the word or concept to the client.

Ask if there are any images, thoughts, emotions or sensations present. Record these elements.

Expansion

During expansion if there is a charge with any aspect, (image, thought, emotion, sensation) record the elements and tell the client to simply accept it as a part of life. These elements may disappear as the process progresses.

Ask, *"How do you feel about your situation now? Tell me how you feel in one sentence. Write this sentence down."*

Write it down yourself.

Have the client close their eyes. Read the sentence to the client.

"How do you feel about your situation now? Tell me how you feel in two sentences. Write these sentences down."

Write them down yourself.

Have the client close their eyes. Read the sentences to the client.

"How do you feel about your situation now? Tell me how you feel in three sentences. Write these sentences down."

Write them down yourself.

Have the client close their eyes. Read the sentences to the client.

"How do you feel about your situation now? Tell me how you feel in four sentences. Write these sentences down."

Write them down yourself.

Have the client close their eyes. Read the sentences to the client.

"How do you feel about your situation now?"

Things to Look for in this Process

The problem could vanish in any phase of Verbal Reduction or Expansion. Usually it vanishes during Reduction.

As the process progresses, elements of experience (image, emotion, sensation, thought) may not be present. If one of the elements is not present simply move on to the next element.

In the phase of **Verbal Expansion** positive emotions normally become stronger and they sometimes are transformed to a mild euphoria. At the end of the process it is advisable to apply the expansion procedure. This will stabilize positive feelings in place of the problem (see Expansion Procedure in the text of the Holographic process.)

Be careful to stop the process at any point where an optimal reaction occurs. It could happen at any point of the process, on two sentences, one, or on the single word. To continue after the optimal point would be overrunning and it would have the negative effect. What would happen in such situation is this: Using this process, in one moment you would pull your client out of the unwanted state and he would feel released and liberated. If you continue doing the process and you overrun it, you could push him back into an unwanted state. If you bypass the optimal point of the process, the result could be similar to overeating. The client was hungry and he ate. At a certain point he felt good. If we continue feeding him, he will soon feel sick. From the optimal point you don't continue the process.

In the majority of methods we do not want to leave a vacuum in the place where a problem used to be. This is because the vacuum has a tendency to suck a similar problem into it, and the experience of a problem returns. Therefore we do the installation of a positive state in its place, or we fill the empty space with the light, which is the most simple procedure. In the **VRE** this filling in of the empty space is not necessary, because in the phase of expansion we automatically fill the vacuum with positive contents.

Result for both of these processes are surprisingly good, sometimes almost miraculous.

Observations

When working with clients with very difficult problems and with depressive people we need to start with 5 or 6 sentences.

Zeljko Radjen, a computer specialist posted on the list this report:

"For long time I am on this list but hope you will forgive me because I waited so long to introduce myself. My name is Zeljko, age of 29, living in Belgrade. For years I am interested in spiritual practice and my first book with which I started was Zivorad`s "Keys of Psychic Magic". From that time I passed many other and important processes as member of Omega group. I would like to share with you all my experience with this new, easy but very efficient process Zivorad mentioned in mail bellow. For a long time after my Primes neutralization did not have any major problems and only thing what was bothering me last couple of days is strange tiredness after

coming home from my work. When I come yesterday to Zivorad I did not have any idea that it is possible at all to solve this except to take good, nice vacation. And than Zivorad solved my problem for couple of minutes. It is almost unbelievable that one so simple process can be so efficient. At the end I was feeling as new, full of energy and when I went home I cleaned snow in front of my building for full two hours alone without stopping. Today I am planning some creative things to start at my work, and as process in one of its stages finish with one sentence I will do the same: After this I fill GREAT!"

The following example presents another typical example of solving a problem with **VRE** method. The client was a woman who has had financial difficulties for much of her life. This problem persisted.

Here are her sentences and process:

Reduction:

Four sentences: *Day after day my problem with money keeps coming. Often it seems to be unsolvable. If there is a solution, it is transient. Financially I'm insecure.*
Image picture: Empty space
Emotion: Feeling of powerlessness
Body sensation: Heart beating
Thought: Perhaps one day it will be better.

Three sentences: *I'm financially insecure. The problem can't be solved easily. I think it will be better.*
Image picture: (none)
Emotion: I'm much calmer than a few moments ago.
Body sensation: I'm almost completely relaxed.

Thought: The problem will be solved for sure.

Two sentences: *It seems strange, but the problem is solvable. It will be solved for sure.*
Image picture: (none)
Emotion: (none)
Body sensation: (none)
Thought: Some indefinite positive thought

One sentence: *This problem is absolutely solvable.*
Image picture: As if something inside of me breaks out on the surface
Emotion: Calmness
Body sensation: Relaxation, no more tension
Thought: (none)
One word: *Calmness*

In the state of calmness there are no other elements. No thought, no other emotions, no body sensations.

The processor asks: "How is the problem we started from? " *"There is no problem!"*

Because money is one of the dominant problems in contemporary society, I quote here notes from another process of this kind. The client is Zoran, a young man but an experienced processor from Zagreb, Croatia. The process lasted only 12 minutes. Pay attention how this client changed an "objective" situation into a subjective one.

Problem: Anger, frustration and dissatisfaction with himself because of his bad financial situation.
Reduction:

Four sentences: *I'm angry because I'm in such a situation. I feel powerless. Taxes irritate me. I feel a lack of understanding of my surroundings.*
Image: Just red specks in front of my eye
Emotion: A mixture of sadness and anger
Body Sensation: Irritation in eye lids and in my throat
Thought: Will the end of this state come?

Three sentences: *Life is unjust. I am the fool. Even the fool is sometimes lucky.*
Image: Bills which should be paid on the table.
Emotion: All this make me sick.
Body sensation: My body is rigid as a stone. I have an urge to vomit.
Thought: Only God can help me.

Two sentences: *I allowed this to happen. There is a hope.*
Image: Image of a green meadow
Emotion: A kind of positive excitement
Body sensation: A pleasant feeling in my body
Thought: (none)

One sentence: *I am the master of my life.*
Image: Image of a band connecting my "I" here and another "I" in some other universe
Emotion: Feeling of my own presence as the miracle of God
Body sensation: (none)
Thought: (none)
One word: Peace

Expansion
One sentence: *All is OK.*
Two sentences: *All is OK. I can do it.*
Three sentences: *I don't know why this was a problem for me? Everything is in my own hands. God loves me.*

Zoran's process ends here.

Pay attention to the following. If these two people want to have permanent good results and change of their financial situation it is necessary for them to create good identities in themselves. Without that, this process would undoubtedly have good effects, but they would be transient.

After the workshop, Zoran sent this report to our discussion group:

"Dear Group, as many of you know Zivo and Alda were in Croatia last week. I attended 'Inner Magic of Words' workshop on Sunday. Although I'm not a newbie in practical spirituality, the experience was quite 'miraculous' and eye-opening. During the workshop Zivo asked if anyone is willing to be a subject for demonstration. I step up and we started. The 'money problems' was the topic I choose because this is a very real problem since I live in a country which is in a state of deep economic turmoil, to put it lightly. When Zivo started I was feeling 'low' and 'bleak'. But not for long. Suddenly my perception of 'my problem' and 'my situation' changed. Where there was once fear and dread, now was the feeling of lightness, deep & profound peace and also the sudden burst of energy & optimism! What was really amazing is the fact that the entire 'session' lasted only twelve minutes!

That was not 'just my case' - the whole group had similar experiences. Yesterday, I tried to 'digest' all that happened but I'm still feeling high. Somehow, I know that everything will be ok. That is really a relief since I was rather depressed about finances lately. And, as everyone knows, when you're 'full of it' it's not easy to be efficient and focused.

Also, during the last 48 hours I received some important calls & e-mails concerning my business, which gave me another 'proof'. Also, the ability for 'creative problem solving' became much stronger and I had some good ideas which I'm planning to try in the months ahead.

Judging from this experience, the 'Inner Magic of Words' has tremendous potential no matter if you work with clients or with your own issues. To put it in short, 'Inner Magic of Words' is real magic."

In some processes, when we do **Verbal Reduction** to one word, it seems the problem has not vanished. But if we continue the other phase, **Verbal Expansion**, the problem will vanish. Here is one such example.

Problem: The client was almost 70 years of age. She complained that she gets tired quickly and is not able to do the usual activities. The process went this way:

Reduction
Four sentences: *I get tired very quickly. I am not able to do things which I would like. It causes my depression. As a matter of fact I can do very little.*
Image: I see myself in my kitchen.
Emotion: I feel empty.
Body Sensation: My body is exhausted.

Thought: Old age is boring.

Three sentences: *I can do very little. I can't fight tiredness. I'm not able to do anything.*
Image: I see myself sitting, tired.
Emotion: Depression
Body Sensation: Heaviness in my body
Thought: There is no exit out of the situation.

Two sentences: *I can hardly move my hand. I'm unsatisfied because I can't do things I would like.*
Image: Dust on the table
Emotion: Apathy
Body sensation: I grit my teeth.
Thought: It will be worse and worse.

One sentence: *I feel hopeless because of my powerlessness*
Image: (none)
Emotion: I feel fear to become unable to take care of myself
Body sensation: Vibrations in my body
Thought: (none)

One word: *Collapse*
Thought: This is the end.
(There were no other elements.)

Expansion:
One sentence: *Everything is collapsing down.*
Image: Everything is gray
Emotion: Indifference
Body sensation: Relaxation

Thought: Then what?

Two sentences: *I get tired anyway. Such is the life.* Everything is empty. There are no elements.

Three sentences: *That is life. I accept it completely. I feel satisfied because I accept life.*

Four sentences: *I feel satisfaction and energy. The energy becomes more and more strong. I feel deep satisfaction and self-confidence. I'm stronger than I think*

The Processor asks: "What's about the problem? Is it still a problem for you?"
The client answers: *What problem? It was my game. Now it is over!*

In this case the problem did not vanish when the client came to one word. The problem vanished during **Verbal Expansion**, on "two sentences." But in the majority of cases positive states appear earlier, and they are often strong and evident. It happens especially when the problem concerns relationships.

What follows is a typical example. The client, a 21 year old girl, complains about her younger sister, Ana. Ana is 12 years old and her behavior is typical for adolescents: she opposes her parents aggressively, criticizes all family members, cuts short communications of others etc. The process went this way:

Reduction:

Four sentences: *Ana makes me nervous. Her behavior makes me nervous. Her presence is unpleasant to me. I can't listen to her impudent words.*
Image: Two of us standing on opposite sides of the living room
Emotion: Nervousness and intolerance
Body sensation: Trembling in my solar plexus
Thought: She should shut up.

Three sentences: *Ana makes me nervous. I dislike her talking. I love Ana.*
Image: Ana and I sit and talk.
Emotion: Some emotional closeness and love
Body sensation: Some warm feeling in my body
Thought: (none)

Two sentences: *I like when I'm with Ana. Sometimes it is strenuous.*
Image: Two of us sit close to each other
Emotion: Calmness and love
Body sensation: I am fulfilled inside
Thought: (none)

One sentence: *I like when Ana kisses me.*
Image: Ana and I sitting close to each other
Emotion: Love
Body sensation: (none)
Thought: (none)

One word: *Love*

The Expansion sentences are missing in this process. At the end of the Reduction, the client feels love all the time, everything else is empty. She says: *"I've got nothing more to say. There is only love."* She was extremely surprised with the unfolding of the process. To her great wonder the image of their relationship changed as if she had viewed it in a short movie. In the beginning she and younger sister are on two distant parts of the room. Then they are seated on the couch closer and finally they sit close to each other. Emotions simultaneously change. Animosity changes to love, and love becomes stronger and more all-embracing.

In this case, when the client said "I've *got nothing more to tell. Love, that's all"*, the processor did well not to insist on **Verbal Expansion**. In this situation it would be over-running or exaggerating. This way the processor left the client filled with love. At the end point he applied the procedure of expansion (spreading the feeling of love to all 6 directions) and that way made possible for her to enter into Pleroma state close to "cosmic love".

Here are some reports from people experiencing this method.

What follows is the report of one of my clients who posted on our discussion list. Serge (Srdjan) Jovanovic, a professional basketball player wrote of his experience with VRE:

> *"My name is Serge. I am 29 and come from Belgrade. I have just finished 10 days of computer lessons, opened my e-mail and I am very happy that finally I can take a part in this forum. I would like to talk about interesting events and experience after I met Mr. Slavinski. I could write for hours because I passed Peat, DP3 and I learned how to use*

JI Dzing, but the main reason of my writing is yesterday's great new experience that I had with a new Slavinski's system - VERBAL REDUCTION. By the way, I am a basketball player and my problem was my relationship with my manager. I had a bad feeling about him and our collaboration. But with VERBAL REDUCTION we successfully solved my problem in less then 10 minutes! At the end my problem was funny to me and I felt very happy and full of positive energy. I could not wait to see my manager again and to talk to him about my future. Finally I saw him yesterday and we had a very friendly conversation. Much, much better then the last couple of years. At this moment I would like to say once again THANK YOU to Mr.Slavinski and his wife Jadranka for the help they gave me in resolving my problems and for everything they taught."

A few days latter Srdjan Jovanovic posted a new report:

"One more time a sensational thing has happened. A few days ago I did "End of Words" with Zivorad about a problem with my ex team. For more than 2 years they owed me large sum of money. I could not collect my debt without going to court. But, just 2 days after I finished Zivorad's "End of Words", my lawyer called me and told me that finally money was paid. I am so happy, that we solved my problem successfully in such short time. Once again thank you Zivo, and best regards to all members."

Although this method is very simple, it is possible to handle very difficult problems with it. It can be used with chronic problems, persisting for years. Here I will quote notes from the process of a young man who felt his situation was without solution. A few years ago his father became a serious alcoholic. Since that time the father had been abusing the client's mother, getting into many affairs with problematic women and acquiring debts that his son had to repay.

Problem: Pay attention to this: His problem, of course, was not his father (this was an objective situation), but feelings and the reactions to father's behavior that he had in that situation. His feelings in the situation were a very strong emotion of powerlessness and a fear that, in his rage, he could injure his father. These are notes from his session:

Reduction
Four sentences: *I feel fear that father will have a stroke. I feel fear of what will happen with my mother. Father will ruin us with his debts. I will do some crazy thing because of his behavior*
Image: Father lying in the bed
Emotion: Some indefinite fear
Body sensation: Feeling of shivering in the body
Thought: Our whole life is purely miserable.

Three sentences: *I feel fear for father's health. I feel fear for my mother. I feel love for my father.*
Image: Same image, father lying in the bed
Emotion: I feel overpowering love for my father.
Body sensation: A tension in my body
Thought: (none)

Two sentences: *I feel fear for father's health. I feel fear for my mother.*
Image: Two of them together.
Emotion: I feel simultaneously fear and love for them
Body sensation: (none)
Thought: (none)

One sentence: *I feel a strong communal spirit of our family.*
Image: A picture from my childhood comes to me
Emotion: Love
Body sensation: (none)
Thought: (none)

One word: *Family*
Image: A picture of four of us together
Emotion: Love
Body sensation: (none)
Thought: (none)

<u>Expansion:</u>
One sentence: *I feel togetherness, relaxation and peace.*

After that sentence the client said there was nothing else, just repeating of the previous sentence. The Verbal Expansion phase was stopped and the expansion procedure was applied.

When asked what had happened to his problem, the client answered: *"It seems to me far away and unreal."*

Be careful! In a situation like this it is necessary to apply circular processing from father's view point (for sure) and probably from mother's and sister's as well if there is a charge on them.

Possible Mistakes in the Application of these Two Methods

Concerning the **"Inner Magic of Words"** you should be careful not to make these commonly occurring mistakes:

1. As was said before, but is repeated here because it is important: Never take any objective situation as a problem, but take the reaction a client has. For example, never accept as a problem, "I am unemployed," or "My mother in law is a bad person". With a couple of questions the processor can shift the statement to the subjective. For example you might ask: "What do you feel because you are unemployed?" or "What do you feel toward your mother-in-law?" or "What is your reaction toward that person?"

2. Some processors begin very well, but during the process they slip bit by bit toward "objective" attitude, instead the "subjective" one. Keep the focus on the client's subjective experience.

3. The problem must be clearly defined in the beginning. An indefinite description of the problem will lead to indefinite and foggy results, rather than concrete results. For example, the client gives us the following problem: "Sadness because I can't help my sister." During a short discussion before the process, the new and much deeper and stronger problem appears: the fear of people (criminals) who threaten his sister and

her children because of money her late husband owes them and also the fear that those people could hurt his own children and him.

4. It is a common mistake during the process to turn from the beginning problem to a similar one. Although the problems could be similar, they are two different problems. To get the most efficient solution we must handle them one at a time, doing a separate process for each problem.

5. If a Processor teaches these two methods, one after another, he/she should always start with **IEW** and after it apply **VRE**. If you do first **Verbal Reduction and Expansion** and after that **Ivana End of Words**, there will be a dropping down effect, too much satiation and possibly a mild disappointment.

6. With an experienced person you can apply **VRE** at once without any preparation. But with an inexperienced person you should first do a couple of exercises in accepting unpleasant experience - all 4 elements, one by one (in **VRE**). Otherwise the inexperienced person won't accept and report unpleasant elements (some or all of them). If there is any kind of resistance the problem will persist and there won't be positive results at the end.

Possibilities for Application of VRE

It is hard to tell what the limits of application are for these two methods. As processors experiment with them they will evidently go on developing and we will have new fields of application. Some people have experiences in areas that I have not even tried to apply them myself. For example, Antonio Frontini, from Luciana, Italy, posted on our List:

> *"For the VRE I had a chance to use it with a client that has speech difficulties. It was very quick and amazing and I think it's best quality is that it gives the client a chance to acknowledge without doubt the changes in the status of the starting problem."*

Another possibility is the application of **VRE** on changing traumatic memories. In this process we not only make a traumatic situation vanish from the mind, but we change it substantially. In other words, at the end of the process instead of trauma we have positive, resourceful experience. I personally tried this and the results were extremely good.

For example, a young man reported as one of his most traumatic situations his experience of being punished by his father in his childhood. His father was a very rigid and rude man. The client did something that made his father mad and in front of the boy's mother the father beat the boy badly. As a young man, now in his late twenties, he remembered that experience with unpleasant and uneasy feelings. And he remembered it very often.

We did **VRE** on that trauma and the situation developed amazingly. In the first 4 sentences we see the whole traumatic situation and the boy is suffering not only because of physical pain, but because his mother is forced to be present and to watch what is happening. But the original scene changes very quickly, becoming more and more positive. At the end, all three of them are standing and hugging each other, father and mother are full of love. "Love" is the last word and the dominating emotion. We can say with the certainty, with Spiritual Technology it's never too late to have a happy childhood.

21

THE SHADOW AND ITS INTEGRATION

On the path of self-realization, especially during processing, sooner or later a practitioner must confront his shadow. In contemporary psychotherapy K.G. Jung was the first to introduce this term and many systems of humanistic and transpersonal psychology took it over from him. So today it is widely accepted.

However, long before Jung, some thinkers knew about shadow under other terms. More important, they knew about the necessity of integration of fragmented parts suppressed into the shadow if one wanted to attain the wholeness of own being. In the hermetism of the 20th century this was called the Guardian of the Threshold and it was considered to lurk in the darkened zones of the being, contained in a kind of psychological cellar. There are interwoven fragmented parts, suppressed sub personalities, rejected aspects, archetypal pictures, long-forgotten childish fears, unacceptable incestuous desires and deep hatred and animosities. Wanting to attain their own goals, each of those parts fights for the attention of the person, no matter how unacceptable for the conscious "I" those goals may be.

As the physical shadow follows our body, so the psychological shadow follows our conscious being. Although it is buried alive in our unconsciousness, it is ready to be resurrected in unexpected moments. We push it into unconsciousness because we feel it is dangerous and destructive for us. But we attempt to suppress its existence and resist it in vain. We can only integrate it in our conscious "I."

The shadow starts to form in the first stage of individual development and its genesis is necessary for the integration and socialization of a young individual. We are constantly exposed to the influence of opposing forces. Confronted with them, our Ego identifies with good, noble and creative polarities and at the same time buries the dark side of our being into unconsciousness so that we are not forced to see it and confront with it. Therefore Ego makes itself idealized and cuts itself off from the negative side of the being. De-identifying from the negative side of polar opposites, our Ego creates a split in the core of our being. The suppressed part is pushed into the psychological underground, where it lives an independent life, trying constantly to break out to the light of consciousness.

Activities of a split off part have destructive results for us and for our surroundings as well. In time, like a steam boiler with a hot steam, the pressure in the split off part becomes stronger. When it gets to the critical point it breaks out on the surface of consciousness like a volcano eruption, causing emotional problems, neurotic symptoms, negative, destructive and chaotic behavior. Often such a split creates a visibly divided personality, which R.L.Stevenson masterly described in his novel as Dr. Jekyll and Mr.Hyde. In such situations two personalities of the same person, unknown to each other, live together with alternating domination.

Constantly trying to set themselves free from their shadows, people use the mechanism of projection. It is a defense mechanism in which the individual attributes to other people impulses, traits, and behavior that he himself has but cannot accept. It is especially likely to occur when the person lacks insight into his own impulses and traits. In the worst cases, people often identify with their nation, religion, or a group of any kind. Out of such identification come the usual and unhappy divisions of "we" and "they." The good, justice and truth are always on our side and on the other side are injustice, evil, and lies.

Many buried fragments are in irreconcilable conflict with other contents of the shadow or with the image we have about ourselves, which we hold out to the world and which we believe to be true. Such conflicts exhaust our energy. Therefore the task of a practitioner is to confront them as soon as possible and to make their tendencies and conflicts conscious. In that way the energy bound in them can be liberated and integrated into the conscious "I". The first step on that path is to get insight into one's own shadow. When a person becomes conscious of their bad emotions and tendencies, anger, envy, malice, greed and narcissistic attitudes, these qualities become diluted and lose their power. By confronting the shadow through the confrontation of the elements of which it consists, we dissolve those toxic emotions and behaviors and make them harmless and integrated.

Every time some conflict from our shadow is made conscious and released, its energy is set free. "I" becomes reorganized on the higher level of integration, so that such work truly represents movement up the path to greater and greater Spiritual freedom.

However, the shadow does not contain only our negative elements, but also positive ones which for many reasons we are not able to accept. In the shadow of every human being sleeps the poet, artist, philosopher or healer, and many of us fight with all our power against their manifestation in the light of consciousness.

The way to heal the Ego is not by investing in efforts to protect it from reality of the shadow, but to come face to face with its dark side. Reconciliation and reconnection with the split off shadow is the key element in psychological and Spiritual maturing. First, we must accept that it is a darkened part of our own being, not the evil part of others. Then we have to be able to integrate it into our self. Only with recognition and integration of the shadow we can become whole and integrated. That does not mean we will surrender to the evil part of our nature, because this would be again supporting opposing polarities. No, we should give up investment of our energy into the idealized image of our self and be able to manifest every behavior which is adequate in a given situation.

Seeing the shadow is a slippery ground, because we have a tendency to ignore its most unpleasant components. Some time ago I created the Magical Mirror, a practical method for integration of the shadow into the wholeness of the being. It is very simple. It is one application of **DP3**. Here it is.

Whenever we feel any aversion or a criticism toward any person or phenomenon in the outside world, we should understand that it is just the reflection of our inner parts. Somewhere inside of us exists that of which we are critical. In the first moment we may think it is impossible, but if we persist in looking, sooner or later we will be able to accept such an unpleasant truth. It is not easy to see the shadow at once, because it is antagonistic to the image we have about ourselves, the image which we show in our communication with the outer world.

No matter how unpleasant that process might be in the beginning, it helps us to go beyond shallow experience of our self into a deeper, more complete and more real experience. That way, instead of spending energy in its repression, we will set the shadow free and at the same time we will be more whole and more human. Recognizing unpleasant characteristics of others in ourselves, we will be more able to identify with other beings, and we will have much wider possibility of choice in our acting and feeling. We will exceed limitations which force us to divide the world into "I" and others, we and they, etc.

It is possible to work on the reintegration of the shadow as a definite exercise, even when initially we do not see anything bad about the other person. You should make an effort to find what you dislike about the other person. Just ask yourself: "What bothers me about this person?" For some time look for a critical content, even though it seems nothing about the other person bothers you. If even the smallest part exists in yourself, you will find it in another for sure!

The theoretical base of this procedure is simple and clear. We cannot see anything negative in people and the world except what exists in us, because the outer world reflects as a mirror our inner world. For a criminal, life is full of hatred and dangers. For him life is a game of winning over others and humiliating them so that you are not defeated and humiliated yourself. On the other hand, for a true saint everything is the God's grace, even life's phenomena which we fear.

This kind of understanding is the application of the basic axiom of the existence of two flows in the universe, which remind one of alternating electrical current. The highest reality is above and beyond this universe, and when it manifests on the physical plane of existence it appears necessarily as positive and negative polarity. Therefore, as long as anything exists in the world around us which disturbs us, which we are critical about, which we judge etc., we must accept that the same dark and negative side of our own nature exists, which is reflected back to us in the cosmic mirror.

The shadow is dangerous and destructive as long as it is ignored, suppressed and unconscious. True development is possible only through integration of opposites in our own being. Our goal is not to remove and destroy negative and evil components of our being, but to integrate them and bring them into balance. Thoughts and feelings which are not integrated and balanced with the opposite thoughts and feelings are distorted. They do not give us a true picture of the world and other beings in it.

Shadow Integration: The Magical Mirror

This process is a simple one, based on the application of **DP3**. If you have got a partner for co-processing, work with a partner. If you mastered self-processing with **DP3**, you can work alone. Just relax and concentrate your thoughts on a person. First, you should choose an unpleasant or repulsive person. Notice the behavior of that person which is to you unpleasant, repulsive, or disgusting. In other words notice that which you feel critical about. You take it for work even if it stimulates only a mild unpleasant reaction.

As soon as you notice such behavior or a characteristic of personality, define it as simply as you can, and put it down on paper. Then direct your attention inside of yourself, trying to find the similar behavior or personality feature in yourself, no matter when it happened. This element is important, because if you do not show such behavior now, it does not mean you did not express it before. Remember, in the shadow has repressed everything that has ever existed in you. Be patient during your search, and be sure the negative element exists in you. If it were not in you, you would not find it in the outer world. When you find it, even in a little measure, do the **DP3** this way:

The first terminal is a person who manifests behavior which of which you are critical. Focus on a specific moment when the person expresses this behavior. (there are moments when the person does not express it). The second terminal is you in the situation when you manifested same or similar behavior.

When, after adequate application of **DP3** on both terminals only emptiness is left, ask yourself (or ask your client if you are processing another person): "What do I feel now toward the behavior of that person? Am I still critical?" Of course, the process is finished when you (or the client) do not feel the critical feeling. There could be some variant of such an answer, for example, "I think such behavior is not OK, but I don't care about it", or "We all have some hang-ups" and similar statements.

You should do this process with a few persons who disturb you with their behavior, speech or even outer appearance. Then pass to a higher level: Choose a person you feel neutral about, or even feel some positive emotions. Now you will need more time to find characteristics that disturb you, but be persistent. As soon as you find something, redirect your attention toward yourself and find such elements inside, either in present or in past time. You will find what you are looking for sooner or later.

What follows is the systematic method for the clearing of the shadow. The previous one was based on your temporary feelings, or was caused by temporary problems you are having with some person. This is a more thorough clearing. Here is what you are going to do next.

Tell your client: "Practice shows us that the three main spheres where human beings engage their attention and energy are 1) sex, love and emotional relationships, 2) power and status in the society and 3) properties and money. Now we are going to clear those spheres:

1. "In sex, love and emotional relationship in general, what are you critical about in some people?"

Go from one to another person, applying the described process, until you exhaust that area. Then pass on the other area:

2. "In the areas of power and status, what are you critical of in some people?"

You can divide one complex area into components. For example, you can ask first about love, then sex and emotional relationship last. Also, you don't have to exhaust one area completely. You can do one process on emotional relationships, then another for money and properties, then power and social status.

Return to Oneness

The next step in the integration of the shadow is searching for behavior that you are critical about on all dynamisms or spheres of activity. In the DP3 section I described the work with spheres of activity. There are 8 spheres. The procedure just described includes the **first sphere of activity or the first dynamism**. Then continue from the second one to the eighth.

Second sphere of activity: Concentrate your attention on your emotional partner or your family as one unit and search for something you are critical about. It could be anything: the way someone speaks or looks, how members of your family treat each other, their attitude toward people outside of their circle...anything. As soon as you find something, turn your attention inward and find the reflection of that defect in yourself. Now the two terminals where you are applying DP3 are: your emotional partner or your family as an unit and you (in situation when you express that what you are critical about them).

Third sphere of activity: Again you are one terminal, and the second terminal is some group you belong to. In the process you treat that group like a unit. It could be professional, religious or national group, sport club, group of people you are relating in your free time...any kind of group. Do DP3 on them in the usual way.

Fourth sphere of activity: Now, the second terminal opposing you is the whole of humanity. I should remind you we are entering into spheres that have some noticeable philosophical elements. You should concentrate on that which you dislike in the whole of humanity as an unit. Do not accept too quickly the conclusion that nothing disturbs you, that you feel just love and other elevated emotion for humanity. Such behavior is typical for some members of the New Age movement. If you carefully search for some dark spots, you will find them; for example, the tendency of humanity to create an evil for itself, the tendency for destructive behavior etc. You can notice that masses of humanity choose dishonest people for their political leaders who are often very popular etc. Or notice qualities of superficiality and selfishness as characteristic of human race, cruelty toward animals and similar behaviors. The process is the same as before.

Fifth sphere of activity: The dynamism dominant in this sphere expresses itself as the tendency to survival of all the living world, all alive beings. The first terminal is you again, and the second one is the whole alive world. Here again you should search for some elements you are critical about. We have a tendency to idealize the alive world, and we forget and suppress elements that disturb us or make us unhappy. For example, there is a lot of beauty in the world of animals, but sometimes we see on TV how animals kill weaker ones to eat them, or sometimes even kill their own young, or how members of the same kind fight to the death for females etc.

Sixth sphere of activity: This is area of survival through the physical, "not alive" universe. It seems to be inert, and it is not easy to find critical statements about it, but it is possible. One simple example: when people stumble on some stone in the darkness and injure themselves, often they feel a rage against it and even curse it as if it were alive. The story of Persian king Kserx is well known. When the stormy sea sank his fleet, he ordered his soldiers to whip the sea. You can also think about big disasters – volcano eruptions, tsunamis, floods in which thousands die: men, women, children. It is the destructive side of the physical universe, which probably you are not cool about.

Seventh sphere of activity: The dynamism of this sphere express itself as urge to survive as a Spiritual being. At first it is not easy to be critical. But perhaps we can think about other side of Spirituality in this dual universe, for example when a man, following the call of his higher being leaves his children and goes to a monastery.

Eighth sphere of activity: This concerns the survival through God or eternity. Some people will hesitate to find any fault with God, but if you remember hard situations from your life it will be clear to you that you have protested God's will. You asked yourself what bad did you do to get such harsh punishments, or you asked God why some children die in a terrible suffering, etc. Then you should turn your attention inside and remember when you yourself caused a suffering of some innocent being, etc.

If in any sphere of activity you are not able to find any reason for criticism, it is OK. You will find it later on for sure. Or perhaps you are a deeply enlightened mystic who sees in all phenomena of life, even extremely disturbing, just God's mercy? If you are such a one, good and fine. This book is not for you nor is any other book. But the rest of us should not be discouraged if now we are not well-polished diamonds in which only the grace of God is reflected. This experience belongs only to saints and great teachers. What is important is that we take this path and we know what is waiting for us at the end of it.

Meditate a bit about the following story. The King of one oriental country heard much contradictory information about the greatest painters in the world. Some people said Greeks were the best, and others said the same for the Chinese. The king was an art-lover and wanted to estimate personally who was the best, so he invited a group of the best painters from China and another group from Greece. Both groups he brought to a large hall in his court. He divided the hall with an opaque curtain and asked them to paint for the whole month on the wall of their part of the room and create the best picture they could.

The Greeks organized the job and incessantly painted for the whole month. At the end of that period the whole wall of their part of the hall was covered with an extremely beautiful picture of vivid colors, which seemed to be alive. The Chinese did not paint at all. They spent all time polishing their wall. They did it first with bare hands, then with linen rags and finally with soft silk. After one month their wall was as smooth as the finest mirror.

At the end of that month the king came with his escort and sat in a chair at the place where the curtain divided the hall and asked artists to remove the curtain. Then in great awe he became speechless. On both walls there was exactly the same beautiful picture, so that neither he nor his escort were able to tell on which wall was the picture and on which was its reflection.

22

LEFT HAND PATHS AND RIGHT HAND PATHS

Out of countless dualities in this world one pair of them serves as fundamental for two different paths to liberation. One is desire for vanishing or non-existence and other is desire for independent existence in the universe. They serve as the criterion for differentiation of Spiritual paths into two main groups, left hand paths and right hand paths.

The right hand path of austerity and renunciation, search's for knowledge of the universe and final Oneness with it, unity with the universe. The right hand path functions on the "out of sight out of mind" principle: by distancing oneself from all that is carnal and worldly, the adept is left free of addictions, compulsions and attachments to this house of glass that we call the world. Thus freed of the lusts of the flesh, the spiritual seeker's opportunity is greatly heightened to arrive at a state of spiritual enlightenment. In such unity, Self disappears. No matter if that unity is in the Christian mysticism, Buddhist nirvana or similar states, in all such systems the desire for Oneness with the universe in which the Self disappears is present.

Left hand paths search for self-knowledge rather than knowledge about the universe. If they look for knowledge about the universe, they search for the relationship of that knowledge to "I". In relationship to the universe "I" is more powerful and it is considered that "I" continues its independent existence after physical death. Everyone has their own personal evolution to experience, to open their mind in a way and form that makes sense only to oneself. You are a unique person. Not only will your evolution not make any sense to anyone else. It doesn't need to. The evolution is within. All healing, liberation, defeat and victory, takes place within. The outer is mere reflection.

The terms Left-hand Path and Right-hand Path come from ancient India. Left handed spiritual traditions are magic, Tantra, worshiping the Great Mother Goddess, Chaos magic, Shamanism, and different branches of Paganism. The typical Left-hand Path is Tantra (although there are Left and Right Tantra), and Right-hand Paths are all the rest of the Paths in Hindu tradition. Buddhism, which originated in India, uses the same terminology. Buddhist systems Hinayana and Mahayana gravitate to extinguishing "I" and its disappearing in nirvana. That process evidently is not the process of self-knowledge, but of disappearing from existence. On the other side, followers of systems such as Shingon in Japan and Scientology in the west search for the knowledge about oneself, so that man would become Buddha alive in this physical body. From that point of view the majority of world religions are Right-hand Paths, because followers experience themselves modestly and glorify the God. The Left-hand Paths do the opposite – they tend to the expansion of Self. They first bow to themselves, and then to any other God.

23

Caution with Depression

Practitioners of any kind of psychotherapy must be cautious with persons who permanently or from time to time suffer from depression. This is the main reason. Depression is a disorder responsible for about 60% of suicides. It occurs twice as often in women as in men. To be depressive is not the same as to be sad or discouraged. These feelings are inseparable part of normal life. Depression is a weakness, serious and hard which could destroy the life of a person suffering from it if the person does not get adequate help.

Depression may look and sound like deep sadness but it lasts longer and has a more profound impact on a person's life. If you're clinically depressed, you live in a state of sadness and hopelessness so severe that it makes normal activities seem impossible. You may lose interest in friends and relatives, hobbies, have suicidal thoughts very often. Suicide may seem to be the only solution for such an unbearable situation.

So a therapist must be careful in handling depressive clients. We meet them pretty often because whenever a person has a hard problem there is a tendency to become depressive. One should check whether such a person has a history of mental illness, a diagnosis, whether they are on medication, to see if their disturbance is a serious one. You see, all so-called "normal people" are depressive from time to time. But our concern should be for people who are seriously depressive. The reason is the possibility of suicide and all the problems that can emerge from such an occurrence.

I'm not going to give you here all details about depression, neither am I qualified to do that. The main point is that such people suffer in the extreme. Their agony is so unbearable that death seems to be the salvation for them.

So, I suggest to you that you avoid doing processes with such people until you have a really sound and long experience processing people. Even when you have long experience be very, very cautious! Before you start to process a depressive client, always ask for agreement from close relatives: marriage partner, parents, brothers and sisters. Also, ask a promise from the client that he/she won't do any harm to herself/himself as long as they are in the process of therapy with you and for a long period after it. It's advisable that the client gives you such a promise in front of other people, or that they give you a written obligation.

Processors are usually very happy when they have the first substantial success - the client goes out of depression, reports that they feel much better, expresses some kind of joy etc. Be careful !!! That's the most dangerous moment for the depressed client! Very often they commit suicide during that period!

Why? You see, they were depressive, and they did not have energy to do anything active. Even to move a little finger for them was unimaginable effort. Now they have a sudden upsurge of energy, and they are able to do something, even to suicide, which could be the fulfillment of their decision from a long time ago.

So, what can you do in such situation?

Return to Oneness

1. In the period of seeming recovery such a client should be under the strict observation of close people. Someone should always take care of them.

2. As soon as possible do the circular processing on him/her from all relevant points of view. That way they understand how their family and friends suffer because of them and what their suicide would do to people around them. It's extremely important to do the process from the point of view of the person who used to love them most of all (even if such person is not alive now).

3. Is advisable to tell them (if they already don't know) a short story and an explanation of reincarnation, to point out to them that human being who kills themselves has to be born again in the similar situation as it is now, but in even worse surroundings. So suicide is not the solution at all.

It is very important that such a client shows a strong intention to do some service for other people, either weak ones, or sick, or spiritually undeveloped etc. When they start doing it with full heart, you can relax. That's the sign of real recovery.

A healthy intake of the B-complex vitamins is important for anyone who wants to keep depression under control. While the whole B-complex apparently plays a role in keeping you emotionally and physically healthy, a few components seem to have particularly strong effects on depression.

Our observation is that with a small number of people, a depressive state can manifest after successful processes, especially after Deep PEAT. Out of many hundreds of cases I had only two or three such cases, but some processors have had more than that. Differing from the majority of therapists who think that depression is anger turned inside, or inability to express aggressiveness toward outer world, John Skaggs, a therapist from Kentucky, USA, has his own pretty original opinion about depression appearing after processing. I give here his experience, because it could be useful:

> *"I am a counseling psychologist and I regularly use a number of the processes Zivorad teaches in his workshops. In fact, I usually have too many things I can do, and then I have to decide which is most likely to be effective. I have had a number of clients describe a depression that occurs in the middle of a session or after a session when they have done some significant work with PEAT or other Spiritual Technology processes. To me depression is a dynamic process that is triggered by an inability to feel sadness. It is not anger turned inward. The sadness usually involves a loss of a part of the self, in other words, the shadow.. A person's shadow is formed early in life and we have little awareness of what we are missing. When people do good work with PEAT, they are able to recognize how they have limited their own lives and that recognition leads to sadness. When a client reports they are sad, I have learned to ask immediately what is "lacking" in their lives. Then I make the connection to how the recently accomplished work allows them to see they have a missing part.*
>
> *Once a client identifies the missing part, I ask for an image, thought, feeling and sensation that represents that part and then do shallow PEAT on it. The FAM I usually use is "Even though I have a missing part of*

myself that is represented by (image, thought, feeling, sensation), I fully....." Usually the sadness disappears with this intervention. If there is any opposition or a negative reaction I do deep PEAT 3 to neutralize it. Hopefully this helps, both to validate that depression and sadness is a typical reaction and that running shallow PEAT is a quick way to get past the sadness by neutralizing it."*

24

Duality in a Session

As long as we are human beings, we must have an Ego. It's our main instrument for surviving in this universe. It evaluates situations and tells us what is good or proper, what is safe or dangerous etc. But when we take a role of processor, Ego could be a very serious cause of all kinds of problems. Working from dualistic, ego-serving rather than truth-serving position, means working in the service of Spiritual separatism. Such an approach can damage both a client and a processor.

Let's take a look at two main elements of the processing situation: Ego and love. Their relationship greatly influences the end result of processing. There are many definitions of Ego, which I'm not going to explain here. The most important thing is to point out to two of Ego's main characteristics: separation from the rest of the world and an irresistible desire to exist. So, if a processor approaches a processing situation from an ego-serving attitude, he/she sees the client as an object in a dualistic situation. The client becomes the object of the therapist's personal desires: for power, for feeling good about himself, self-affirmation etc. Of course, such desires could seem to be noble, but they are burdened with a real danger of losing one's way.

Is there a means to correct such a situation? It is the emotion which we identify using the old fashioned word "LOVE." When I use this term, I do not mean love toward all people, all beings and the cosmos, which is mostly ungrounded. No, it is the concrete love for your client in the session. Why is that love for another the strong lever for the realization of a successful session? Because, love is the only emotion in which the well-being of another is more important that our own well- being.

When we love, our limits disappear, and we embrace another. Because limits disappear, separation from the rest of the world vanishes, separation from the client vanishes, and momentarily Ego disappears as well. True, Ego vanishes for a short period of time, but it's enough if it is absent during our PEAT session.

However, the processor should be always on guard, because Ego uses everything to survive and makes itself stronger. It is one's Ego that could distort love for the client into something personal and useful and make it again an object of its feeding. Thus love as a therapeutic means should be somehow impersonal, a love for anything and everything, which, just for a moment, is concentrated on the client.

25

"The Freedom For" and "The Freedom From"

Once more I will repeat that the main positive result of integration/neutralization of polarities reduces down to the concept of freedom. By integrating certain polarities we get freedom for a definite way of behavior and, at the same time, the freedom from it. One of my close associates, Vladimir Stojakovic, described such a result very well, so I have nothing to add to his description, which follows. I give it here with small changes:

The process of liberation of a human being can be seen from two points of view. One is energetic, other is behavioral. It concerns the behavior of a person who attained such a result. Energetically, we have two poles, plus and minus, and the tension between them, which comes from the difference of their energetic polarity. That charge is the reason why we are not able to see them as two sides of the same whole. When, during the processing we remove that charge and poles merge, unite and become one, they are integrated into the consciousness. In other words, they vanish into void, which is the true essence of human being. Then energy is set free and from that comes the feeling of relief and of higher energy after integration. Two opposing ideas are two sides of the same phenomenon.

Neutralization also affects behavior. Such an individual attains freedom of behavior. More then once I used an example the polarities of giving and receiving, and Vladimir also used it as a good example.

It is an experiential fact that some people give to others with ease, but they have a lot of problems in receiving – material goods, favors...anything. The other group has the opposite problem. They receive easily, but have difficulties giving to others. Evidently both groups have a problem because they are bogged down in one of the opposing polarities. In other words they have not got freedom. In life there are some situations when we should be able to give and situations when we should be able to receive. We should be free to give or receive and also have the freedom to not give and not receive.

It is the freedom to behave in harmony with our free decisions, not as our charge forces us to behave. This is the meaning of the expression freedom for something and freedom from something. Exactly that happens when polarities of giving and receiving merge and become one. After that happens the individual has got the freedom to behave in the optimal way depending on the situation he/she is in. To give and receive at one's own will, not to give or receive when it is expected, when one of polarities forces him/her to do that. In such a situation you decide about your behavior. Behavior is not decided by the charge existing on your polarities. When there is no more charge, when polarities are integrated in your consciousness, you attain the full freedom to behave freely in harmony with your own decisions.

26

PERMANENCY OF PROCESSING RESULTS

One question is woven like a thread through all systems of spiritual and psychological development: How do we get permanent results? Is it possible to keep stable our wins, without losing them after some time?

A great majority of system originators state just that. Their systems of development, they tell us, give permanent results: Good feelings, positive attitudes toward life, ability to cope with problems, higher level of understanding of life and huge expansion of consciousness etc. The fact is, they don't. As the old Chinese Book of Change or I Ching taught humans thousands of years ago – only change is permanent.

I was stimulated to write this because recently one PEAT Processor asked me that old question: How can he anchor the Pleroma state to make the satisfaction and happiness of his clients permanent?

The fact is that permanency and development are mutually exclusive ideas. With many systems you can get relatively permanent states. But if you wish to continue developing, spreading into new dimensions, spaces and dynamisms, you encounter new problems and your previous satisfaction and happiness disappear.

When one experiences the state of Pleroma, Peak experience or ecstasy as the result of processing, such states last for some time, but very soon one starts to spread into other dynamisms or spheres of activities (see 8 spheres of activities of human being). Through such expanding the person starts to experience other people as oneself, so much so that problems of other people become his/her own problem. With such a development one experiences "I" as wider and expanded. One starts to suffer because of the problems of other people, other alive beings, the whole world, existing universe etc. That circle of entities which one experiences as oneself becomes wider and wider.

If a man succeeds in anchoring a Pleroma state for some time, he prevents the further expansion of his being, he inhibits his return to All-source, Oneness. Expansion of the Being is one side of a coin in relationship with realized positive states. As I said, they cannot be stable and eternal and after some time another expansion of being happens. Through the new barriers, their overcoming and our experiencing bad states, finally we remove them. Then what happens is a new expansion. We come to new frontiers where new experiences and previously unknown problems are waiting for us. That is the real development of a being.

There was a long period of time when I practiced Gnostic Intensive with many different groups of people. We considered it to be the deepest and most valuable method of Spiritual development. Gnosis, Enlightenment or Direct Experiences of Truth which we used to get were wonderful, deep and all-embracing. But they were not permanent. After some time they would become more and more pale and would lose their power. After about 10 years of hard struggle Alda and I finally made a breakthrough – we entered a stable state of consciousness or Meuna (in Algolic or cosmic language it means "I am one"). In such Meuna state one is always who one is, another human being is always what another is, life is life, God is God.

After entering Meuna, we seemed to be unable to do any spiritual, psychological or developmental work. There was no point in putting any effort, to struggle, to fight for anything. Everything was given as it should have been. We were driven by the huge river of life and it was ridiculous to make any effort to change it, to swim left or right or to stop it. I had a deep insight about my life. The whole of my life I have been trying to discover the true or correct way of living. Finally, when I was 53, I discovered it was exactly the way of life I have been already living.

Problems lost their sharpness. If you got sick, well...it was an inseparable part of life and you would accept it without much resistance. If you were without money, it was evident you were not going to die, you would go on living anyway.

We felt we came to the end. It was really the end of games. There were no problems, but also no challenges; no defeats, but no victories as well. That state lasted about one and a half year.

At the end of that period I noticed a phenomenon which I called "spiritual itch". You become uneasy and start looking for a new game. True, you were empty and stable and out of problems, but you notice that other beings around you are not. And their problems become your problems. It was as simple as that! I did not care very much about my pneumonia, but I deeply cared about some hungry and dying children in Africa. I would get tears in my eyes watching some dog with a broken leg on the street. Friends use to tell me: "Is it OK to be so weak? Mind your own business. You have good life.

You don't have any real problem." But it is in vain. Perhaps hunger was the problem of African children, but it was my problem for sure!

So, you see, you can attain some relatively stable higher states, but after that, if you want to continue expanding into new spheres and dimensions, you start to experience other beings' problems as yours, because with expansion of your being you embrace them. You are them and they are you.

If you could for some time anchor Pleroma state, you would surely prevent and stop expansion of your own being and delay your return to the Spiritual homeland.

Expansion and ascension of beings is only one part of a coin, another is confronting with new dimensions and worlds, which means new obstacles, difficulties and problems. Then we create new systems to cope with them, and so we continue our development.

Judith Daniel, PEAT Trainer, writes about the consequences of much processing:

"I am writing about an experience I am having that I am not worried about, but I am wondering what it means. I have been using PEAT for myself and with clients pretty regularly. Recently, as in the last month, I feel that I am having trouble using PEAT for myself. I sit down to do DP3 with a polarity in mind that I want to work with, but I am having trouble feeling any distinctions in the two polarities. I am thinking of past times in which I experienced each of the poles, but as I focus on them they feel the same in my body and emotions. Sometimes there will be slightly different thoughts that go with them, but

they do not seem like real thoughts, but like a role, not things I truly believe. Any distinctions seem very subtle or not existing at all. So there seems nothing to pendulate back and forth between. I do not know if the polarities are already neutralized, or if I am resisting somehow.

I have experienced this with everything I have tried to do DP3 with in the last month, things like money-no money and all the money polarities you suggested in your email, and beliefs about myself, like I am good, I am bad.

I also have had the experience when I am trying to choose a polarity to work on, of seeing that all the polarities are the same. They seemed each to be really one big polarity, just this and that, or really this and this, because they were the same. Just a way of breaking things up but so we can talk about them. I could not figure out how to work on these. So I just stopped."

27

Spiritual Honeymoon

Vladimir Stojakovic, whose valuable observations I already quoted, sent the following article to our discussion list on Spiritual technology. Exactly and in detail he described what is happening with a self-realizing person on their Spiritual path. I just omitted a few details from his article.

When a spiritual aspirant encounters a new effective spiritual tool or a new teacher, the state of euphoria that follows this rendezvous is often referred to as a spiritual honeymoon. This euphoria is a characteristic feature of the human being, when a long awaited and craved for goal is achieved or a wish fulfilled. However, in Spiritual Technology, there is more to this phenomenon.

When you do 3-day PEAT Processor seminar, 1 day DP3 seminar and PF Rundown (a session), much charge and a number of your problems will vanish, you will neutralize your Primes, delete Past and Future. Many long time problems are gone, traumas and incidents deleted, you wonder whether they ever existed and feel on top of the world. Everything seems possible now and the future is bright. This is truly the honeymoon.

To understand what happens after the honeymoon, you need to understand firstly kind of restructuring which happens in the reactive mind while processing (ego, subconsciousness.). The reactive mind consists of layers of mind content, and these chaotic layers are on different levels of unconsciousness".

The reactive mind has its surface area. It is like an iceberg. The part of the iceberg that is above the water is equivalent to the surface of the reactive mind. The surface of the reactive mind is the part of it that is closest to you, to your consciousness. The surface of the reactive mind is in contact with you the same way your body is in contact with clothes you wear. The problems that you process or are bothered with are stored in that surface part. Simply, the surface area of the reactive mind is mostly in touch with you, with your consciousness.

When you do this processing, and when you get into the state wherefrom you cannot experience any of your problems any longer, that means that you just vanished the surface of your reactive mind, its surface layer. Now, you discharged a few problems, and the part of the reactive mind that is mostly in contact with you does not exist any longer, therefore you cannot experience your other, deeper problems. That does not mean that they do not exist, you just cannot feel them at this stage. And you cannot experience your other, existing problems, because where the surface of the reactive mind was, it is emptiness now, and emptiness is what you experience.

So what happens now? What happens with an iceberg when its surface layer is removed? The next layer that was just below the surface comes up, and replaces the removed layer. The same happens with our reactive mind. It only takes a bit longer than for an iceberg.

So, after so many seminars/sessions done, apart from the fact the we discharged some major problems, and found new great tools, opened the doors of perception, the doors of ethereal worlds and some different future, an additional reason for all that euphoria and elation is the fact you experience emptiness mostly, due to the fact that what was on the surface on the reactive mind is deleted, many problems are gone, and the contact with the rest of them is temporarily lost. Of course, not only the surface part of the mind is vanished, some deeper parts are gone too, but that only contributes to the whole experience. When people do these seminars, and then write to the list, stating how all their problems are gone and display all that euphoria, I know that most likely, we will hear from them a bit different story, quiet soon.

After a while, a few day, a week or two, as with the mentioned iceberg, another layer will appear from the reactive mind, to replace the vanished surface layer. When this happens, this now new surface layer will bring up some new problems and guess what, the honeymoon is over.

What happens now? Nothing special. It's now the time to apply what you learnt on those seminars and to make step number 2 on your spiritual or healing path. When you make that step and vanish the new recently appeared surface layer, what happens next? The same. New layer comes up, and you are about to make step number 3. And so on. That is called Spiritual Development.

This is a VERY simplified description of the process. There isn't much "space" in a post, but there are a few important points that have to be understood. We vanish problems, and then we have new ones and so forth. This sounds like we don't make any progress at all? That's not correct. The reactive mind is a sum of many problems, tensions and unwanted states, etc. With every element of the reactive mind you vanish, you reduce that sum and make your life better. Also, you removed problems, and release abilities, therefore improving your life.

These new problems, when they surface from the reactive mind, are they new or old? Good question. They are actually and mostly old, older than the problems you vanished in the previous layer. There is something called downward and upward spirals of evolution. In the downward spiral, you descend from the perfect being to this material universe. On the way down you create problems. When you hit the ground and start going up (Spiritual Development), you will first encounter the problems you recently created, and then on every next layer, older problems will come up. This is also applicable to a single life, from birth to a moment you become an adult and start you spiritual development. You are to become again what you were when a child, but this time you will have something you the child did not have: awareness.

Removing layers and layers of the reactive mind - that's Spiritual Development or Life Repairing. Bringing to light all those enslaved parts of your being and liberating them. Becoming whole again. You may call it Spiritual Development, or simply improving my life and liberating myself.

So, don't be discouraged when the honeymoon is over. When a new layer of problems and suffering comes up, keep in mind one thing - the elation, happiness and freedom you will experience after you vanish these new problems are equivalent to the suffering these problems now produce..

28

ON BEING A PROCESSOR

Often people, especially beginners in the spiritual milieu ask how to be a master, a processor, a group leader? Who can be such a one? What are the characteristics of such person? What training does one need, etc.

Speaking about it we come to a well-known formula: BE - DO - HAVE. In everyday life people usually turn that formula upside down. They believe that you must HAVE something to BE someone. If you want to be a doctor, you have to go to medical university, study medicine for many years and finally, as most important, get the certificate. If you want to be a painter, besides talent, you've got to have a studio, many acquaintances which want to buy your pictures, money to organize exhibitions, you must wear velvet trousers, have a beard, canvas, colors etc.

In spiritual work we have an opposite order. You have to BE someone to be able to DO something and to HAVE something. It's wide spread delusion that you have to know something, or to have something to BECOME someone. For example, take a real painter. In a fire he can lose all his belongings: studio, paintings, academy degree etc. Will he stop experiencing himself the painter. Of course not! If in such circumstances one feels one is not a painter any more, one has never been a painter.

In Spiritual work this applies even more then in art. If you ARE the Processor, Master, group leader, you don't need anything to do your job. BEing is enough!

A Processor or a Master can get information about his job, he can use experiences of other people, he can learn to relax in tense situations etc. but first of all he must BE a Processor or a Master. For that there is no substitute.

However, there are some characteristics of such a person. In my experience, these characteristics are as follows:

The Master (Processor) is Self-confident and certain that he or she can lead people to the desired result.

The Master (Processor) must be authentic. That means they must speak out of themselves. He or she must be him or her self. They can make mistakes, small, major and drastic ones. They can fall and rise. But it must be the Master (Processor) who falls and rises. It won't be someone who tries to be a Master.

He/She must be devoted to his/her people! During a workshop or training he/she must forget about their own problems and must leave them for the time after the job has been done.

Such a person doesn't make a compromise with the knowledge he is transferring to other people. If a best friend, brother, or sister makes mistakes, the Master (Processor) says the Truth about it. In a way, he/she must put the Truth above everything.

The Story of Two Friends

Very often people complain of being in bad or unfavorable circumstances for effective spiritual work, practice and development. But practice shows that often in bad surroundings we do a better job than in comfortable ones. The following yoga story tells us a lot about it.

In India, there were two friends. For many years they had been inseparable, always going everywhere together, doing the same things etc. One day they talked about how to spend that evening. One proposed. "Let's go to the temple of great sage. Every evening he teaches people about moral life, death, destiny. We will learn something valuable."

The other did not agree. "I am fed up with all those wise words. Better we go to the whorehouse. I heard they have new, beautiful girls. We will have a lot of fun."

They could not agree and each one went one's own way.

The man who went to the ashram of wise man was satisfied for some time because he chose spiritual advancement instead of carnal desires. He was seated close to feet of the Master trying to follow his words, fully concentrating, but his thoughts were escaping persistently to the whore house. In his imagination he saw his friend having a lot of fun. Those images became more and more vivid and exciting, thus he slipped slowly into a meditation about sexual pleasure.

The other friend started to feel remorse as soon as he entered the whorehouse. He compared himself with his friend: "Alas, I am sitting here in dirt with prostitutes and drunkards and my friend is listening to elevated words of a great sage." Then wise words which he had heard before and read in sacred books started to flood his consciousness and soon he entered the deep meditation about meaning of human life.

29

PARADOX AND HUMOR IN SPIRITUAL WORK

In Spiritual tradition humor has at least three functions: Humor embraces opposites, it turns over and brings the collapse of opposing categories. It is the expression of enlightenment, that is, the integration of opposites and the liberation from their shackles. We meet humor most often in Zen and Sufism. In the Sufi tradition it is usually embodied in the character of Mula Nasrudin, which acting as a fool and ignorant, speaks the deepest truths about life and man.

In one educative story, at the twilight Nasrudin kneels in the grass in front of his home, as if looking for something.

"What are you doing here, Nasrudin? his neighbor asks. *"I'm looking for a key which I lost in the wood?"* Nasrudin replies. *"Why don't you look for it in the wood?"* says the neighbor, wondering at Nasrudin's folly. *"Because there is much more light here"*, answers Nasrudin.

His answer, at first sight crazy, speaks about people who do not search for the Truth about themselves in the only place they could find it – in themselves.

People following Sufism in the West recently developed so called absurd humor, which uses paradoxes. One such example is paradoxical riddle: *"What is the difference between one chicken?"* The answer to that question is consistently paradoxical: *"The difference is this: It's both legs are same, especially the left one."*

In Zen the humor, which points to deeply hidden truth, is often crude and direct. To the question of his disciple, *"What is Buddha?"* the Teacher answers, *"Buddha is dog shit!"* It does not mean he is degrading Buddha, it means that a deeply enlightened person sees Oneness in everything existing, even in such opposing ideas as Buddha and dog shit.

In another anecdote, a young Zen monk just experienced satori, permanent enlightenment, and he sees in everything One and undivided Truth. Angry, he enters a temple where a group of religious people kneel around a golden statue of Buddha, praying, and he spits on the statue. "Lunatic, what are you doing?" people screamed at him, "You are spiting at the Buddha, the Truth Itself." *"Let someone of you show me where there is no Truth, I will spit there,"* answered enlightened young man.

Zen insists on absolute directness. To the question of a disciple," What is Zen?" the famous teacher answered, *"When I'm hungry I eat, when I'm thirsty I drink, when I'm sad I cry, when I'm joyful I laugh."* Sometimes they even make jokes about such an attitude. On one religious assembly, followers of many different teachings gathered. One Zen Teacher, well known by his custom to confuse his disciples with simple questions, approached the Tibetan Rinpoche (Teacher) who was playing with his rosary. Disciples of the Zen Master gather around expecting a well-known performance. The Zen Teacher pulled an orange out of his kimono.

He showed it to lama and asked him aloud: *"What's this?"* Lama did not answer. He went on playing with his rosary. *"What's this?"* insisted the Zen Teacher, pushing the orange under lama's nose. Lama leaned toward the translator and for a couple of minutes they whispered.

Then the translator said to the whole group: *"Rinpoche says, What is the matter with this man? Don't they have oranges there where he comes from?"*

A psychiatrist, studying and meditating in a Zen center, wanting to get as much knowledge as possible, asked a Zen Teacher, *"How do you deal with neurotics?"* The Zen Master replied, *"I get them to the point where they can't ask any more questions."*

As I said, practitioners of Zen are able to make jokes about themselves. Here is such one: *"How many Zen Buddhists does it take to change a light bulb?"* The answer is: *"Three. One to change it, one to not-change it and one to both change and not-change it."*

The following story speaks about hope of every disciple that one day their Teacher will uncover the deepest secret about man, life and cosmos which he has kept hidden so far. A Zen Master lies dying. His monks, from the senior monk to the novice monk, have gathered about his death bed. The senior monk leans over to ask the dying master if he has any last words for the assembled monks. The old Master replies in a whisper, *"Tell them, Truth is like a river."* This bit of wisdom is then passed around the room from monk to monk and everybody pretends to hear the deep wisdom. When it reaches the novice monk, who did not learn to pretend yet, the novice asks, *"What does he mean, 'Truth is like a river?'"* The question is passed back up the room to the senior monk, who then asks the master, *"Master, what do you mean, 'Truth is like a river?"* Slowly the master opens his eyes and in a weak voice whispers, *"Okay, Truth is not like a river."*

30

LAST WORD

At the risk of boring all readers of this book, I repeatedly have emphasized the fundamental dual nature of this world. As the shield has two sides and we are not able to use just one without other, so the whole universe in which we live has two sides and two energetic flows.

Even in Christian teaching, which seemingly gravitates only to good and stresses it, one side is necessary for the existence of the other side. Christ, the son of God, is tortured, humiliated and crucified on the cross because of our sins. Pay attention to this simple truth, which many people do not see: if our sins had not existed, he would not have been able to manifest his extreme sacrifice and his divine nature.

A few years ago my wife Alda did one process which opened my eyes to a component of life which evaded me up to that moment. In that process she was supposed to imagine an ideal world in which she would like to live. Besides many details, she was supposed to find an ideal activity which she would devote herself to in that world. She chose an activity which at the first sight matched that ideal world: She wanted to devote her whole life helping unhappy people. Then she experienced a real shock! She realized that she created an ideal world in her imagination in which there were unhappy human beings and as her ideal activity helping them. For her, having an ideal activity, to be able to be doing an ideal thing, meant that unhappy people were necessary!

Even an ideal world must be built on duality. The world filled with great happiness must have its opposite in the existence of unhappy people. If it is given as completely perfect, what could noble people do in it, which goals would they have to fight for? Therefore the majority of world religions hold out to man the idea of paradise in which there is no unhappiness, sickness, old age, jealousy and suffering. But none of them succeeds to create the paradise without its dual opposite. As its shadow hell appears in which is everything negative, painful and unhappy. Again the Codes of the whole human race appear before us, good and bad.

Differing from a typical Western religious and philosophical point of view, which directs us incessantly only to the positive side of phenomena and experiences, there have always been independent thinkers in the West with an all-embracing attitude. Creative professionals tend to think in the language of opposites! When administered a free association test, Nobel Prize winners are more likely to respond to a stimulus word by supplying its opposite. Albert Einstein had been greatly perplexed as to how he could develop an all-encompassing general theory of relativity similar to his special theory of relativity applied to light. The idea came to him that if a man was falling from a building he would be in motion and yet at rest relative to an object falling from his pocket. The reconciliation of this paradox led to Einstein's most famous theory.

Fortunately enough, some wise ones, the missionaries of higher consciousness, long ago pointed out the way we should follow if we want to get free of this world torn by dual forces. It is necessary to attain the transcendence of polarities in one's own consciousness. Only then does the reflection in the cosmic mirror essentially change. It is a long and strenuous way but it leads out of this labyrinth.

Those wise men created systems which teach us how to find the way out, serving as valuable maps and guideposts. A person walking this path gradually surpasses this world and stops playing its compulsive and futile games. Although his roots are in the depths of dark and condensed matter, his consciousness gradually but surely rises into the light of the integrated Being. Such a one becomes the live integration and synthesis of the deepest and highest, light and darkness, material and Spiritual, free will and destiny, limitation of individual and limitlessness of the universe. Buddhist philosopher Nagarjuna pointed to the Enlightened state as our final goal: *"The completely Enlightened One is neither being, nor not-being. He is beyond all opposites."*

LITERATURE

Andre Breton. *On Surrealism in its Living Works.* 1953.

Arnold Kezserlink. *From Sufferening to Fulfillment.*

Audrey Cook and Rick Bradshaw. *Toward Integration. One Eye at a Time.* Vancouver, Second Edition, 2000.

Bojana Mihajlović. *Memento. Sećanje prošlih života.* Beograd, 1999.

David Kenyon Nelms. *Inner-Fire Kindling.* 2004.

Ernesto Rossi. *Psychology of Mind Body Healing.* 1986.

Funch, Flemming. *Transformational Dialogues. Facilitator Training Manual #1: An instruction manual of practical techniques for facilitating personal change.* Transformational Processing Institute. 2004.

Geoffry Filbert. *Excalibur Revisited.* (private edition).

Hale Dwoskin, *The Sedona Method.* Sedona, AZ. 2003.

Gregg Braden. *Awakening to Zero Point.* Eelleve, WA. 1977.

Julie J. Nichols, Ph.D., and Lansing Barrett Gresham. *Ask Anything, and Your Body Will Answer.* 1999.

Lev Vygotsky. *Thinking and Speaking.* 1934. Revised edition under the title *Thought and Language.* Alex Kozulin (Editor). 1986.

Leslie Templ-Thurston. *The Marriage of Spirit: Enlightened Living in Today's World.* 2000.

Lisa Sarasohn. *The Woman's Belly Book: Finding Your Treasure Within*. 2003.

Michael J. Gelb. *Da Vinci Decoded*. 2004.

Dr Randolph Stone, *Polarity Therapy The Complete Collected Works Volume 1*. 1986.

Sandra Ingerman. *Soul Retrieval: Mending the Fragmented Self through Shamanic Practice*. 1991.

Stephen Wolinsky. *Tao of Chaos: Essence and Enneagram*. 1994.

Tarthang Tulku. *Openness Mind*. Darma Publishing, Berkeley, USA. 1978.

Vladimir Stojaković. Articles on the Spiritual Technology discussion List

Made in the USA
Lexington, KY
30 November 2011